NATIONAL
GEOGRAPHIC
KiDS

ALMANAC 2016

A lion cub lounges in Masai Mara
National Reserve in Kenya.

ALMANAC 2016

NATIONAL GEOGRAPHIC
WASHINGTON, D.C.

National Geographic Kids Books
gratefully acknowledges the following people for their help with the
National Geographic Kids Almanac 2016.

Anastasia Cronin of the
National Geographic Explorers program and
Chuck Errig of Random House

Amazing Animals

Suzanne Braden, Director, Pandas International

Dr. Rodolfo Coria, Paleontologist, Plaza Huincul, Argentina

Dr. Sylvia Earle,
National Geographic Explorer-in-Residence

Dr. Thomas R. Holtz, Jr., Senior Lecturer, Vertebrate Paleontology,
Department of Geology, University of Maryland

Dr. Luke Hunter, Executive Director, Panthera

Dereck and Beverly Joubert,
National Geographic Explorers-in-Residence

Nizar Ibrahim, National Geographic Emerging Explorer

"Dino" Don Lessem, President, Exhibits Rex

Kathy B. Maher, Research Editor,
National Geographic magazine

Kathleen Martin, Canadian Sea Turtle Network

Barbara Nielsen, Polar Bears International

Andy Prince, Austin Zoo

Christopher Sloan

Julia Thorson, translator, Zurich, Switzerland

Dennis vanEngelsdorp, Senior Extension Associate,
Pennsylvania Department of Agriculture

Super Science

Tim Appenzeller, Chief Magazine Editor, *Nature*

Dr. Rick Fienberg, American Astronomical Society,
Press Officer and Director of Communications

Dr. José de Ondarza, Associate Professor,
Department of Biological Sciences, State University
of New York, College at Plattsburgh

Lesley B. Rogers, Managing Editor (former),
National Geographic magazine

Dr. Enric Sala, National Geographic Visiting Fellow

Abigail A. Tipton, Director of Research (former),
National Geographic magazine

Erin Vintinner, Biodiversity Specialist,
Center for Biodiversity and Conservation at the
American Museum of Natural History

Barbara L. Wyckoff, Research Editor (former),
National Geographic magazine

Wonders of Nature

Anatta, NOAA Public Affairs Officer

Dr. Robert Ballard,
National Geographic Explorer-in-Residence

Douglas H. Chadwick, wildlife biologist and contributor to
National Geographic magazine

Susan K. Pell, Ph.D., Science and Public Programs Manager,
United States Botanic Garden

Culture Connection

Dr. Wade Davis, National Geographic Explorer-in-Residence

Deirdre Mullervy, Managing Editor,
Gallaudet University Press

Going Green

Eric J. Bohn, Math Teacher, Santa Rosa High School

Stephen David Harris, Professional Engineer,
Industry Consulting

Catherine C. Milbourn, Senior Press Officer, EPA

Brad Scriber, Senior Researcher,
National Geographic magazine

Paola Segura and Cid Simões,
National Geographic Emerging Explorers

Dr. Wes Tunnell, Harte Research Institute for
Gulf of Mexico Studies, Texas A&M
University—Corpus Christi

History Happens

Dr. Sylvie Beaudreau, Associate Professor,
Department of History, State University of New York

Elspeth Deir, Assistant Professor, Faculty of Education,
Queens University, Kingston, Ontario, Canada

Dr. Gregory Geddes, Lecturer, Department of Global Studies,
State University of New York–Orange,
Middletown-Newburgh, New York

Dr. Fredrik Hiebert, National Geographic Visiting Fellow

Micheline Joanisse, Media Relations Officer,
Natural Resources Canada

Dr. Robert D. Johnston,
Associate Professor and Director of the
Teaching of History Program, University of Illinois at Chicago

Dickson Mansfield, Geography Instructor (retired),
Faculty of Education, Queens University,
Kingston, Ontario, Canada

Tina Norris, U.S. Census Bureau

Parliamentary Information and Research Service,
Library of Parliament, Ottawa, Canada

Karyn Pugliese, Acting Director, Communications,
Assembly of First Nations

Geography Rocks

Glynnis Breen, National Geographic Special Projects

Carl Haub, Senior Demographer,
Conrad Taeuber Chair of Public Information,
Population Reference Bureau

Dr. Mary Kent, Demographer, Population Reference Bureau

Dr. Walt Meier, National Snow and Ice Data Center

Dr. Richard W. Reynolds,
NOAA's National Climatic Data Center

United States Census Bureau, Public Help Desk

Dr. Spencer Wells,
National Geographic Explorer-in-Residence

Contents

Super Science

100

Wonders of Nature

136

Fun and Games

158

Culture Connection

178

Going Green

History Happens

Geography Rocks

At the 2016 Olympic Summer Games in Rio de Janeiro, Brazil, golf returns after a 112-year absence, and rugby will be contested for the first time since 1924. Here players compete in the 2014 Premiership Rugby 7s Series in Northampton, England.

Your World
2016

Almanac Explorer!

I am the largest of my **k**ind.

This is clue #1!
Collect them all and unscramble the letters to find the secret animal. Enter the animal name at kids.nationalgeographic.com/almanac-2016!

SUPERLAB
AT SEA

This cutting-edge vessel may change how we explore the oceans.

S taring out of your bedroom window, you watch as a great white shark swims by. Soon an octopus shoots into view, followed by a swarm of jellyfish. You're aboard the SeaOrbiter, a high-tech research vessel set to launch in 2016.

The 190-foot (58-m)-tall craft, which is being built with support from the National Geographic Society, is designed so that the top half towers above the ocean's surface while the bottom half plunges into the water. The vessel will sail to remote parts of the ocean, then drift with currents as scientists conduct research. Check out the SeaOrbiter's coolest features.

SUPERFAB LAB The egg-shaped marine lab will be lined with several aquariums filled with fish and crustaceans collected from the ocean. That way, scientists can examine the marine animals up close. They can also perform chemistry experiments on seawater to test things like pollution levels.

HANGAR HANGOUT
The hangar will hold Remotely Operated Vehicles (ROVs), devices that let scientists explore underwater peaks and canyons without leaving the SeaOrbiter. ROVs can travel thousands of feet deep while sending live video back to the vessel.

SOUND OFF The SeaOrbiter is designed to be ultraquiet and less likely to scare animals, while supersensitive recorders will capture sounds from marine life like whales swimming far below the craft.

THE SUITE LIFE With room for 22 people, the living area on the SeaOrbiter will be five-star quality. Bedrooms will come complete with TVs and computers. Inhabitants can exercise at the fitness center or play the pipe organ in one of the vessel's classrooms. And big underwater windows will be like personal aquariums.

DEEP-SEA DIVERS LEAVE THE PRESSURIZED AREA FOR THE OCEAN.

RE-CREATION
OF TUT'S FACE

MUMMY SECRETS
REVEALED

Scientists find NEW EVIDENCE about how KING TUT may have died.

For decades archaeologists have studied King Tut's reign hoping to learn more about the ruler. They've uncovered a lot about his life, but a riddle remains. No one knows exactly how the king died.

A SICK KING

To solve this ancient mystery, researchers are relying on modern technology. While various theories about Tut's death have emerged over the years—including the notion that he was murdered—new research has led to a new conclusion. Using more than 2,000 computed tomography scans of King Tut's mummy, scientists conducted a "virtual autopsy." The findings: Tut's death was most likely a result of his overall weakened state—he had a foot disease and was suffering from malaria, according to genetic testing.

CRASH TEST MUMMY

An older theory suggests Tut died in a chariot crash. To reach this conclusion, researchers created a life-size image of Tut using x-rays taken of Tut's mummy. They got a replica Egyptian chariot from a company that makes props for movies, hitched it to horses, and took it out for a spin to record how the vehicle maneuvered at its top speed. They compared this data with the x-ray image to develop their theory.

Perhaps no one will ever know for sure what happened to this legendary leader. But these theories bring us one step closer to understanding the truth.

KING TUT'S
COFFIN

GATOR GETS NEW TAIL

Mr. Stubbs looks like any other gator—except for one thing. The Arizona, U.S.A., reptile has a tail made of rubber. The first alligator known to wear a prosthetic tail, he lost his appendage after it was bitten off by a bigger gator. Without it, Mr. Stubbs couldn't walk or swim properly, which eventually hurt his back. So a team of engineers stepped in to offer the reptile relief. After measuring the gator and studying his movements, the scientists used silicone rubber to build an artificial tail that attaches to Mr. Stubbs' back legs with nylon straps. Soon, the gator could propel himself across the pool. Looks like this tail has a happy ending.

HEY, WHEN
DID I GROW
SO LONG?

FAKE TAIL

Once Upon a RHINO

"When there are so few of us, it's hard to find friends to play with. This is sad to me. So I'm here to tell you about my life and ask for your help."

This is the voice of a Sumatran rhino named Andatu, as imagined by fifth graders at P.S. 107 John W. Kimball Learning Center in Brooklyn, New York, U.S.A. The creative kids penned a book about the animal called *One Special Rhino* to raise money for the Sumatran rhino cause. And rhinos like Andatu definitely need the help: Given rapidly decreasing numbers due to habitat loss and poaching, scientists estimate that there may be no more than a hundred Sumatran rhinos left in the world.

So how did the young authors connect with Andatu? It all started with a schoolwide effort to save Sumatran rhinos. Students made rhino piggy banks out of recycled coffee cups, collected spare change, and posted a YouTube video about Andatu, the first Sumatran rhino born in captivity. But they wanted to do more. So, with teachers and parents pitching in, the students collaborated on the story, which peeks at life at the Way Kambas rhino sanctuary, where Andatu lives, plays, wallows in mud, and eats—a lot.

Fortunately, Andatu is thriving. And others will too, thanks to *One Special Rhino* and other initiatives supporting all species of rhinos. For example, National Geographic Explorers-in-Residence Dereck and Beverly Joubert, through their rescue mission *Rhinos Without Borders*, are airlifting the animals from South Africa to Botswana, where the poaching levels are low. The Jouberts aim to protect and sustain species that may otherwise be lost forever within a decade—and, hopefully, give Andatu more friends to play with.

Ice Orchestra

It's a scene straight out of the movie *Frozen*: musicians, playing instruments made almost entirely from ice, performing in an igloo. But this is no fairy tale. It's an actual orchestra in the remote Swedish town of Luleå, just beneath the Arctic Circle. With temperatures in the concert hall kept at a frigid 23° Fahrenheit (-5°C), the audience is encouraged to bundle up to hear the *ice*-struments play!

Whiz Kid! Jack Andraka

Jack Andraka, of Crownsville, Maryland, U.S.A., was 13 when a close family friend died of pancreatic cancer. Since then, he's made it his mission to stop the spread of the deadly disease. At just 15, he invented an inexpensive blood test that can detect pancreatic cancer far earlier and faster than ever before. And while Andraka's test is still being developed, the National Geographic Emerging Explorer has already been tapped as one of the top cancer researchers of our time.

NEON SHARKS

Researchers recently made a really bright discovery in the northern Atlantic Ocean: glow-in-the-dark sharks! More than 180 species of fish and sharks—including the deep-sea-dwelling chain catshark—are biofluorescent, meaning they have the unique ability to absorb light and emit it as neon red, green, or orange under a blue light. Scientists think that these fish have filters in their eyes to help them see each other's neon hues in the deep blue sea.

DOG FACIAL RECOGNITION

Oh, no! Your pet pooch ran off down the street and you haven't seen him for hours. You've hung flyers around your neighborhood. Now what? Simply go online and see if he's turned up at a nearby shelter. Using facial recognition technology, the website and app Finding Rover compares photos of lost dogs with those at local animal shelters. As soon as you report your dog lost and post a pic, the app tracks eight facial markers, including the size of their eyes and their position near the snout, to match mutts. Pretty doggone smart!

HOT MOVIES in 2016*

FINDING DORY

BATMAN v SUPERMAN

ANGRY BIRDS

- *Ice Age: Collision Course*
- *Batman v Superman*
- *Finding Dory*
- *Angry Birds*
- *Ninjago*

*Release dates and titles are subject to change.

14

2016 Olympics

BRAZILIAN PERFORMERS AT THE 2012 SUMMER OLYMPIC GAMES CLOSING CEREMONY IN LONDON, ENGLAND

Rio2016™

Bring on the rings! When the 2016 Olympics hit Rio de Janeiro in August, it will mark the first time a South American nation has ever hosted the games. But Brazil is no stranger to major events: After all, the country recently hosted the 2014 FIFA World Cup (attended by more than three million soccer fans), and it welcomes millions of revelers to Rio's Carnival festival each year. With thousands of people from 204 countries expected to compete, Brazil will soon be rocking once more with athletes all going for the *ouro* (that's gold in Portuguese, the official language of Brazil).

Dino Robot

You may not be able to go back in time to visit dinosaurs, but toymaker Martin Grossman has invented the next best thing. His company makes Megasaurs, jumbo-size dinosaur toys programmed to act like the real thing. Each creature can swish its tail and open its mouth to unleash monstrous bellows. Dinos such as *Triceratops* and *T. rex* are available, and some are even life-size—though the price may be just as big. The *T. rex* sells for about $10,000!

Cool Events in 2016

Clean Monday Flour War

Partyers in Galaxidi, Greece, mark the start of spring by playfully **pelting each other with colored flour.**

March 14

International Day of Happiness

There's plenty to smile about today, so get to grinning!

March 20

Earth Hour Day

Recharge the planet by powering down your electronics from 8:30 to 9:30 p.m.

March 26

Harry Potter's Birthday

Calling all muggles! Put on your Gryffindor robe and celebrate the beloved books today!

July 31

Olympic Summer Games

Rio de Janeiro, Brazil, is the place to be for thousands of Olympic athletes aiming to shine.

August 5–21

World Lion Day

Rawr!
Honor the King of the Jungle in this *mane* event for lions.

August 10

Redhead Days

Redheads from all over the world gather in Breda, the Netherlands, to celebrate being ginger.

September 2–4

Paralympic Summer Games

Physically challenged Olympians from around the world compete in events like wheelchair basketball and paratriathlon.

September 7–18

Elephants
ON PARADE

Packs of baby pachyderms are popping up in cities around the globe to raise awareness and support for Asian elephants. In each location, different designers, artists, or celebrities hand-paint the life-size sculptures of elephants, which go on display in places like malls, neighborhoods, and city plazas. But the colorful sculptures aren't just sitting pretty: They're also for sale, with proceeds going toward elephant conservation in the hopes of boosting the animal's dwindling numbers in the wild, mostly due to habitat loss and poaching. A herd of 31 sculptures in Hong Kong recently sold at auction for more than $277,000. Now that's huge!

Water polo players compete for the ball during an Olympic competition between Serbia and Italy in Beijing, China.

Angie Skirving (bottom) of Australia and Jin-Kyoung Kim of South Korea dive for a ball at an Olympic field hockey competition.

Paul Nicklen, a National Geographic photographer, shot this photo of a diver exploring an underwater cave near Akumal, Yucatán, Mexico.

Awesome Adventure

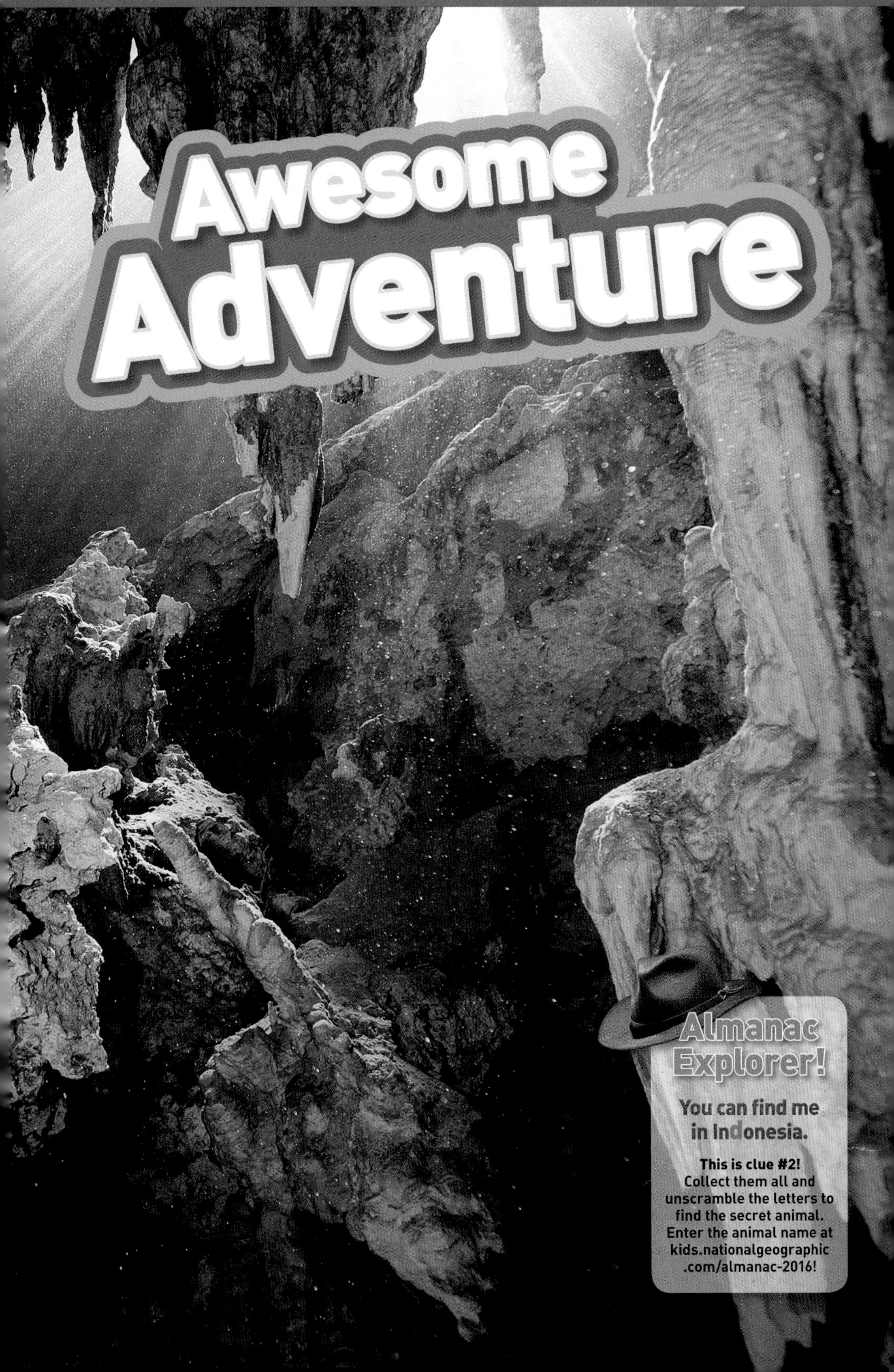

Almanac Explorer!

You can find me in Indonesia.

This is clue #2!
Collect them all and unscramble the letters to find the secret animal. Enter the animal name at kids.nationalgeographic.com/almanac-2016!

DARE to EXPLORE

Do you have what it takes to be a great explorer? Read these stories of four adventurers, and see how you can get started on the exploration path.

KENNETH SIMS
Geologist / geochemist

"Don't ever let fear of failure get in the way of your goals. There are no defeats, only setbacks."

A SWELTERING LAVA LAKE

SIMS REACHES A CRATER'S RIM.

"My job is to investigate something called radioactive isotopes. These are unstable atoms that are found in volcanic rock and lava. Researching them can give us clues about how volcanoes work and help us predict future eruptions.

"Collecting samples to study can be dangerous but exciting. I've climbed down ropes into the mouths of volcanoes, dived to volcanic vents on the ocean floor, and traveled to a frozen peak in Antarctica where molten lava bubbles within. To stare into an active volcano is like standing at the top of a football stadium filled with seething lava.

"Some of my experiences have been scary. But I try to stay unafraid. You do the best you can to keep safe while getting the job done. It's important to live life to its fullest."

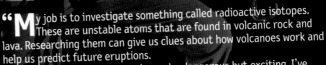

EARTH HAS ABOUT 1,500 ACTIVE VOLCANOES.

MEAVE AND LOUISE LEAKEY

WANT TO BE A PALEONTOLOGIST?

STUDY: Geology, biology, and chemistry

WATCH: National Geographic's *Mysteries of Mankind*

READ: *The Skull in the Rock* by Lee R. Berger and Marc Aronson; *The Tree of Life: Charles Darwin* by Peter Sís

LOUISE

MEAVE

"Important lessons about **our existence** today can only be learned by studying the past."

LOUISE LEAKEY WORKING IN THE FIELD

"**S**earching for clues to our human ancestry is a lot like putting together complex, 3-D puzzles in which all the pieces are buried deep in the ground.

"One particular morning my mother and I had been out collecting fossils. Our bags were heavy, our water had run out, it was hot, and we still had a 20-minute walk to the car. But we stopped to look at the two final points on our list. We found the fossil of a piece of a skull barely visible on the surface and we dug out the large block of sandstone containing what we hoped was the entire fossil to carry back to camp. After several months of cleaning the fossil under a microscope, we realized what we'd discovered: the preserved, small skull of *Homo erectus*, one of the closest relatives to today's human beings.

"Paleontology requires patience and concentration, a love of the outdoors, and a deep curiosity about our past and what life was like before humans. In the field, you need to be comfortable with a rugged existence, away from all the comforts of home—and most important: You have to be a team player."

A 4.1-MILLION-YEAR-OLD JAW

A MORE THAN 3-MILLION-YEAR-OLD SKULL

OLD.

KIRA SALAK
Adventurer and writer

"Don't let doubt get in the way of your goals. Persistence is a powerful thing. Just keep trying and you'll make your dreams a reality."

TRAVELING BY CAMEL IN LIBYA, AFRICA

KAYAKING IN MALI

"I was kayaking down the Niger River in Mali, Africa, when lightning ripped through the sky and heavy rains began to fall. My goal was to paddle for 600 miles (965 km), and it was only the first day of my journey. As the thunderstorm raged, winds stirred up huge waves that threatened to capsize my boat. It took all of my strength to steer the kayak along the thrashing waters. Finally, the storm passed.

"I've traveled to every continent on Earth, trekking through some of the world's harshest environments and writing about my experiences. I love telling true stories that introduce people to distant places and cultures. My trips are often challenging—and they leave me sore! I've cycled across Alaska to the Arctic, hiked more than 200 miles (322 km) along the Himalaya in Asia, and ridden camels through the Sahara in Africa. Wherever I go, I meet amazing people. They've taught me that we can look at the world in many ways."

THE NIGER RIVER IS SHAPED LIKE A BOOMERANG.

JOEL SARTORE
Nature photographer

WANT TO BE A PHOTOGRAPHER?

STUDY: Any topic that interests you and inspires you to snap pictures

WATCH: *March of the Penguins* and NatGeo's *Great Migrations*

READ: *Rare: Portraits of America's Endangered Species* by Joel Sartore

"Saving threatened animal species will help preserve the future for humans as well."

PENGUIN PHOTO SHOOT!

SARTORE'S STUNNING IMAGES

"One day while in Alaska, I took a helicopter to a tiny coastal island to photograph two bull musk oxen that lived there. I knew I was in trouble as soon as the helicopter dropped me off and flew away. The bull musk oxen spotted me and began charging. These animals are huge, shaggy, and sport very sharp horns—you don't want to mess with them! So I took off running. But the animals kept coming at me. Finally I waded into the water and climbed on a rock. I stayed there until the helicopter returned later that day.

"Even during dangerous moments, I love my job. My goal is to inform the public about threatened species through photography. I once took pictures of a Rabbs' fringe-limbed treefrog, the last of its kind. It's amazing and sad to know that once this one animal is gone, its species will be extinct. But capturing the frog's image is like giving it a voice. Once people see an animal and learn its story, they want to help."

EARLY CAMERAS USED SILVER TO PROCESS PHOTOS.

SECRETS OF THE

DARING SCIENTISTS SEARCH FOR

A bizarre world lies under the sparkling Atlantic Ocean off the islands of the Bahamas, a world few have seen. Here, a system of super-deep underwater caves called blue holes contain odd-looking creatures, six-story-high rock formations, and even ancient human remains. Scuba-diving scientists must dodge whirl-pools and squeeze through narrow tunnels to study blue holes—but their risky expedi-tions uncover amazing secrets.

CREATURE FEATURE

FANGED CRUSTACEAN

WEIRD WATER

NEON PINK CAVE WATER!

Dive about 30 feet (9 m) into some blue holes, and the water turns pink. It looks nice—but it's poison-ous. Because of a weak current here, rainwater and salt water mix in a way that traps a layer of toxic gas where pink bacteria thrive. To avoid getting ill, divers do not linger here.

In other blue holes, ocean tides can whip up whirlpools that look like giant bathtub drains. Scientists must circle carefully, or else risk being sucked in.

Farther down, the caves become dark and twisty. Anthropologist and National Geographic explorer Kenny Broad and his team have found many odd species here, including a tiny, transparent crustacean that is venomous (above).

Blue holes also contain fossils of animals— even birds. During the last ice age, these areas were dry and made perfect perches for the fliers. In one watery cave, a 12,000-year-old owl's nest was found surrounded by lizard bones—leftovers from the owl's meals.

BLUE HOLES

CLUES ABOUT UNDERWATER CAVES.

HOW BLUE HOLES FORMED

During past ice ages— the most recent about 18,000 years ago—water levels dropped and new land was exposed. Rain ate away at the land, forming holes that became deep caves. The caves filled with water after sea levels rose again. The deepest known blue hole is about 660 feet (200 m) deep.

BONE-CHILLING DISCOVERY

The most amazing find in the blue holes? Human skeletons. Scientists were able to trace the remains back 1,400 years to the time of the Lucayans—the first people believed to live in the Bahamas. No one is sure how the bones ended up in the submerged caves. But the team thinks the Lucayans might have used these areas as burial sites for their dead. With more investigation, the mystery of the skeletons may soon be solved. But scientists believe that other secrets are waiting to be uncovered in blue holes. "There are hundreds left that no human has seen," Broad says. "It's a whole other world for exploration."

A BLUE HOLE OFF BELIZE

25

Bet you didn't know

8 deep facts about caves

1 Certain ice caves in Iceland are filled with hot springs.

2 1,000-year-old popcorn was found in a Utah cave.

3 Cave bears, which are now extinct, weighed around 1,500 (680 kg) pounds.

4 A cave in American Fork Canyon was used as a dance hall during World War II.

5 Caves can be formed by earthquakes.

6 Many cave-dwelling fish don't have eyes.

7 Ancient cave paintings in Australia show an almost 8-foot-tall (2.4-m) bird.

8 Some doctors in the 1800s thought cave air could cure illness.

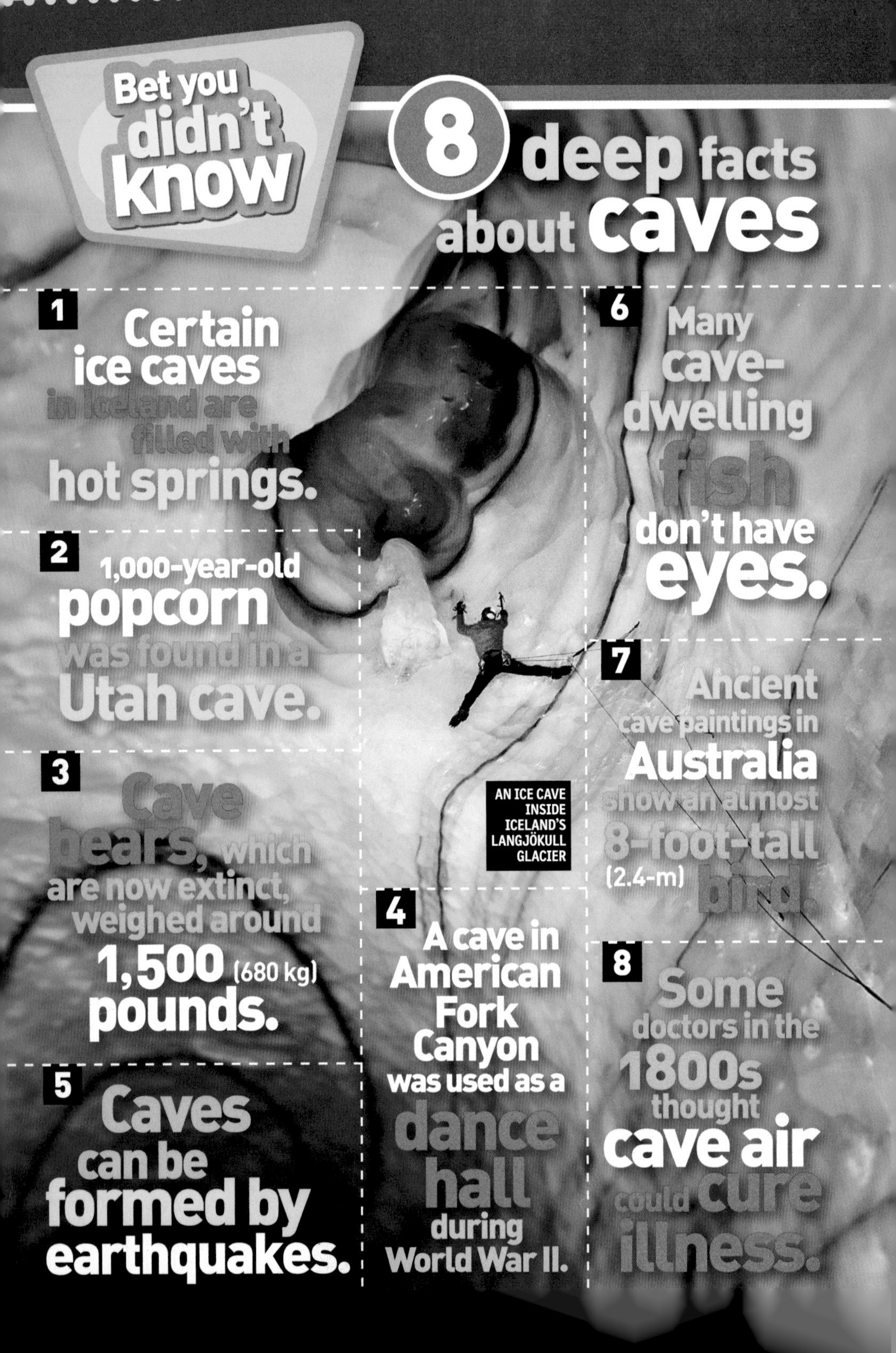

AN ICE CAVE INSIDE ICELAND'S LANGJÖKULL GLACIER

MYSTERY IN THE SKIES

What happened to Amelia Earhart?

PILOT AMELIA EARHART AND HER COPILOT FRED NOONAN REVIEW A FLIGHT CHART.

A Lockheed Electra airplane took off into the sky over the Pacific, with no sign of trouble ahead. At the controls was famous American pilot Amelia Earhart, the first woman to fly solo across the Atlantic Ocean. Alongside her sat Fred Noonan. Together, they planned to fly 2,556 miles (4,113 km) from the island nation of Papua New Guinea to Howland Island in the South Pacific Ocean, the third-to-last leg in a trip around the world. The date was July 2, 1937. That was the last time anyone ever saw them.

Earhart's disappearance remains a mystery. Now, more than 75 years later, new research is shedding light on what may have happened during that fateful flight.

SPLASH AND SINK

The most widely accepted explanation for what happened to Earhart is that her plane crashed into the ocean. According to a U.S. Coast Guard boat keeping radio communication with the Electra during the flight, Earhart said she was searching for the island but could not find it—and that she was running low on fuel. No underwater wreckage has been found, but searches continue. A recent expedition used a deep-sea sonar system to scan a wide area around which the Electra likely went down, but it did not find any sign of a plane.

CRASH LANDING

Others think the Electra landed on the remote Pacific atoll Nikumaroro and that Earhart and Noonan lived as castaways. Newly discovered evidence found on Nikumaroro—such as fragments of glass made in the U.S. and a cosmetics jar—have caused speculation that Earhart lived there for an unknown amount of time before she died. But despite multiple expeditions to the island, no plane or other conclusive evidence has been found.

LEGACY

Other less likely theories—including one claiming that Earhart acted as a spy during World War II and then changed her identity—are still floating around, offering extra ideas for what happened. As the search for answers continues, one thing remains certain: Amelia Earhart will always be one of the most celebrated aviators in history.

GETTING the SHOT

Capturing good photographs of wild animals can be tough. To get amazing pictures of them, nature photographers often tap into their wild side, thinking and even acting like the creatures they're snapping. Whether tracking deadly snakes or swimming with penguins, the artists must be daring—but they also need to know when to keep their distance. Six amazing photographers tell NG KIDS the behind-the-scenes stories of how they got these incredible shots.

MY SHOT

EARN BADGES FOR YOUR CRITTER PICS.
ngkidsmyshot.com

FANG FOCUS

PHOTOGRAPHER: Mattias Klum
ANIMAL: Jameson's mamba
SHOOT SITE: Cameroon, Africa

"The Jameson's mamba is beautiful but dangerous. It produces highly toxic venom. My team searched for weeks for the reptile, asking locals about the best spots to see one. At last we came across a Jameson's mamba peeking out from tree leaves. Carefully, I inched closer. It's important to make this kind of snake think that you don't see it. Otherwise it might feel threatened and strike you. At about four and a half feet (1.4 m) away, I took the picture. Then I backed up and the snake slid off."

SECRETS FROM
AMAZING WILDLIFE PHOTOGRAPHERS

Usually solitary creatures, oceanic whitetip sharks have been observed swimming with pods of pilot whales.

SHARK TALE

PHOTOGRAPHER: Brian Skerry
ANIMAL: Oceanic whitetip shark
SHOOT SITE: The Bahamas

"I wanted to photograph an endangered oceanic whitetip shark. So I set sail with a group of scientists to an area where some had been sighted. Days later, the dorsal fin of a whitetip rose from the water near our boat. One scientist was lowered in a metal cage into the water to observe the fish. Then I dived in. Because I wasn't behind the protective bars, I had to be very careful. These nine-foot (2.7-m) sharks can be aggressive, but this one was just curious. She swam around us for two hours and allowed me to take pictures of her. She was the perfect model."

LEAPS and BOUNDS

PHOTOGRAPHER: Nick Nichols
ANIMAL: Bengal tiger
SHOOT SITE: Bandhavgarh
National Park, India

Fewer than 2,500 Bengal tigers are left in the wild.

"While following a tiger along a cliff, I saw him leap from the edge to his secret watering hole and take a drink. I wanted a close-up of the cat, but it wouldn't have been safe to approach him. Figuring he'd return to the spot, I set up a camera on the cliff that shoots off an infrared beam. Walking into the beam triggers the camera to click. The device was there for three months, but this was the only shot I got of the cat. Being near tigers makes the hair stand up on my arm. It was a gift to encounter such a magnificent creature."

National Geographic Emerging Explorer **Jill Pruetz** studies savanna chimpanzees in Senegal, Africa.

So what does she pack when she heads out to the field? Find out ...

1 BANDAGES
"WITH ALL OF THE WALKING I DO, I ALWAYS HAVE BLISTERS. BANDAGES HELP ME KEEP UP WITH THE CHIMPS EVEN WITH SORE FEET."

2 WATER BOTTLE
"I walk up to 20 miles (32 km) in a day, depending on where the chimps are. It's crucial to drink throughout the day."

3 POCKETKNIFE "YOU NEVER KNOW WHEN YOU MIGHT NEED THIS ALL-PURPOSE TOOL. I GAVE MYSELF A REALLY BAD HAIR-CUT WITH A POCKETKNIFE ONCE IN THE FIELD."

16 THINGS IN AN EXPLOR

4 CAMERA
"I share my pictures with other people so they can enjoy chimps as much as I do."

5 SNACKS
"In Senegal, we don't have access to many packaged foods, so I usually bring snacks like cookies, peanuts, and canned meat to eat on the go."

6 DATA BOOK
"I FILL THE PAGES OF THESE BOOKS WITH DATA. I CARRY THEM BACK HOME WITH ME ON THE PLANE BECAUSE I DON'T WANT THEM TO GET LOST WITH CHECKED BAGGAGE!"

7 ALLERGY MEDICINE
"CHIMPS LOVE HONEY, AND THEY RAID BEEHIVES FREQUENTLY. THE BEES GET AGGRESSIVE! IN CASE I GET STUNG, ANTIHISTAMINE REDUCES THE SWELLING."

8

FLASHLIGHT

"For walking in the dark and to make sure I see venomous snakes that come out at night."

9

MOSQUITO HEAD NET

"Mosquitoes can be bad during the wet season. A net protects me from bites and malaria."

10

BINOCULARS

"I USE THESE TO SEE DETAILS LIKE EXACTLY HOW MANY FRUITS THE CHIMPS EAT, OR WHAT PARTS OF A PLANT ARE EATEN."

11

MIRROR "HAVING A LITTLE MIRROR HANDY IS KEY TO HELPING ME REMOVE A BEE'S STINGER. THE LONGER IT STAYS IN YOUR SKIN, THE MORE VENOM IS GOING INTO YOUR BODY."

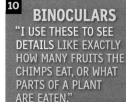

12

TOURNIQUET AND PAIN MEDICINE

"I MAY FACE A POISONOUS SNAKE, A LEOPARD, OR RISK FALLING DOWN A RAVINE. I LIKE TO BE PREPARED FOR ANY SORT OF DANGER."

ER'S BACKPACK

13

GPS WITH 2-WAY RADIO

"THIS LETS ME TRACK THE CHIMPS' MOVEMENTS THROUGHOUT THEIR HOME RANGE—AND HELPS ME FIND MY WAY HOME IN THE DARK!"

14

RAIN JACKET

"THIS IS ESSENTIAL TO STAYING WARM AND DRY DURING THE RAINY SEASON. I JUST HAVE TO MAKE SURE IT'S NOT A BRIGHT COLOR, WHICH BOTHERS THE CHIMPS."

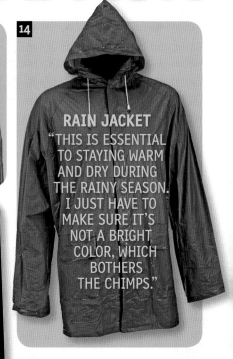

15

WATERPROOF PENS "I follow the

chimps even when it rains. The only way to take data is to use waterproof notebooks and pens."

16

CELL PHONE

"I'll use it in case there's an emergency, or to text the whereabouts of the chimps to my research assistant."

SURVIVAL STORY

ORANGUTAN
TO THE RESCUE

After getting lost in the rain forest, National Geographic explorer Agustín Fuentes receives some very unlikely help. Read on to find out how Fuentes found his way home.

All Agustín Fuentes wanted to do was find the rare maroon leaf monkey. He'd been spending some time at Camp Leakey, an orangutan research camp on Borneo, a large, mountainous island in southeast Asia, and he got the urge to take a day trip into the dense rain forest to seek one out. So he packed up his compass, headlamp, and small backpack, and off he went.

After four hours of following marked trails, Fuentes thought he caught a glimpse of a maroon leaf monkey. But then it scampered away into the rain forest. He had a decision to make: Should he stay on the trails and hope he sees the monkey again? Or should he follow it?

"I took a risk and went off trail," Fuentes says.

Bad move. Forty-five minutes later, Fuentes found himself deep in the rain forest, with no maroon leaf monkey in sight. He used his compass to make a guess as to which direction he was heading and kept walking.

"Another 30 minutes passed, and I began to get a little nervous," says Fuentes. "Darkness was coming on quickly."

Fuentes tried to find comfort in the fact that he was in a place where another human had likely never been. As he looked around the rain forest, there was so much to admire.

"At one point, I spotted a shimmering metallic blue pool in an opening. I moved closer, and the blue image vibrated. Suddenly, hundreds of blue butterflies took flight before me," he says. "They had been feasting on wild pig droppings on the ground a few feet away."

Pulling out his compass, Fuentes headed south, thinking he'd eventually hit the river, if not a trail first. It paid off. After about 20 minutes, he saw an unmarked trail. Seconds later, he heard a rustling. He shone his headlight toward the sound. It was an orangutan! And not just any orangutan: Fuentes recognized right away that she was one of the tribe being rehabilitated at camp.

"We looked at each other, and she held out her hand to me," he says. "Then she led me, hand in hand, to camp. Just like me, she was heading back for the evening."

HOW TO
SURVIVE A
KILLER BEE ATTACK!

1 Buzz Off
Killer bees—or Africanized honey-bees—only attack when their hive is being threatened. If you see several bees buzzing near you, a hive is probably close by. Heed their "back off" attitude and slowly walk away.

2 Don't Join the Swat Team
Your first instinct might be to start swatting and slapping the bees. But that just makes the buzzers angry. Loud noises have the same effect, so don't start screaming, either. Just get away.

3 Don't Play Hide-and-Seek
Hives are often near water, but don't even think about outlasting the bees underwater. They'll hover and attack when you come up for air, even if you try to swim for it.

4 Make Like Speedy Gonzalez
Killer bees will chase you, but they'll give up when you're far enough away from the hive (usually about 200 yards [183 m]). Take off running and don't stop until the buzzing does.

5 Create a Cover-Up
Killer bees often go for the face and throat, which are the most dangerous places to be stung. While you're on the run, protect your face and neck with your hands, or pull your shirt over your head.

HOW TO SURVIVE A
BEE STING!

1. De-Sting Yourself
First, get inside or to a cool place. Then, remove the stinger by scraping a fingernail over the area, like you would to get a splinter out. Do not squeeze the stinger or use tweezers unless you absolutely can't get it out any other way.

2. Put It on Ice
Wash the area with soap and water and apply a cool compress to reduce swelling. Continue icing the spot for 20 minutes every hour. Place a washcloth or towel between the ice and your skin.

3. Treat It Right
With a parent's permission, take an antihistamine and gently rub a hydrocortisone cream on the sting site.

4. Hands Off
Make sure you don't scratch the sting. You'll just increase the pain and swelling.

5. Recognize Danger
If you experience severe burning and itching, swelling of the throat and/or mouth, difficulty breathing, weakness, or nausea, or if you already know you are allergic to bees, get to an emergency room immediately.

33

QUIZ WHIZ

How much do you know about all things adventure? Quiz yourself and find out!

ANSWERS BELOW

① **What journey was Amelia Earhart about to complete when she disappeared?**
a. a flight across the U.S.A.
b. a flight from New York to London
c. a flight to the North Pole
d. a flight around the world

② **True or false?** If you dive about 30 feet (9 m) into some blue holes, the water turns pink—and poisonous.

③ **Which extinct cave-dwelling animal weighed around 1,500 pounds (680 kg)?**
a. mammoth bat
b. cave bear
c. Icelandic tortoise
d. woolly tiger

④ **You've been stung by a bee. Ouch! What's the first thing you should do to treat the sting?**
a. Swat and slap the bee away.
b. Remove the stinger with your fingernail and apply ice to the affected area.
c. Squeeze the stinger out with tweezers.
d. Ignore the sting and hope the pain goes away.

⑤ **What does a geochemist study?**
a. the chemical makeup of rocks, planets, and oceans
b. how rocks react to different chemicals in a lab
c. the history of Earth
d. maps of the world

Not **STUMPED** yet? Check out the *NATIONAL GEOGRAPHIC KIDS QUIZ WHIZ* collection for more crazy **ADVENTURE** questions!

ANSWERS: 1. d; 2. True; 3. b; 4. b; 5. a

HOMEWORK HELP

How to Write a Perfect Essay

Need to write an essay? Does the assignment feel as big as climbing Mount Everest? Fear not. You're up to the challenge! The following step-by-step tips will help you with this monumental task.

1 **BRAINSTORM.** Sometimes the subject matter of your essay is assigned to you, sometimes it's not. Either way, you have to decide what you want to say. Start by brainstorming some ideas, writing down any thoughts you have about the subject. Then read over everything you've come up with and consider which idea you think is the strongest. Ask yourself what you want to write about the most. Keep in mind the goal of your essay. Can you achieve the goal of the assignment with this topic? If so, you're good to go.

2 **WRITE A TOPIC SENTENCE.** This is the main idea of your essay, a statement of your thoughts on the subject. Again, consider the goal of your essay. Think of the topic sentence as an introduction that tells your reader what the rest of your essay will be about.

3 **OUTLINE YOUR IDEAS.** Once you have a good topic sentence, you then need to support that main idea with more detailed information, facts, thoughts, and examples. These supporting points answer one question about your topic sentence—"Why?" This is where research and perhaps more brainstorming come in. Then organize these points in the way you think makes the most sense, probably in order of importance. Now you have an outline for your essay.

4 **ON YOUR MARK, GET SET, WRITE!** Follow your outline, using each of your supporting points as the topic sentence of its own paragraph. Use descriptive words to get your ideas across to the reader. Go into detail, using specific information to tell your story or make your point. Stay on track, making sure that everything you include is somehow related to the main idea of your essay. Use transitions to make your writing flow.

5 **WRAP IT UP.** Finish your essay with a conclusion that summarizes your entire essay and restates your main idea.

6 **PROOFREAD AND REVISE.** Check for errors in spelling, capitalization, punctuation, and grammar. Look for ways to make your writing clear, understandable, and interesting. Use descriptive verbs, adjectives, or adverbs when possible. It also helps to have someone else read your work to point out things you might have missed. Then make the necessary corrections and changes in a second draft. Repeat this revision process once more to make your final draft as good as you can.

Almanac Explorer!

I eat alMost any kind of meat.

This is clue #3! Collect them all and unscramble the letters to find the secret animal. Enter the animal name at kids.nationalgeographic.com/almanac-2016!

Amazing Animals

Four koalas gather in a line in Australia.

16
Cutest Animals of 2016

From arctic foxes to zebras, baby animals easily qualify as some of the cutest creatures on Earth. Here's NG Kids' roundup of cuddly critters that are sure to make you say *awww*.

1

BLUE-EYED LEMUR

It's pretty hard to look away from Dimbi, a member of the critically endangered blue-eyed black lemur species. Born in France's Mulhouse Zoo, Dimbi belongs to one of only two groups of primates besides humans that can have blue eyes in addition to brown.

2

RHINO RUN

A rhino's feelings wouldn't get hurt if you called it a name. (Not that you would.) Rhinos have thick skin—literally. About an inch (2.5 cm) thick, rhino skin is built to protect the animal from thorns and biting flies in its African home. A rhino's size is nothing to mess with either. One of the world's biggest babies, rhinos can weigh 140 pounds (63.5 kg) at birth!

3

SAY CHEESE

Nice fur coat! Snow leopards live in some of the coldest parts of Asia, where they need the fluffiest, fuzziest fur to keep warm. These rare cats have large, fur-covered paws that act like snowshoes so they don't sink into deep snow. Snow leopards also beat the chill by sleeping with their tails wrapped around them like a blanket.

4

WILL SQUIRT FOR FOOD

Billy the porcupine puffer fish is one of about 30 creatures in his tropical tank at the Blue Reef Aquarium in Tynemouth, England. When he's hungry, he squirts water at his keepers to let them know he wants to eat first.

5

HANGING OUT

Hang in there, buddy! Opossums have some cool secret powers, including expert climbing skills. They're also immune to rattlesnake venom. Plus, opossums have 50 teeth, more than any other North American land mammal.

6

APE-DORABLE

This young chimp looks sort of like a human baby (with *way* more hair). Africa's chimpanzees do many things humans do—they live in families where they kiss, hug, and tickle each other, and even laugh when they play!

7

FUR BABY

Fluffy cottontail rabbits, found in North and South America, get their name from their adorable cotton-ball tails. But it doesn't get much cuter than their perky ears, which constantly move in all directions to listen for predators.

8

ON THE LOOKOUT

Native to parts of Africa, meerkats are constantly on alert for predators such as jackals and falcons. Clever critters, meerkats share the group's work—including guard duty and babysitting. Everything gets taken care of by working as a team. *Hakuna matata!* No worries!

9 SWEET SIBLINGS

These recently hatched baby gentoo penguins look ready to explore their home in the Antarctic area, but they'll actually stay with Mom at the nest for up to a month. Gentoo penguins build nests of pebbles and moss. Some gentoos even bring their partners pebbles as gifts.

10 COOL 'DO

Galápagos sea lion pups are born with long hair called lanugo, which helps them keep warm until they develop blubber, or fat. By the time a sea lion is two years old, it will be one of the fastest mammals in the ocean, zipping through the water at bursts of up to 25 miles an hour (40 km/h).

11 BAMBOO BREAK

Bamboo, *delish!* Red pandas, or "fire foxes," as they're sometimes called, dine on bamboo like their black-and-white namesake does. But unlike giant pandas, Asia's red pandas have cute white whiskers. The sensitive hairs help the pandas navigate narrow spaces, especially at night.

13

VERY CHEEKY

The Eastern chipmunk, a North American rodent, stays alert while it fills its cheek pouches with everything from seeds and nuts to worms and bird eggs. If danger comes along, it calls out to warn others.

12

NOT-SO-SCARY BEAST

There's not much not to "like" about Beast, the Hungarian sheepdog. The fluffy pup from Palo Alto, California, U.S.A., has more than 2 million fans on Facebook!

14

BEAR-Y CUTE

North America's black bears weigh as little as a hockey puck when they're first born and even purr as they nurse from their mother. After they stop nursing, hungry bears munch on almost anything—insects, nuts and berries, even grass.

15

BABIES ON BOARD

When common loon chicks hatch, they're almost immediately on the go—Mom carries her little ones on her back to protect them from predators. Once grown, loons can dive down nearly 250 feet (76 m) and hold their breath for up to eight minutes as they fish.

16

SNOW SWEET

These pink-faced Japanese macaques——also called snow monkeys——are found only in Japan. During the freezing winter, some groups treat themselves to a resort-style dip in natural hot springs. Others wash their food in salt water to give it a little extra flavor.

HOW TO SPEAK DOG

C'MON! CATCH ME IF YOU CAN!

Watch a group of dogs playing at a park. These pups don't know each other, yet within a few minutes of meeting, they'll start playing a doggie game. As they wrestle and chase, it's obvious they're "talking." But instead of words, they're using body language. Learning to "listen" to your pup's body language will help you get closer to your pet. Check out what your dog may be trying to tell you through these five behaviors.

A dog's tail should never be pulled. Pulling it could dislocate the bones and cause nerve damage. Then the tail won't move anymore.

THE PLAY-BOW

The play-bow means your pup is ready for fun with another dog. She'll crouch down with her "elbows" almost touching the ground, her tail waving madly, and her rump in the air. After holding this pose for a few seconds, she'll take off running, checking over her shoulder to make sure the other dog is following. When her new playmate comes bounding after her, the two dogs will race and chase. If one dog bangs into the other too hard, it'll do a quick play-bow to say, "Oops!" So the next time your dog play-bows, let the games begin!

THE SHOWY TAIL

A dog strutting around with his tail held high is showing he's in charge. This works even better if the dog has a tail that's easy to see. Maybe that's why wolves have big bushy tails, and why many dogs have tails with lighter-colored hair on the underside. The light color shows when their tails go up, a perfect signal flag.

WANT MORE?

Check out the National Geographic book *How to Speak Dog.*

THE BEGGING STARE

That sweet little beggar staring directly at you while you eat isn't starving. He's controlling you. A staring dog is communicating with you. Outside, he might be telling you that he's the boss so you'd better not come too close. But at the dinner table, he's probably begging for a scrap. And if you sneak him a bite, he might think he's got you well trained—and taking orders from *him!* So ignore a staring, begging dog. Make sure that nobody else feeds him from the table, either. Eventually the pooch will realize *you're* in charge and that begging doesn't work. Next time you tell him to go lie down, he might just do it.

Scientists say dogs are four times more likely to steal food when they think you're not looking.

A dog can make about 100 different facial expressions.

THE BUTT-SNIFF

Dogs sure have a weird way of saying hello. Instead of shaking paws, they sniff each other's rear ends! One dog lets the other sniff him. Then they switch positions. Why? Dogs identify friends by the way they smell, not by looks. It's the anal glands—located in a pooch's bottom—that give each pup a signature scent. To a dog, another pup's personal smell carries as much data as an ID card. This information tells if a dog is healthy or sick, young or old, and even what he ate for dinner.

THE BELLY-UP

Time for a belly rub! That's what it looks like a dog is saying when she rolls onto her back with her front legs bent and her belly exposed. When you start rubbing, sometimes one hind leg will kick, and she'll look super-content. The kicking leg is just a reflex—kind of like what happens when the doctor taps your knee with a rubber hammer. But the real meaning of this dog's position is submission and trust. She's saying that you're in charge, and she's OK with that.

45

5 SiLLY Pet Tricks

1 GOAT SKATEBOARDS

Jumping on her skateboard, Happie the goat zips down driveways and cruises along sidewalks. The animal first showed her zeal for wheels when she tried to leap on a bicycle that owner Melody Cooke was riding. Cooke decided to get Happie her very own skateboard and train her to ride. After a lot of practice and goodies, the goat learned some sweet boarding moves: Happie can coast for more than 100 feet (30 m) without stopping. Talk about being on a roll.

2 HORSE PLAYS B-BALL

Before he makes a slam dunk, Amos the miniature horse looks around to see if people are watching. "Amos definitely likes an audience," owner Shelly Mizrahi says. To teach him to "play" basketball, Mizrahi gave Amos carrot slices each time he touched his nose to a hoop set on a short stand. Later Amos learned to pick up a small ball with his teeth and place it in the hoop. Scoring baskets has become the horse's all-time favorite activity. The hoofed athlete once dunked the ball a hundred times in a row. "Amos can also paint and play a xylophone with a mallet," Mizrahi says. "But if I place a paintbrush, a musical instrument, and a basketball in front of him, he always goes for the basketball."

Why won't you see Jax the cat's paw prints on the floor? Because the kitty can move around on a large, rolling ball! "Jax has always loved perching on narrow surfaces," owner Samantha Martin says. "I thought she'd like even cooler balancing acts." To prepare for the trick, Jax practiced standing on a smaller ball set in a bowl so it couldn't move. Then Martin placed her on a bigger ball at one end of a short track. On the other end were yummy cat treats. The clever kitty quickly figured out that if she inched backward on the ball, she could move it down the track—and get her delicious reward.

CAT WALKS ON BALL 3

Mudslinger the pig can be a real hog when it comes to music. He enjoys creating tunes with horns, and once he gets started, he sometimes doesn't want to stop. Trainer John Vincent introduced the pig to the horns by tooting some in front of him. After watching his owner, the curious pig tried squeezing the instruments with his mouth to make noise. Whenever he continued, Vincent fed him juicy grapes to keep him motivated. The curly-tailed rock star creates new sound patterns whenever he plays.

5 MACAW TAKES UP SKIING

Luna the hyacinth macaw loves to fly—down a ski slope! Owner Mark Steiger knew the eight-year-old bird would be a natural skier. "Hyacinth macaws like Luna have strong legs," he says. First, Luna practiced walking while clutching handles on tiny skis with her claws. Then Steiger taught her to slide down a custom-made four-foot (1.2-m)-tall slope on the skis, rewarding the bird with treats at the bottom. The macaw even learned to take a "ski lift" up her slope. With her hardy beak, she grasps onto a metal ring that her owner uses to pull her up the slide. Just before Luna whooshes back down, she leans forward like a competitive skier. "She picked that up all on her own," Steiger says. "Luna's a total pro."

NauGHty PETS

CAUGHT ON CAMERA

NAME **King Floppy**

FAVORITE ACTIVITY
Weighing himself to judge how much more can fit in his belly

FAVORITE TOY **An oversize food bowl to fit big treats**

PET PEEVE
Being called cute

I DEMAND A BIGGER SCALE AND GIANT CARROTS!

AND THEY WONDER WHY THERE'S ALWAYS HAIR IN THE SINK.

NAME **Landry**

FAVORITE ACTIVITY
Going for a swim in the sink

FAVORITE TOY
Floating hair balls

PET PEEVE **Plastic kiddie pools**

I'LL GET RID OF THIS HOMEWORK SO SHE HAS MORE TIME TO PLAY WITH ME.

NAME **Sadie**

FAVORITE ACTIVITY
Chewing up school essays

FAVORITE TOY **Erasers**

PET PEEVE **Computer assignments**

REAL ANIMAL HEROES!

THESE ANIMALS SHOW AMAZING BRAVERY.

DOG SAVES KID FROM TRUCK

Geo the German shepherd mix follows ten-year-old Charlie Riley everywhere. Naturally the pup goes along on family walks. One day Charlie, his mom, and two younger brothers are standing at a street corner. Geo is sitting at Charlie's side. Suddenly ...

"We hear a roar," Charlie's mother says. An out-of-control pickup jumps the curb. It's heading straight for Charlie!

But Geo makes a flying leap. "He hits me so hard I fall over," Charlie says. The speeding truck slams into Geo instead. They rush an injured Geo to the animal hospital for emergency surgery.

"My dog could have died," Charlie says. And my son could have too, thinks his mother. But he didn't—thanks to Geo.

CAT DETECTS LOW BLOOD SUGAR

Patricia Peter is asleep when her cat, Monty, bites her hand. "It's the hand I poke to test my blood sugar level," she says. Peter has diabetes, a serious disease that requires frequent blood testing. Peter pushes the cat away, but Monty bites harder. Peter gets up and Monty leads her to the kitchen, then jumps on the counter beside Peter's testing kit.

Peter tests, and her sugar level is dangerously low. She pops some sugar pills, and her level returns to normal. According to Peter's doctor, Monty knew something was wrong by smelling her breath and tasting her skin. "He's my guardian angel," Peter says.

PUP DETECTS SEIZURES

Zoe the pit bull mix is Gretchen Jett's best gift ever. Born deaf, the 11-year-old girl from Nevada, U.S.A., also has epilepsy, a brain disease that causes seizures. Because of this, she usually has to play indoors. So her dad gets a dog to keep his daughter company.

Just two nights later, Zoe bursts into Gretchen's parents' room. "I get up, thinking she needs to go outside," Gretchen's dad says. "Instead, Zoe runs in a circle and bolts straight into Gretchen's room. She's suffering a bad seizure." Circling and running becomes Zoe's signal. "When she does that we know something is wrong with Gretchen," her dad says. Zoe knows that Gretchen needs her.

49

PAW ENFORCEMENT

★★★★★★★★★★★★★★★★★★★★★★★★★★

DOGS ON DUTY SNIFF OUT SMUGGLERS.

NON-POISONOUS GOPHER SNAKES **ARE USED FOR TRAINING.**

Walking his beat at the Honolulu International Airport in Hawaii, Taylor stops to observe two women waiting for a flight to the U.S. mainland. Taylor's partner, Inspector Edna Tanaid, has no reason to believe the women might be smugglers, but Taylor smells trouble. He's a skilled, no-nonsense detective that works for the federal government. There's only one thing Taylor likes more than busting smugglers—the mouthwatering flavor of meaty dog treats. Taylor is a beagle mix. And you're in trouble if he sits down next to you and wags his tail so hard it looks ready to fly off.

BUSTED BY A DOG

"Where are your fruits?" Tanaid asks.

"We aren't carrying any," the women reply. Taylor excitedly wags, pants, and aims his sensitive nose back and forth at the women's

jacket pockets. Sure enough, they have mangoes in their pockets. Tanaid seizes the contraband, or illegal goods, and gives Taylor some extra petting along with his meaty reward.

Sniffing around may sound like fun—and for Taylor, it is—but it's important work. Mangoes could contain the larvae of the Mediterranean fruit fly, a variety that lives in Hawaii but not in the continental United States. If these fruit flies reach the mainland, they could devastate American crops, costing billions of dollars.

Taylor was born with his great nose, but before putting it to work, he and his canine colleagues get about three months of training at the National Detector Dog Training Center in Georgia. There the new recruits learn the basic scent of contraband and how to find it in bags, boxes, and pockets—an advanced game of hide-and-seek.

CANINES AT WORK

In addition to sniffing around travelers and baggage, dog teams examine U.S. and international mail, which is a huge job. Janelle Michalesko checks out arriving cargo and mail with her canine partner, Khaz, at JFK Airport in New York City. Khaz is equal parts Chesapeake Bay and Labrador retriever, a big energetic mix that makes him perfect for patrolling long warehouses and inspecting big boxes.

GOOD JOB

Along with the fruits and vegetables they discover, Khaz and Michalesko regularly find mailed meat products that could carry diseases. The handler guesses that it would take her a full day to search a warehouse that Khaz can clear in 15 minutes. Other breeds do different jobs. Tiny, fearless Jack Russell terriers, for instance, are perfect for finding brown tree snakes in cargo leaving Guam, a U.S. island in the Pacific Ocean. If stowaway snakes spread to Hawaii, it could doom the state's rare birds.

SMART PUPS

For sniffing baggage and passengers at airports, beagles are the ideal breed. "They're very friendly and people usually aren't intimidated by them," says Andrew Bateman, a Customs and Border Protection (CBP) handler who, with pup partner Cayenne, guards the Hartsfield-Jackson Atlanta International Airport. Detector dogs don't just smell well; they're trained to smell the difference between contraband and safe snacks.

Someone might assume a dog as valuable as Cayenne was raised in a special kennel and trained from birth. "She was actually found on the side of the road on a highway," Bateman says. All detector dogs that deal with agricultural items were adopted. Many, like Cayenne, are found at animal shelters, while others are donated by owners or breeders.

"I couldn't for the life of me figure out why somebody would give away a dog that's so handsome," says handler Jonathan Saito about his stocky beagle partner, Bruno, a former pound dog. "He's just an incredible dog to work with. We say 'work,' but actually, it's a game for the dogs."

Tanaid agrees. "Taking in one of these dogs and giving it a second chance at doing an important public service is great. And the dogs love what they do."

DOGS SEARCH CARS AND LUGGAGE.

IN ONLY TWO DAYS, TAYLOR FOUND ALL THIS.

Protecting American Agriculture

51

EXTRAORDINARY Animals

BLIND PUP HAS GUIDE DOG

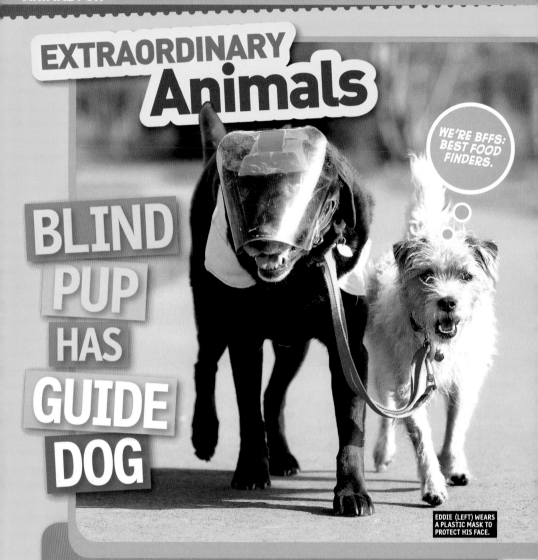

WE'RE BFFS: BEST FOOD FINDERS.

EDDIE (LEFT) WEARS A PLASTIC MASK TO PROTECT HIS FACE.

Cardiff, Wales

Eddie the Labrador retriever loves splashing in a creek near his home. But often the blind dog is unable to find his way back to the bank. That's when Milo the mixed terrier steps in, barking so Eddie can follow his voice to the creek edge. The "guide dog" then grabs on to the Lab's protective face shield to lead him to dry land.

Eddie and Milo have been best buds for years. When Eddie lost his sight, Milo acted as the pooch's very own guide. Indoors, Eddie follows Milo's scent, which helps Eddie to avoid bumping into furniture. If the blind pooch wanders away outside, Milo runs off to find him and lead him home. The terrier even sits protectively on Eddie's back while the Lab sleeps.

"Eddie and Milo have a strong bond," dog behaviorist Mary Burch says. "Milo cares for Eddie, and Eddie pays more attention to sounds and smells so he can follow Milo." The pair uses teamwork even at play. "They love running around together holding the ends of a giant branch in their mouths," owner Angie Baker-Stedham says. "Eddie would be lost without Milo."

MAKE SURE TO GET MY GOOD SIDE.

Seawalker GREEN ISLAND AUSTRALIA

PHOTOBOMBING FISH!

MY FAVORITE GAME IS ANGRY BIRDS.

Green Island, Australia
When divers off of Green Island plunge underwater to check out coral reefs, Gavin the parrotfish prepares for his close-up. As a photographer snaps pictures of the tourists, Gavin sneaks in front of the camera lens and poses with people.

The fish has been "photobombing" visitors for a couple of years. "Gavin is probably in eight out of every ten snapshots taken," says marine life expert David Joyce of Seawalker Green Island, a company that leads eco-friendly tours of the reefs where Gavin lives and photographs guests on dives. But this parrotfish isn't practicing to become a gilled supermodel. He's just attracted by bubbles from the divers' helmets, camera flashes, and his reflection in the lens.

JEREMY PLAYS ON HIS iPAD.

JEREM

PENGUINS PLAY WITH iPAD

Long Beach, California
Forget about catching fish. Jeremy and Newsom the Magellanic penguins are all about catching mice—on an iPad.

Jeremy and Newsom's caretakers introduced them to a digital game to keep the birds entertained at the Aquarium of the Pacific. Designed for cats, the game features mice zipping across the screen. Players get points for tapping on the critters before they disappear. "It challenges them," penguin keeper Sara Mandel says. Newsom and Jeremy take turns perched in front of their iPad, pecking on the virtual rodents with their beaks. Newsom once racked up 1,600 points!

"He's in it to win it," Mandel says.

ANIMAL RASCALS

(5) mischief-makers you'll never forget

Do you know people who are clever or sneaky, who enjoy pulling crazy pranks or fooling you? Sometimes animals exhibit this same type of behavior. See for yourself with these five stories about animal tricksters.

1

UP AND OVER

One day, Mavis Knight, of Toronto, Canada, spots a raccoon on her garage roof. From there he climbs a nearby tree until he reaches the utility lines. Then he stands up on the bottom of the wire, holds the top one, and side-steps across—all the way to a neighbor's backyard. A week later, he does it again.

Why? A tall, wooden fence separates the properties. Instead of taking time to run around the barrier, this furry daredevil has found a quicker "highway" over the top. "He's very clever," Knight says. "I'm no longer angry at him. I just enjoy him." It's like having front-row seats at the circus.

A RACCOON USES A HIGH WIRE TO GET FROM YARD TO YARD.

2

PULLING TEETH

Bill Exner of Waterville, Maine, U.S.A., is eating a peanut butter sandwich in bed when he gets sleepy. So he takes out his false teeth, sets them on the nightstand, and falls asleep.

The next morning, his teeth are gone! He searches under the bed and behind the dressers. No pearly whites. Then, Exner remembers seeing a mouse near his bed the night before. He pries off the baseboard, shines a flashlight into the space behind the wall, and ... ah ha! Exner spots his dentures—safe and licked clean. He livetraps two sneaky little mice, then releases them on a college campus. Luckily, it's not a law school.

3

GONE FISHIN'

Bailey the Labrador retriever has eaten something he shouldn't. "His owners see it poking out behind his rib cage, but they don't know what it is," says Gary Sloniker, a veterinarian in Spooner, Wisconsin, U.S.A. The vet takes the dog in for an x-ray. What do they see? A 24-inch (61-cm) ice-fishing pole!

Sloniker thinks Bailey was chewing the handle when he stretched his neck, making the pole slide right into the puppy's mouth. His swallowing reflex kicked in, and down it went.

The vet reaches down Bailey's throat with long-handled tweezers and "fishes" out the hookless pole.

THIS X-RAY OF BAILEY'S INNARDS SHOWS THE ICE-FISHING POLE HE SWALLOWED.

THE ROD THAT BAILEY SWALLOWED WAS SIMILAR TO THIS ONE BUT DIDN'T HAVE THE REEL ATTACHED.

4

SWEET THIEF

Huh? Jo Adams opens her candy store in Estes Park, Colorado, U.S.A., to find dirt on the checkout counter and a candy tin on the floor. Curious, she plays the video from her surveillance cameras.

A small black bear can be seen sliding his claws under the locked front door and jiggling it open. The store is packed with yummy treats, but the bear chooses to chow down on only peanut butter cups, English toffee, fudge balls, and rice cereal treats. Then he tops it all off with four big cookies called—drumroll, please—cookie bears.

5

NIGHT MUSIC

It's a humid July evening in Katonah, New York. At the Caramoor Music Festival, an opera is being performed on an outdoor stage. The audience falls silent as one of the female stars begins to sing. *Tra-la-la ... CROAK! Tra ... CROAK! La ... CROAK!*

Operagoers look at each other. They shift in their seats. "The croaking sounds very loud and very close," says Paul Rosenblum, managing director of the festival. By Act 2, Michael Barrett, head of Caramoor at the time, can't stand it anymore. Wearing dress clothes, he leaves his seat and goes backstage. He climbs a ladder onto the roof of the nearest building. And there's the culprit: a lone frog no bigger than a golf ball. Barrett catches the little loudmouth and releases him in the woods. The opera continues. And the famous soloist no longer sounds like she has a frog in her throat.

Incredible
Animal Friends

YOU QUACK ME UP.

OWL SNUGGLES
WITH DUCK

CHOP SUEY

LARCH

North Yorkshire, England
Someone forgot to tell Larch the long-eared owl that owls sometimes hunt ducklings. His best friend is a white-crested runner duck named Chop Suey. The two birds spend hours preening—or grooming—each other's feathers at the Kirkleatham Owl and Endangered Species Centre, where they both hatched.

Paired up because neither had siblings, the birds immediately bonded. Chop Suey's fondness for water can be a problem, though. Owl feathers aren't waterproof like duck feathers, so it's hard for owls like Larch to get dry once they're wet.

As the pals grow up, they'll spend less time together. Chop Suey will sleep at night, while the owl will snooze during the day. But until then, the winged friends continue to flock together.

RUNNER DUCK

RANGE Every continent except Antarctica

NAME GAME Runner ducks don't waddle. Like their name says, they can run.

ALSO KNOWN AS A male duck is a drake. A female duck is a hen.

QUACK ATTACK Only hens make quacking sounds; drakes make whispering noises.

LONG-EARED OWL

RANGE North America, Europe, Asia, and parts of Africa

CAMO-OWL Long-eared owls can blend into tree limbs to protect themselves from predators such as eagles and other owls.

X MARKS THE SPOT White feathers form an x between these owls' eyes.

NIGHT HUNTER Even in pitch black, long-eared owls can catch mice, thanks to their excellent hearing.

CAPYBARA

WEIGHT 66 to 155 pounds (30 to 70 kg)

RANGE South America

CLAIM TO FAME The capybara is the world's largest rodent.

LISTEN UP Capybaras bark when they're in danger. They can also purr and whistle.

CAPYBARA PLAYS WITH PUPPIES

Midway, Arkansas

Like a mother duck leading her babies, Cheesecake the capybara is at the head of a parade. But her followers aren't ducklings, or even baby capybaras. They're abandoned dachshund puppies. The seven pups love to wrestle with their rodent babysitter. When they tire of playing, the dachshunds march into Cheesecake's heated pen and curl up next to the capybara in a supersize puppy pile.

The day the orphaned dachshunds arrived, Rocky Ridge Refuge owner Janice Wolf didn't have much time to prepare. Cheesecake's pen was the only place to keep the tiny pups. "Cheesecake was thrilled to have the puppies," Wolf says. But if the pups are naughty—like when they try to grab hay out of the capybara's mouth—Cheesecake isn't afraid to discipline them. "She makes a cute little squeaky noise to scold them," Wolf says.

Capybaras are semiaquatic animals with partially webbed feet. So Cheesecake spends much of her time in water when she's not playing with her pups. "I made her a pen outside with a pool," Wolf says. This way, the pups could watch Cheesecake play in the water. The dachshunds have since been adopted, but a new litter of orphaned pit bull pups have arrived. "I keep an eye on them," Wolf says. "But Cheesecake does all the work. She's the best nanny ever."

> I'M CUTE ENOUGH FOR BOTH OF US.

DACHSHUND

ORIGIN Most experts believe that dachshunds were first bred in Germany to hunt badgers.

MAKES SENSE In German, *dachs* means "badger" and *hund* means "dog."

HOT DOG Because of its shape, this pup is sometimes called a "sausage dog."

FIRST POOCH President Grover Cleveland had a pet dachshund in the White House.

DO ANIMALS LOVE EACH OTHER?

It's a boy! Romani the Asian elephant has just given birth. After nursing, the baby falls asleep and his mom positions herself directly over him. All is quiet in the barn, and the elephant keeper dims the lights. Then this first-time mom does something remarkable: Like a human mother tucking her child into bed, she gently covers her baby with hay.

Is it love? Scientists used to say that love belonged only to humans. Now they aren't so sure. Jaak Panksepp, a neuroscientist at Washington State University, believes that feelings such as love are hardwired into animals' brains and control their behavior.

The most important sensation is the need to feel good. Like people, many animals feel good when they have something to look forward to—and somebody they care about. Keep reading for more stories of animal love.

MOM, LEAN DOWN ... I'VE GOTTA TELL YOU A SECRET.

CARE BEAR

One day, Else Poulsen, a zookeeper at the Detroit Zoo, puts extra branches in Triton the polar bear's enclosure. Why? Poulsen is playing matchmaker. She's bringing a second bear, a female named Bärle, to live with Triton. One look at Bärle turns Triton to mush. It takes a while, but he eventually wins her over with gifts of sugar maple branches.

Later, their cub is born. In the wild, Triton would be long gone. Male polar bears don't stick around once mating season is over, and they do not help raise their young. But Triton continues to bring Bärle gifts, including a plastic toy that Poulsen fills with small treats such as raisins. "They have a strong bond," Poulsen says.

A PRESENT? FOR ME? YOU'RE SO THOUGHTFUL!

HOW COME YOU ALWAYS GET TO SIT UP FRONT?

SISTER ACT

Glitter and Golden are the oldest twin chimpanzees known to survive in the wild. And they're very close. How close? Their bond is so strong that they even share food—a rare sight in the wild.

Take, for instance, when Golden and their mother are pigging out on freshly hunted monkey meat, a special treat for chimps in the forests of Tanzania. But no fair—Glitter doesn't have any! A frustrated Glitter holds out her hand and begs. While the mom ignores her pleas, Golden hands over some of her meat. She has no reason for doing that, unless, of course, she truly loves her twin.

DEVOTED DAD

In India's Ranthambore National Park, two orphaned Bengal tiger cubs are missing. Their mother died, and the cubs' den is empty. Has the ruling male tiger killed the defenseless babies?

Forest rangers set up camera traps and catch a photo of a male tiger named Zalim. But one of the missing cubs is also in the picture! Zalim isn't preying on them; he's traveling with them. It turns out he's taken over the role of the mother. For example, when the cubs kill a goat, Zalim lets them eat it instead of taking it for himself as most males would do. And when another tiger threatens one of his "kids," Zalim makes the bully back off. This is one big cat that's really earning his stripes.

I'M STARVING! DID DAD TELL YOU WHAT'S FOR DINNER?

UM, YEAH. YOU DEFINITELY HAVE FISH BREATH.

SPECIAL DELIVERY

It's lunchtime at the Philadelphia Zoo. A keeper brings a bucket of catfish to the otter exhibit, and an otter mom and her five hungry pups come running. But not Banjo, the pups' dad. At 19, Banjo is one of the world's oldest otters.

The otters start chowing down, except Banjo. He never worries about getting fed, because his pups always take care of him. One of them races over and drops a fish at Banjo's feet. The pup scampers off and Dad eats.

Does Banjo's caring family contribute to his long life? "Absolutely," says carnivore curator Tammy Schmidt. "That's part of his secret."

WHAT IS Taxonomy?

Since there are billions and billions of living things, called organisms, on the planet, people need a way of classifying them. Scientists created a system called **taxonomy**, which helps to classify all living things into ordered groups. By putting organisms into categories we are better able to understand how they are the same and how they are different. There are seven levels of taxonomic classification, beginning with the broadest group, called a domain, down to the most specific group, called a species.

Biologists divide life based on evolutionary history, and they place organisms into three domains depending on their genetic structure: Archaea, Bacteria, and Eukarya. (See p. 125 for "The Three Domains of Life.")

Where do animals come in?

Animals are a part of the Eukarya domain, which means they are organisms made of cells with nuclei. More than one million

Chinese stripe-necked turtle

species of animals have been named, including humans. Like all living things, animals can be divided into smaller groups, called phyla. Most scientists believe there are more than 30 phyla into which animals can be grouped based on certain scientific criteria, such as body type or whether or not the animal has a backbone. It can be pretty complicated, so there is another, less complicated system that groups animals into two categories: vertebrates and invertebrates.

SAMPLE CLASSIFICATION
RED PANDA

Domain:	Eukarya
Phylum:	Chordata
Class:	Mammalia
Order:	Carnivora
Family:	Ailuridae
Genus:	*Ailurus*
Species:	*fulgens*

TIP
Here's a sentence to help you remember the classification order:
<u>D</u>ear <u>P</u>hillip <u>C</u>ame <u>O</u>ver <u>F</u>or <u>G</u>ood <u>S</u>oup.

BY THE NUMBERS

There are 11,682 vulnerable or endangered animal species in the world. The list includes:

- **1,199 mammals**, such as the snow leopard, the polar bear, and the fishing cat.

- **1,373 birds**, including the Steller's sea eagle and the Madagascar plover.

- **2,172 fish**, such as the Mekong giant catfish.

- **902 reptiles**, including the American crocodile.

- **954 insects**, including the Macedonian grayling.

- **1,961 amphibians**, such as the Round Island day gecko.

- **And more**, including 158 arachnids, 725 crustaceans, 858 sea anemones and corals, 170 bivalves, and 1,759 snails and slugs.

Vertebrates Animals WITH Backbones

Fish are cold-blooded and live in water. They breathe with gills, lay eggs, and usually have scales.

Amphibians are cold-blooded. Their young live in water and breathe with gills. Adults live on land and breathe with lungs.

Reptiles are cold-blooded and breathe with lungs. They live both on land and in water.

Birds are warm-blooded and have feathers and wings. They lay eggs, breathe with lungs, and usually are able to fly. Some birds live on land, some in water, and some on both.

Mammals are warm-blooded and feed on their mothers' milk. They also have skin that is usually covered with hair. Mammals live both on land and in water.

Bird: Bald eagle

Fish: Clown anemonefish

Invertebrates Animals WITHOUT Backbones

Sponges are a very basic form of animal life. They live in water and do not move on their own.

Echinoderms have external skeletons and live in seawater.

Mollusks have soft bodies and can live either in or out of shells, on land or in water.

Arthropods are the largest group of animals. They have external skeletons, called exoskeletons, and segmented bodies with appendages. Arthropods live in water and on land.

Worms are soft-bodied animals with no true legs. Worms live in soil.

Cnidaria live in water and have mouths surrounded by tentacles.

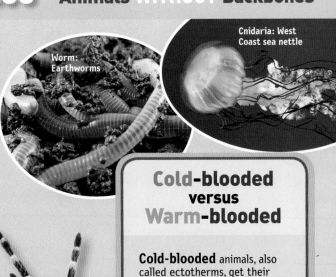

Worm: Earthworms

Cnidaria: West Coast sea nettle

Cold-blooded
versus
Warm-blooded

Cold-blooded animals, also called ectotherms, get their heat from outside their bodies.

Warm-blooded animals, also called endotherms, keep their body temperature level regardless of the temperature of their environments.

Name That

Dolphin

Bottlenose dolphins live all over the world—near shore, far out to sea, and in warm water in both hemispheres.

Surprising new evidence suggests that each bottlenose dolphin creates its own name.

Bottlenose dolphins eat fish, squid, and shrimp.

A bottlenose dolphin is 8 to 12 feet (2.4 to 3.7 m) long.

With a flick of its tail, a young bottlenose dolphin races through the ocean. The powerful dolphin easily cuts through water. At the surface, where it's sunny and clear, visibility is great—it's easy to see for miles. But deeper underwater, where the dolphin swims, visibility is down to a few feet. Yet the dolphin swiftly and easily zooms around boulders, dodges puffer fish, and avoids an enormous sea turtle without hesitation.

When it discovers a huge school of fish, the hungry dolphin whistles excitedly. In the distance a dolphin trills a reply. The two whistle back and forth, as the second dolphin rushes to locate its friend. Soon the two share a secret communication as they twist and turn in unison, eating, leaping, and gliding through the school with the perfect precision of ballet dancers.

Dolphins live in a dark, murky, underwater world. It's often impossible to see each other or anything else around them, so sound plays an essential role in their survival. To communicate with each other, dolphins produce a variety of whistles, squeaks, trills, and clicks.

Only other dolphins understand what the squeaks and squawks mean. Biologists haven't cracked their secret communication, except for one kind of whistle. It might last less than a second, but this whistle is a big deal. Why? Because these whistles are actually names of dolphins—and every bottlenose dolphin has one.

A mother dolphin whistles repeatedly to her newborn for several days after it's born. Biologists believe that this enables the calf to learn to recognize her through sound.

DOLPHIN RINGTONE

Think of a signature whistle as a special ringtone. When other dolphins hear it, they know which dolphin is calling or chattering. It's sort of a "Yo, it's Bob. I'm over here" kind of message. Other group members may reply with their own signature whistles, like a dolphin's version of Marco Polo.

Dolphins often hunt and explore solo, but they need to stay connected to the group. Their signature whistles allow them to check in with other dolphins who may be nearly five football fields away.

BABY NAMES

Many animal species have distinctive or shared calls. But a specific name for an individual is rare. Only humans, some parrot species, and a few other kinds of dolphins are known to have names for individuals.

Scientists believe that the calf itself comes up with the signature whistle. Like human babies, a calf plays with sounds throughout its first year, and dolphins have their own version of baby babble. So, while testing its sound skills, a baby dolphin is actually figuring out its signature whistle— and it may be nothing like its mother's or a group member's whistles. By the time the calf is a year old, its signature whistle is set.

Deciphering dolphin names is just the beginning of figuring out what dolphins communicate about with all their trills and squeaks. Do they chat about sharks? Discuss the tides? Maybe they even have a name for people. Someday scientists hope to decipher the rest of the mysteries of dolphin communication.

Dolphin Dictionary

BEHAVIOR	RUBBING FINS AFTER BEING APART	S-SHAPED BODY POSTURE	APPROACH FROM BEHIND	TAIL-SLAPPING	TOUCHING FIN TO SIDE OF ANOTHER DOLPHIN
WHAT THE DOLPHIN IS SAYING	HELLO! I MISSED YOU.	WATCH OUT!	LET'S PLAY!	BACK OFF!	HEY, GIVE ME A HAND.
SIMILAR BEHAVIOR IN HUMANS	SHAKING HANDS	WAVING CLENCHED FIST IN THE AIR	STARTING A GAME OF TAG	HAND UP, SIGNALING "STOP, KEEP AWAY"	TAPPING SOMEONE ON THE SHOULDER

OCEAN SUPERSTARS

The fascinating lives of 6 sea turtle species

Think all sea turtles are the same? Think again! Each of these species stands out in its own way.

1 GREEN SEA TURTLE: THE NEAT FREAK

In Hawaii, U.S.A., green sea turtles choose a "cleaning station"—a location where groups of cleaner fish groom the turtles by eating ocean gunk, like algae and parasites, off their skin and shells. In Australia, the turtles rub against a favorite sponge or rock to scrub themselves. Neat!

2 KEMP'S RIDLEY: THE LITTLE ONE

They may be the smallest sea turtles, but they're not so tiny: Adults weigh as much as many ten-year-old kids, and their shell is about the size of a car tire. They're speedy, too: It takes them less than an hour to dig a nest, then lay and bury their eggs.

3 OLIVE RIDLEY: THE ULTRA-MOM
Every year, hundreds of thousands of female olive ridley sea turtles take over beaches to lay their eggs and then bury them before disappearing back into the sea. Call it safety in numbers: With thousands of turtles swarming the shoreline, they're sure to overwhelm any predator.

4 LEATHERBACK: THE MEGA-TURTLE
These giants among reptiles have shells about as big as a door and weigh as much as six professional football players! Their size doesn't slow them down, though. A leatherback can swim as fast as a bottlenose dolphin.

5 HAWKSBILL: THE HEARTY EATER
What's the hawksbill's favorite snack? Sponges! These turtles gobble about 1,200 pounds (544 kg) of sponges a year. The turtles can safely eat this sea life, which is toxic to other animals. That means there are plenty of sponges to snack on!

6 LOGGERHEAD: THE TOUGH GUY
The loggerhead sea turtle's powerful jaws can easily crack open the shells of lobsters, conchs, and snails to get at the meat inside. Some loggerheads swim a third of the way around the world to find food.

Parenting, PUFFIN Style

Tips for bringing up these little clowns of the sea

There comes a time, if you're a puffin, that **your beak changes** from dull gray to outrageous orange. **Your feet, too.** That means one thing—it's time to become a puffin parent. Here are **six pointers** for new puffin moms and dads.

1 Touch Down Carefully

When you're ready to become a parent, return to the islands of the North Atlantic where you hatched years before. Remember, landing on rocks isn't like your usual soft watery splashdown. So don't fly in at your full speed of 55 miles an hour. (88 km/h).

2 Show Your Affection

Sometime, maybe in the last year, you met that special someone. Each April you'll reunite. After racing toward each other, show your devotion by rubbing and tapping beaks. Other puffins will gather to enjoy this public display of affection.

3 Develop a Routine

Fly, dive, fly back, drop off fish. Repeat. Each day, you and your mate will make several trips to sea, easily diving 276 times. The usual catch is about ten fish per trip. By the time the chick is ready to leave the nest, each of you will have made 12,420 dives.

4 Land and Run

When returning from sea with a beak full of fish, don't forget to land close to the burrow, then race inside. Herring gulls would rather steal a quick meal from you than hunt for their own food.

"FLYING" THROUGH WATER

5 Prepare for Lots of Fishing

Congratulations! It's a *puffling!* This little fluffy ball of feathers needs you. It can't fly, swim, or hunt. To keep up with its ravenous appetite, it will take both you and your mate to bring it enough baby food: fish.

6 Let Your Puffling Go

You did it—you raised a puffling. Now it must survive on its own, so you have to let it leave the nest. Plus it's time for you to return to life at sea. See you next year!

A MESSAGE TO PUFFLINGS:

You're 45 days old; it's time to leave Mom and Dad. You've got sturdy, smooth feathers now—perfect for flying or diving into the cold sea. To avoid predators hanging around the burrow, be sure to fly or swim away in the dark. In four to six years, you'll return and become a puffin parent, too.

67

5 COOL THINGS ABOUT KOALAS

A koala doesn't look like the kind of creature that keeps campers awake at night or dines on food that would give you a serious stomachache. There's a lot more to these living "teddy bears" than cotton-ball ears and a laid-back lifestyle. Check out five amazing things about these wild, loud, and lovable creatures from Australia.

1. Loudmouths

Imagine a burp so loud it brings you to your knees, followed by a snore that rattles the rafters. Combine them and you have the typical bellow of a koala. Why so noisy? Male koalas grunt with gusto to broadcast their whereabouts to distant females or to scare rivals.

2. Toxic Diet

Koalas eat one to two pounds (450 to 900 g) of eucalyptus leaves each day. The leaves are not only poisonous—they're also tough to digest and provide little nutrition. But koalas have a specially adapted digestive system that extracts every drop of energy from the leaves while neutralizing their toxins.

3. Mistaken Identity

The Europeans who first settled in Australia mistook these tree dwellers for a type of bear, and the name "koala bear" stuck. However, a koala is actually a marsupial—a type of mammal that protects and nurtures its tiny newborns in a pouch.

4. Feisty Guys

A koala may look like a stuffed animal, but you'd be sorry if you tried to cuddle a wild one. Their long, sharp claws—supremely adapted for climbing trees— are used as daggers when two male koalas argue over territory or a mate.

5. Awesome Moms

Born blind, hairless, and no bigger than a jelly bean, a baby koala, or joey, spends six months sleeping and drinking milk in its mother's pouch. Eventually, it will poke its head out to eat pap—a poopy soup from its mother that builds resistance to eucalyptus poison. When the joey leaves the pouch, the mama koala carries it on her back or belly as she climbs trees and teaches the tiny koala by example.

FOXES ON ICE

Clever arctic foxes survive snow, ice, and freezing cold temperatures.

Not far from the North Pole, an arctic fox trots across the endless sea ice on a winter walkabout. It's been days since her last meal, and the whipping wind is relentless. She digs a hollow in the snow, curls up her cat-size body, and wraps her tail across her body and face to stay warm. Her fur acts like a warm sleeping bag, keeping her snug as temperatures dip well below zero degrees. But warm fur alone might not keep this fox alive during the polar winter. Other freeze-defying strategies make this animal a champion of the cold.

FINDING FOOD

Arctic foxes prefer to eat small rodents called lemmings, but when times are tough, they'll take what they can get. This may be scraps of a seal that a polar bear has killed, or crabs and algae stuck to the bottom of ice. Sometimes, they'll stash dead lemmings near their dens for leaner times.

LEMMING

KEEPING WARM

In the toughest temps, this female fox digs a snow den and hunkers down for up to two weeks. She can slow her heart rate and metabolism to avoid burning more energy—similar to hibernation but not as long lasting. The fox's short legs provide heat exchange between warm blood flowing down from the body and cold blood flowing up from the legs.

When the fox emerges, she listens for scurrying sounds under the snow. Quietly, she takes a few steps, and then dives into the snow. Her head emerges with a brown fur ball in her mouth. With the energy tank refilled, this arctic fox has a better chance of making it through the long, dark winter.

FREAKY frogs!

Nearly 6,000 species of frogs hop, burrow, climb, swim, and even soar in exotic ecosystems around the world—and your own neighborhood. Their sometimes startling adaptations make them remarkable survivalists. Here are some frogs whose freakish good looks and bizarre lifestyles will make you become a frog fan.

WARNING LABEL

From the top, the Oriental fire-bellied toad from Korea, China, and southeastern Russia appears to be a mild-mannered frog. If threatened, though, it flashes its brightly colored belly to warn predators. "Look but don't touch." Not only is it toxic, it's also covered with sharp warts.

An amphibian is a **frog**, **toad**, newt, **salamander**, or caecilian.

CLEARLY SEE-THROUGH

From Central and South America, glass frogs are translucent (kind of see-through, like fogged glass). This type of camouflage makes them appear nearly invisible or like a bump on a leaf. Some even have green bones to blend in and trick predators. If you flip over a glass frog, you can see its heart beating through its skin.

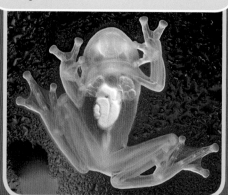

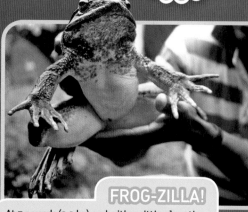

FROG-ZILLA!

At 7 pounds (3.2 kg) and with a sitting length of 12.5 inches (31.8 cm), the Goliath frog from Cameroon and Equatorial Guinea is bigger than a Chihuahua. The world's largest frog, it can leap ten times its body length, or about 10 feet (3 m) each hop. Its body and legs can stretch 29.5 inches (75 cm) long, a little longer than a tennis racket.

FLYING FROG

Why hop when you can fly?
These amphibians, which live high
up in the rain forest canopy in Indonesia,
Malaysia, and Thailand, glide from tree to tree to
escape predators or search for food. With its webbed
feet and side skin flaps, this four-inch (10-cm)-long frog can
glide up to 50 feet (15 m). That's like flying from the pitcher's
mound to home plate on a Little League field.

Frogs live on **every** continent **except** Antarctica.

BIG GULP

Go ahead and yell, "Hey, bigmouth!" The
Amazon horned frog won't be offended. That's
because its mouth is 1.6 times wider than its
entire body length. It eats anything it can fit
inside that mega-mouth, including rodents,
snakes, lizards, and even other frogs. And it
swallows the prey whole. Sometimes its eyes
are bigger than its stomach. Some Amazon
horned frogs have attempted to eat prey that
was larger than themselves.

KISS ME AND CROAK

A golden poison frog has enough poison on its skin to kill several
men. This tiny toxic frog from Colombia doesn't make its own
poison. It absorbs toxins from the insects that it eats. Unlike most
frogs, it boldly rests out in the open for everyone to see. Its color
warns enemies to leave it alone. Being armed with enough poison
to drop half a football team means there's no need to hide.

BURPING UP BABY

The male Darwin's frog of Argentina and Chile gives
"birth," but in his own weird way. After the female lays
eggs, the male guards them for about 20 days. Then he
swallows them, and the tadpoles grow and morph into
frogs inside his throat pouch. After 50 to 60 days, Daddy
belches up more than a dozen baby frogs. Yum!

THE BIGGEST SMALLEST DISCOVERY

In 2009, on the rain forest floor in Papua
New Guinea, scientists discovered the planet's
smallest frog species, known only by its
scientific name, *Paedophryne amauensis.*
How small is it? A couple of them could sit
on a dime and still have room!

Weird but true!

Check out these outrageous facts.

ANYONE HAVE SOME FOOT DEODORANT?

Squirrels sweat through their feet.

A chameleon's **tongue** can travel as fast as **13** miles an hour. (21 km/h)

I'M EAR-RESISTIBLE.

A basset hound weighs about as much as an **elephant's heart.**

Rhinos may communicate **by leaving each other** **dung piles.**

A NINE-BANDED **ARMADILLO** CAN **JUMP** UP TO **4 FEET** (1.2 M) **VERTICALLY** OFF THE GROUND.

Ants
AS BIG AS THIS TOY CAR ONCE MARCHED ON EARTH.

WOLVERINE!

How to track a wild, mysterious super-predator

Wolverines are small but ferocious bearlike animals. They're so mysterious that scientists don't even know how many there are in the wild. But researchers like Gregg Treinish are working to help this wild species continue to survive.

"It's February and I'm on the top of a mountain in Montana, U.S.A., all alone. The snow-caked forest is silent. All of a sudden I spot a wolverine track. I start following his trail.

"Tracking a wolverine is like following a ghost through the forest. They're so fast—covering 20 miles (32 km) in a day—and stealthy that I've never seen one in the wild. But if I pay close attention to the trail this one left, I can learn a lot about him.

"The tracks are grouped side-by-side instead of one after the other, showing that the wolverine was bounding fast, hunting something. I see another set of wolverine tracks. Then two more, crossing each other. Something was going on here. Ahead, I spot a four-foot (1.2-m) hole in the snow. Dirt and blood are scattered around the edge. I peer in to see an elk leg—a tasty meal for the wolverine.

A WOLVERINE CHOWS DOWN ON A LARGE ANIMAL'S LEG BONE.

Wolverines are highly intelligent. People have reported seeing them climb trees, wait, and then pounce on deer that walk by.

"I search the hole and find two wolverine hairs, which I place in a bag. Later, scientists will extract DNA from the hairs and that will help them discover how many wolverines live in this area, what they're eating, and how far they're traveling.

"As climate change warms the planet, wolverines' snowy habitat is disappearing. The clues I find will help scientists track the population to learn whether we need to take action to prevent these phantoms of the forest from disappearing forever."

Animal Rescues

FLYING FOX

NEW SOUTH WALES, AUSTRALIA

Wildlife rehabilitator Lib Ruytenberg gets a call for help: A newborn gray-headed flying fox has been found on the side of a road. She names the baby bat Ruben, warms him up with a heating pad, and feeds him half a teaspoon of cow's milk.

Days later, another newborn flying fox pup, also found on the ground, has arrived. Ruytenberg names this pup Hannah. She suspects these bats might have fallen from a tree while their mothers were feeding them.

COMFORTING THE PUPS

To keep these winged babies warm and fed, Ruytenberg wraps them in blankets and puts pacifiers in their mouths so they feel secure. She also wears a special shirt with pockets on the front that Hannah and Ruben like to snuggle in (hanging upside down, of course).

FLYING FREE

At 16 weeks old, Hannah and Ruben are ready to transition to an aviary, a large enclosure for birds, where they can practice flying and climbing. It also lets them get used to the colony, where they'll live among thousands of tree-dwelling bats.

When placed outside the aviary, at first they return for food every night. But then their visits become infrequent. "When they stop coming back, that's when I know they've gone completely wild again," says Ruytenberg.

FRAIL PUP

SEAL

MANASQUAN, NEW JERSEY, U.S.A.

A ten-day-old gray seal pup leaves her mother for the first time, venturing into the ocean to search for food on her own. Suddenly, a shark sinks its teeth into one of her rear flippers. She manages to escape but, exhausted, she washes up on the beach at Manasquan, New Jersey.

Someone spots the gray seal pup and calls the Marine Mammal Stranding Center. They send a rescue worker to the scene, who scoops up the seal and places her in a plastic dog carrier.

Back in Brigantine, New Jersey, a vet draws blood, gives the seal antibiotics, and cleans her wound.

STRANDED AND HURT

DISAPPOINTING NEWS

Several months pass, and the seal still has an infection at the site of her wound. An x-ray reveals a broken bone in her flipper, requiring surgery. A veterinary surgeon performs the surgery for free.

HAPPY ENDING

After nine months at the center, the seal is finally healthy enough to be released. At a nearby beach, she's placed close to the water. After a few pauses, she leaves the carrier, looks around, sniffs the water, and swims back into her ocean home.

WOLF
NAPLES, FLORIDA, U.S.A.

FEEDING FRENZY

Three tiny gray wolf pups huddle against each other, fenced in behind a home in southern Florida. They are hungry and their bodies are riddled with infections.

Alerted to the situation by concerned neighbors, a wildlife officer arrives on the scene and confiscates the babies. Other officials will return later to rescue the adult wolves, purchased as pets, and deal with the neglectful homeowner. But right now the officer must focus on getting the pups medical treatment.

A vet spots an itchy fungus growing on their skin and potentially deadly parasites living in their guts. It's a miracle they're alive.

CANINE COMEBACK

The animals receive daily medicated baths to treat the fungus and antibiotics to eliminate the parasites. They guzzle goat's milk formula from bottles. They're also hooked up to an IV, which delivers strengthening nutrients through tubes directly to their bloodstreams.

Five days later, the pups seem stable and more energetic. A volunteer teaches the pups—now named Tien, Chocowa, and Indy—to lap formula from a bowl. Later they start eating solid foods.

A NEW HOME

After about six weeks, the healthy siblings are moved into their permanent home at Shy Wolf Sanctuary. Because the pups won't have the survival skills to live in the wild, Shy Wolf is the next best place for them. They'll stay in large living areas with other rescued wolves. As the pups are released, something clicks. They know they're home.

CHOCOWA

ALL GROWN UP

HEALED AND FREE

HEALING

If you see a wounded seal or other marine mammal, do not go near it. Contact your local stranding

According to an ancient Indian legend, the Raven turned one out of every ten bears white to remind people of a time when Earth was covered by snow and ice.

Secrets of the Spirit Bear

A rare animal creates a mysterious sight in the forest.

O n a cold, rainy October night in the rain forest, a hulking white form with a ghostly glow appears in the distance. No, it's not the ghost of a black bear. It's a spirit bear, also called a Kermode bear, which is a black bear with white hair. Kermode bears live almost exclusively in one place: the Great Bear Rainforest along the coast of British Columbia, Canada. Researchers want to figure out why the bears with white coats have survived here. Fewer than 200 spirit bears call this area home.

WHITE COAT CLUES

For many animals, unusual white coloration can make it hard to survive since they may have trouble hiding from predators. But the Kermode bears' coloring may actually help them survive and give them an edge while catching salmon.

"A white bear blends into the background during the day and is more successful catching fish," explains biologist Thomas Reimchen. "There is an advantage to one bear in some conditions and to the other in different conditions."

TALE OF TWO ISLANDS

Canada's Gribbell Island has the highest concentration of Kermode bears, followed by neighboring Princess Royal Island. These isolated islands may be another key to the bears' survival since there's no competition from grizzly bears, and wolves are the only natural threat. The islands' trees provide shelters, and rivers are filled with salmon.

Even though spirit bears have flourished on these islands, new threats such as logging worry scientists and the members of the Native American Gitga'at First Nation, who have lived with and protected spirit bears for centuries. That's why researchers are working hard to understand the biology of the spirit bear. As they do, they can find the best ways to ensure its survival.

PANDA PARTY

THE WORLD CELEBRATES THE FIRST SET OF **GIANT PANDA TWINS** BORN AT A U.S. ZOO IN 26 YEARS.

IN KEEPING WITH CHINESE TRADITION, THE CUBS ARE NAMED WHEN THEY'RE 100 DAYS OLD. ON OCTOBER 23, 2013, CUB B BECAME MEI HUAN (ABOVE, LEFT) AND CUB A BECAME MEI LUN.

The cubs have older brothers: Mei Lan (7), Xi Lan (5), and Po (3). Their father is Lun Lun's mate, 16-year-old Yang Yang.

BABY PANDA TIME LINE

It's a boy! No, wait, Lun Lun the giant panda gave birth to twin cubs in July 2013. Luckily her home is at Georgia, U.S.A.'s Zoo Atlanta, where both cubs have a better chance of surviving than they would in the wild.

Wild panda mothers have a hard time caring for two cubs, and one often dies. But Lun Lun gets help taking care of her cubs, and they're thriving under the attention of the zoo's staff.

Each birth of a giant panda brings new hope for this endangered species. Scientists who study giant pandas believe that as few as 1,600 of the creatures live in the wild. Logging, building highways, and other human activities have severely reduced their habitat in the mountains of China. But more than 350 giant pandas live in captivity in zoos and breeding facilities around the world, and some of these pandas may one day be introduced to protected areas in the wild. So every panda birth is a reason to celebrate.

BIRTHDAY: July 15

DAY 14: July 29

DAY 23: August 7

DAY 77: September 30

DAY 100: October 23

Return of the Missing
LYNX

How this wild cat is making an unexpected comeback.

Dodging campfires, sprinting from vicious dogs, and hiding in caves, the last Eurasian lynx in the British Isles lived a dangerous life. Starting in the late fifth century A.D., people here chopped down forests to clear land for their farms and pastures, leaving these elusive cats with few places to hide—and fewer prey to stalk. Once they began pouncing on livestock, lynx became public enemy number one. Their numbers dwindled, and they soon vanished from the British Isles.

Today, scientists want to bring the cat back.

SECRETIVE LYNX

The largest of the four lynx species, the Eurasian lynx is also one of the widest ranging. These solitary cats slink through forests from western Europe across Russia and into Central Asia. They rely on stealth, keen vision, and super-hearing to stalk rabbits, rodents, birds, and deer four times their size. But without a thick cover of trees and shrubs to hide them, Eurasian lynx have a tough time ambushing prey, and they struggle to survive. In some cases, they've disappeared altogether.

But not for good. Wildlife conservationists in Switzerland, Germany, France, and other countries have taken Eurasian lynx from elsewhere in their range and reintroduced them to these old forest haunts. Now scientists are looking to do the

NORTH AMERICA
ATLANTIC OCEAN
ARCTIC OCEAN
BRITISH ISLES
EUROPE
AFRICA
ASIA
PACIFIC OCEAN

Where Eurasian lynx live

LYNX KITTENS BECOME INDEPENDENT BY THE TIME THEY'RE A YEAR OLD.

KITTENS WILL HAVE SPOTS LIKE MOM BY THE TIME THEY'RE 14 WEEKS OLD.

same thing in the British Isles. Returning the cat would do more than just boost the numbers of this once threatened species. A win for the lynx is also a win for the forest.

BALANCING ACT

Imagine if you popped the hood of your parents' car and started pulling out parts. It wouldn't take long for the engine to sputter or burn too much gas or belch smoke. The forests of the British Isles went similarly out of whack when the Eurasian lynx disappeared. Deer populations skyrocketed without cats to hunt them.

Deer nibble on the leaves of trees and bushes for food, and soon large areas of British forest couldn't keep up with the deer's appetites. Birds and rodents that relied on shelter provided by

the lower level of forest vegetation fell prey to foxes, which lynx also hunt. "The system is now clearly unbalanced, even to the untrained eye," says Paul O'Donoghue, the conservation biologist who founded the Lynx UK Trust project to reintroduce lynx to the British Isles. "We have forests where regrowth has stopped because of all the deer."

Bringing this cat back to the British Isles will restore balance to the forests by controlling the deer population. "And the lynx is an ambassador for other endangered animals," O'Donoghue says. "It will inspire people to protect not just the lynx but other species."

The reintroduction of Eurasian lynx to the British Isles may pave the way for a comeback of other long-gone predators to the area, including the gray wolf and brown bear.

LAND OF THE LYNX

Once the lynx are released back into the wild, they'll be tracked with GPS collars, allowing scientists to monitor their location and health. Eventually the cats will meet up and have kittens of their own.

BIG CATS

A young male jaguar

What are big cats? To wildlife experts, they are the four living members of the genus *Panthera:* tigers, lions, leopards, and jaguars. They can all unleash a mighty roar and, as carnivores, they survive solely on the flesh of other animals. Thanks to powerful jaws; long, sharp claws; and daggerlike teeth, big cats are excellent hunters.

WHO'S WHO?

FUR

BIG CATS MAY HAVE a lot of features in common, but if you know what to look for, you'll be able to tell who's who in no time.

Most tigers are orange-colored with vertical black stripes on their bodies. This coloring helps the cats blend in with tall grasses as they sneak up on prey. These markings are like fingerprints: No two stripe patterns are alike.

TIGERS

JAGUARS

A jaguar's coat pattern looks similar to that of a leopard, as both have dark spots called rosettes. The difference? The rosettes on a jaguar's torso have irregularly shaped borders and at least one black dot in the center.

LEOPARDS

A leopard's yellowy coat has dark spots called rosettes on its back and sides. In leopards, the rosettes' edges are smooth and circular. This color combo helps leopards blend into their surroundings.

LIONS

Lions have a light brown, or tawny, coat and a tuft of black hair at the end of their tails. When they reach their prime, most male lions have shaggy manes that help them look larger and more intimidating.

JAGUAR
100 to 250 pounds
(45 TO 113 KG)

5 to 6 feet long
(1.5 TO 1.8 M)

LEOPARD
66 to 176 pounds
(30 TO 80 KG)

4.25 to 6.25 feet long
(1.3 TO 1.9 M)

BENGAL TIGER
240 to 500 pounds
(109 TO 227 KG)

5 to 6 feet long
(1.5 TO 1.8 M)

AFRICAN LION
265 to 420 pounds
(120 TO 191 KG)

4.5 to 6.5 feet long
(1.4 TO 2 M)

LION

MISSION ANIMAL RESCUE

NATIONAL GEOGRAPHIC KiDS

Save ANIMALS >> Save the WORLD

Caged and neglected, an orphaned cub gets a second chance.

The female lion cub cowers in the corner of a cramped cage in a village in Ethiopia, Africa. People are paying money to see her up close, and she's hissing and snarling out of fear. While visiting the village, American humanitarian aid worker Jane Strachan hears rumors about the cub. When she catches sight of the terrified animal huddled on the dirt floor, Strachan becomes very worried. There's a chain circling the cub's neck, held by a padlock, and no one can find the key. One day the leash will interfere with her breathing. "If she stays here, she'll die," Strachan says.

SAVING THE LION

Rushing back to Ethiopia's capital, Addis Ababa, Strachan contacts the Born Free wildlife rescue team and tells them about the captive lioness. Soon after, a rescue worker and a federal wildlife officer confront the feline's keepers, informing them that it's illegal to house a lion. The keepers hand over the cub, and the worker places her in a pet carrier, then drives her to his rescue center.

Caretakers name the cub Safia and perform a checkup. They're concerned that the cub hasn't received enough calcium. "It's likely that Safia's mom was killed by hunters before the cub was done nursing, so she didn't get all the nutrients she needed," says Stephen Brend, who runs the center. Otherwise the 60-pound (24-kg) seven-month-old seems healthy.

CAGED CUB

LET FREEDOM ROAR

Since Safia never learned survival skills from her mom, she can't be released back into the wild. But her new home at the center will be a grassy area with bushes and trees, similar to a lion's natural habitat. When Safia is placed in her enclosure, she cautiously explores, diving for cover at every little noise. Soon, she gets playful, chasing birds and batting a plastic ball. Gobbling up two meat meals a day with calcium supplements helps Safia gain strength.

After nearly a year and a half, the now 275-pound (125-kg) Safia is released into another, permanent home. Safia meets Dolo, her big cat "roommate." Soon the two are close friends and spend their days playing and lounging together. And when Dolo lets out a mighty roar, Safia joins in. "Safia's finally happy in the way she deserves," Strachan says.

The largest population of wild lions is in Tanzania, Africa.

PLAY BALL!

Lions spend about 20 hours a day resting.

THE LION QUEEN

Lions begin growing their manes at about three years old.

MISSION: LION RESCUE

ALL ABOUT LIONS AND HOW TO SAVE THEM

SAVE ANIMALS, SAVE THE WORLD!

National Geographic Kids has a new initiative called **Mission: Animal Rescue** to show kids how to save lions and other threatened animals. Try out these activities to help the majestic lion.

Create a photo album of pet cats and lions from a local zoo. Share the album with friends to teach them about lions.

Find celebs with pet cats. Write a letter asking them to join the effort to help save their pets' big-cat relatives.

Get more lion rescue activities in the National Geographic Kids book **Mission: Lion Rescue.** To make a contribution in support of the **mission** initiative, grab a parent and go online. kids.nationalgeographic.com/mission-animal-rescue/

CHEETAHS: Built for SPEED

This wild cat's body makes it an incredible predator.

Breathing deeply, the cheetah prepares her body for the chase. Head low, eyes focused on an impala, she slowly inches forward. In three seconds this streamlined, superfast cat is sprinting at 60 miles an hour (96 km/h), eyes locked, laserlike, on the fleeing impala.

Long, muscular tail for balance in tight turns

The legendary Jamaican runner Usain Bolt is the world's fastest human. Bolt ran 200 meters in 19.19 seconds, about 23 miles an hour (37 km/h), but that's slow compared with the cheetah. Cheetahs can run about three times faster than Bolt. At top speed a sprinting cheetah can reach 70 miles an hour (113 km/h). Next time you're in a car on the highway, imagine a cheetah racing alongside you. That will give you an idea of how fast this speedy cat can run.

Several adaptations help cheetahs run so fast. A cheetah has longer legs than other cats. It also has a

Small, short face with enlarged nostrils to take in lots of air

long, extremely flexible spine. These features work together so a running cheetah can cover up to 23 feet (7 m) in one stride—about the length of five ten-year-olds lying head to feet in a row.

Most other cats can retract their claws when they're not using them. Cheetahs' claws stick out all the time, like dogs' claws. Cheetahs use these strong, blunt claws like an athlete uses cleats on track shoes—to help push off and quickly build up speed. The large center pad on the cheetah's foot is covered with long ridges that act like the treads on a car tire. A sprinting cheetah needs to be able to stop fast, too. It is able to spread its toes wide, and its toe pads are hard and pointed. This helps a cheetah turn quickly

Strong, blunt claws and ridged footpads to grip the ground

and brake suddenly. It can stop in a single stride from a speed of more than 20 miles an hour (32 km/h).

All of these body adaptations add up to extraordinary hunting abilities. A cheetah stalks up close to a herd of impalas, then streaks forward with lightning speed. As the herd bolts, the cat singles out one individual and follows its twists and turns precisely. As it closes in on its prey the cheetah strikes out with a forepaw, knocks the animal off its feet, and clamps its jaws over the prey's throat.

Snow Leopard SECRETS

High-tech tools help scientists understand how to save these big cats.

On a cool summer night, a snow leopard curiously sniffs an overhanging boulder for a strong scent sprayed by other cats. He rubs his cheeks on the boulder, scrapes the ground with his hind paws, and then urinates.

This act—called scraping—is how snow leopards communicate with one another. A scrape tells other snow leopards what they're doing and may reveal whether a snow leopard is male or female, has cubs, or is looking for a mate.

Recently, researchers studying the 4,000 to 7,000 snow leopards in the wild have set up motion-activated cameras at scraping sites in an effort to gather more information on these elusive cats and expose new details about how many snow leopards there are, how long they live, and how we can protect them.

Even though snow leopards live in some of the most rugged mountain terrain on Earth, people pose the biggest threat to their survival. Poachers can sell a snow leopard's hide and bones for thousands of dollars. Herders often kill any snow leopard that attacks their livestock. Hunters target ibex, wild sheep, and other animals for food and trophies—removing important snow leopard prey.

Like a snow leopard reality show, the cameras expose everything that happens. The images also help researchers count the number of snow leopards in an area and reveal whether prey animals, livestock, or poachers are nearby.

Other researchers will gently trap the wild cats and put satellite radio collars on them to track where the cats roam and to learn new things about how and where they live. Technology like this is essential to help researchers protect snow leopards in the wild and preserve their habitat.

Despite their name, snow leopards are not snow-colored. Their spotted gray or beige fur actually stands out against a snowy background—but blends in with rocks.

MARKING TERRITORY

TWO CUBS

CHASING DOWN PREY

1

A LADYBUG MIGHT EAT MORE THAN **5,000** **INSECTS** IN ITS **LIFETIME.**

2

Periodical cicadas are LISTED AS INGREDIENTS IN SOME PIZZA RECIPES.

3

Fruit flies have **TRAVELED** with astronauts into **space.**

4

ALCON BLUE CATERPILLARS ARE RAISED BY **ANTS** UNTIL THEY **COCOON.**

16 COOL THINGS ABOUT

5

THE RED POSTMAN BUTTERFLY DEVELOPS ITS OWN POISON BY EATING TOXIC PLANTS.

6

TO HIDE FROM ENEMIES, THE SPITTLEBUG COVERS ITSELF IN A FROTHY, SPITLIKE LIQUID.

7

TO BREATHE UNDERWATER, THE WATER SCORPION USES A SNORKEL-LIKE TUBE ON ITS ABDOMEN.

8

MOSQUITOES ARE ATTRACTED TO SMELLY FEET.

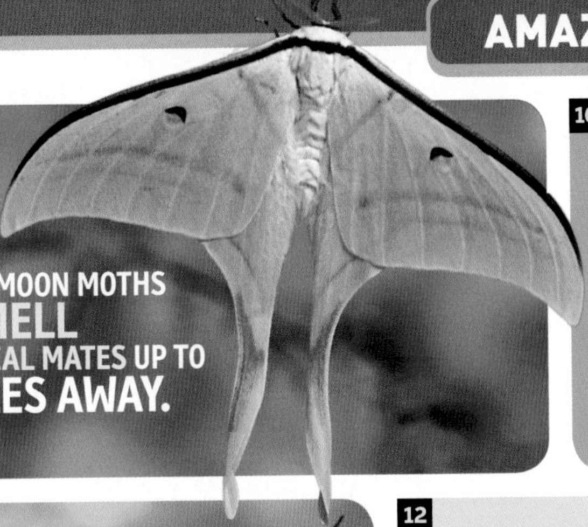

9 INDIAN MOON MOTHS CAN **SMELL** POTENTIAL MATES UP TO **6 MILES AWAY.** (9.7 km)

10 BULLDOG **ANTS** CAN **LEAP** FROM THE GROUND ONTO THE BACKS OF FLYING BEES.

11 GRASSHOPPERS HAVE SPECIAL **ORGANS** IN THEIR HIND KNEES THAT STORE ENERGY FOR JUMPING.

12 A SINGLE HONEYBEE COLONY CAN PRODUCE AROUND **200** POUNDS (91 KG) OF **HONEY** EACH YEAR.

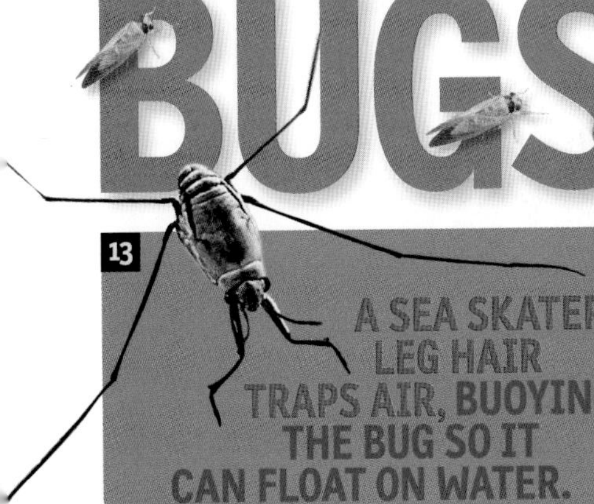

BUGS

13 A SEA SKATER'S LEG HAIR TRAPS AIR, BUOYING THE BUG SO IT CAN FLOAT ON WATER.

14 GIANT DARNER DRAGONFLIES SOMETIMES PREY ON SMALL FROGS.

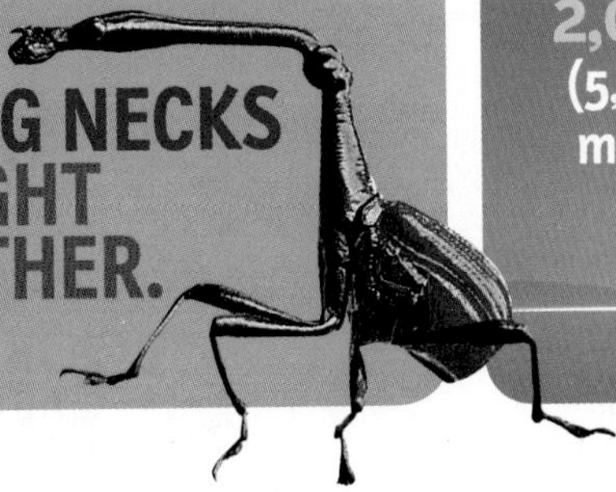

15 MALE GIRAFFE WEEVILS USE THEIR **LONG NECKS TO FIGHT EACH OTHER.**

16 A swarm of locusts covering about 2,000 square miles (5,200 sq km) reportedly moved over the Red Sea in 1889.

Make a SPIDERWEB

GAIN A GREATER APPRECIATION FOR ALL THE WORK SPIDERS PUT INTO THEIR WEBS BY MAKING YOUR VERY OWN!

SPIDERS HAVE CLEAR BLOOD.

SOME SPIDERS EAT THEIR OWN WEBS.

MOST SPIDERS HAVE EIGHT EYES.

GET OUTSIDE GUIDE

CHECK OUT THE BOOK!

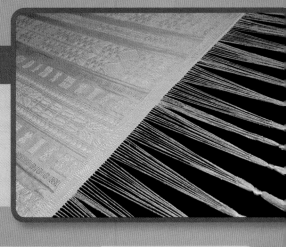

fun fact

A spider's web may look delicate, but it's strong! Spider silk is five times as strong as steel of the same diameter.

SUPPLY LIST

- A notebook and pencil
- Yarn or string

STEPS

1. Before you do anything, go on a hunt for spiderwebs. Spiders spin all kinds of designs. Spend some time studying one and sketch out the design in a notebook. Webs can be found everywhere, from crevices of trees to in between grasses to inside shrubs. Look high and low!

2. Next, start spinning your web. There's no limit to the size—just find two trees and start unwinding your "silk" (your yarn or string). Try to copy the pattern you sketched.

3. Compare your web to the spider's web. Try making a large web and a tiny one.

Time: about 25 minutes

HOW DO SPIDERS AVOID GETTING TANGLED?

Spiderwebs are sticky business, so how come spiders don't get caught in their own webs? It turns out that a spider's web isn't all sticky—the spiral parts are generally sticky, the spokes are not. But spiders do have to touch the sticky parts while building the web. To get around that, their legs have tiny hairs that prevent them from getting stuck. Spiders also have an oily substance on them that repels the sticky stuff.

Prehistoric TIME LINE

HUMANS HAVE WALKED on Earth for some 200,000 years, a mere blip in Earth's 4.5-billion-year history. A lot has happened during that time. Earth formed, and oxygen levels rose in the millions of years of the Precambrian time. The productive Paleozoic era gave rise to hard-shelled organisms, vertebrates, amphibians, and reptiles.

Dinosaurs ruled the Earth in the mighty Mesozoic. And 64 million years after dinosaurs became extinct, modern humans emerged in the Cenozoic era. From the first tiny mollusks to the dinosaur giants of the Jurassic and beyond, Earth has seen a lot of transformation.

THE PRECAMBRIAN TIME

4.5 billion to 542 million years ago

- The Earth (and other planets) formed from gas and dust left over from a giant cloud that collapsed to form the sun. The giant cloud's collapse was triggered when nearby stars exploded.
- Low levels of oxygen made Earth a suffocating place.
- Early life-forms appeared.

THE PALEOZOIC ERA

542 million to 251 million years ago

- The first insects and other animals appeared on land.
- 450 million years ago (m.y.a.), the ancestors of sharks began to swim in the oceans.
- 430 m.y.a., plants began to take root on land.
- More than 360 m.y.a., amphibians emerged from the water.
- Slowly the major landmasses began to come together, creating Pangaea, a single supercontinent.
- By 300 m.y.a., reptiles had begun to dominate the land.

What Killed the Dinosaurs?

It's a mystery that's boggled the minds of scientists for centuries: What happened to the dinosaurs? While various theories have bounced around, a new study confirms that the most likely culprit is an asteroid or comet that created a giant crater. Researchers say that the impact set off a series of natural disasters like tsunamis, earthquakes, and temperature swings that plagued the dinosaurs' ecosystem and disrupted their food chain. This, paired with intense volcano eruptions that caused drastic climate changes, is thought to be why half of the world's species—including the dinosaurs—died in a mass extinction.

DINO TIMES

THE MESOZOIC ERA

251 million to 65 million years ago

The Mesozoic era, or the age of the reptiles, consisted of three consecutive time periods (shown below). This is when the first dinosaurs began to appear. They would reign supreme for more than 150 million years.

TRIASSIC PERIOD

251 million to 199 million years ago

- Appearance of the first mammals. They were rodent-size.
- The first dinosaur appeared.
- Ferns were the dominant plants on land.
- The giant supercontinent of Pangaea began breaking up toward the end of the Triassic.

JURASSIC PERIOD

199 million to 145 million years ago

- Giant dinosaurs dominated the land.
- Pangaea continued its breakup, and oceans formed in the spaces between the drifting landmasses, allowing sea life, including sharks and marine crocodiles, to thrive.
- Conifer trees spread across the land.

CRETACEOUS PERIOD

145 million to 65 million years ago

- The modern continents developed.
- The largest dinosaurs developed.
- Flowering plants spread across the landscape.
- Mammals flourished, and giant pterosaurs ruled the skies over the small birds.
- Temperatures grew more extreme. Dinosaurs lived in deserts, swamps, and forests from the Antarctic to the Arctic.

THE CENOZOIC ERA—TERTIARY PERIOD

65 million to 2.6 million years ago

- Following the dinosaur extinction, mammals rose as the dominant species.
- Birds continued to flourish.
- Volcanic activity was widespread.
- Temperatures began to cool, eventually ending in an ice age.
- The period ended with land bridges forming, which allowed plants and animals to spread to new areas.

DINO Classification

Classifying dinosaurs and all other living things can be a complicated matter, so scientists have devised a system to help with the process. Dinosaurs are put into groups based on a very large range of characteristics.

Scientists put dinosaurs into two major groups: the bird-hipped ornithischians and the reptile-hipped saurischians.

Ornithischian

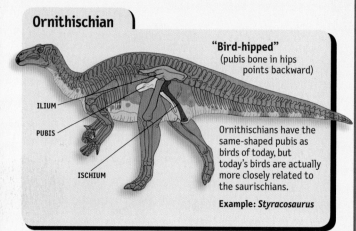

"Bird-hipped"
(pubis bone in hips points backward)

ILIUM

PUBIS

ISCHIUM

Ornithischians have the same-shaped pubis as birds of today, but today's birds are actually more closely related to the saurischians.

Example: *Styracosaurus*

Saurischian

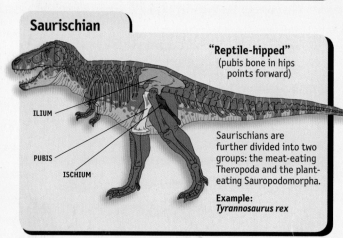

"Reptile-hipped"
(pubis bone in hips points forward)

ILIUM

PUBIS

ISCHIUM

Saurischians are further divided into two groups: the meat-eating Theropoda and the plant-eating Sauropodomorpha.

**Example:
*Tyrannosaurus rex***

Within these two main divisions, dinosaurs are then separated into orders and then families, such as Stegosauria. Like other members of the Stegosauria, *Stegosaurus* had spines and plates along the back, neck, and tail.

Who Ate What?

Herbivores
- Primarily plant-eaters
- Weighed up to 100 tons (91 t)—the largest animals ever to walk on Earth
- Up to 1,000 blunt or flat teeth to grind vegetation
- Many had cheek pouches to store food.
- Examples: *Styracosaurus, Mamenchisaurus*

Carnivores
- Meat-eaters
- Long, strong legs to run faster than plant-eaters; ran up to 30 miles an hour (48 km/h)
- Most had good eyesight, strong jaws, and sharp teeth.
- Scavengers and hunters; often hunted in packs
- Grew to 45 feet (14 m) long
- Examples: *Velociraptor, Gigantoraptor, Tyrannosaurus rex*

Bet you didn't know

9 *dino*-mite facts about **dinosaurs**

1 **T. rex** could gulp (45 kg) **100 pounds** of meat at once.

2 Concho- raptor's **strong beak** could crack open **conch shells.**

3 **Meat- eating dinos** laid **long, thin eggs;** plant-eaters laid **round** ones.

4 **Mamenchi- saurus' neck** stretched up to **35 feet.** (10.7 m)

5 Some dinosaurs were **no bigger than chickens.**

6 **Micro- raptor** had **feathered wings** but **couldn't fly.**

7 **Velociraptor** could **run** about **25 miles an hour.** (40 km/h)

8 **Shantungo- saurus** sported **378 teeth.**

9 **Most dinosaurs could swim.**

Dynamite
DINO AWARDS

Spiky body armor. Razor-sharp teeth. Unimaginable strength.
No doubt, all dinos are cool. But whether they were the biggest, the fiercest, or the biggest-brained of the bunch, some stand out more than others. Here are seven of the most amazing dinos ever discovered.

Supersize Appetite

Shortest Name

Scientists think that **Tyrannosaurus rex** could gulp down 500 pounds (227 kg) of meat at a time—that's like eating 2,000 hamburger patties in one bite!

Minmi, a small dinosaur—which was covered in a bony armor—gets its brief name from Minmi Crossing, a creek in Australia where it was first discovered.

Weighing more than 14 African elephants and with thigh bones taller than an adult human, **Titanosaur** is, according to scientists, the largest creature to ever roam the Earth.

Biggest

Quetzalcoatlus's wingspan reached up to 35 feet (11 m), making it the largest creature to ever take to the skies. Despite its big wings, it weighed only around 200 pounds (90 kg), allowing it to fly long distances.

Longest Wings

Longest Nose

Nicknamed "Pinocchio rex," the **Qianzhousaurus sinensis** had a snout some 35 percent longer than other dinosaurs of its size. Scientists think it may have used its long snout to snag prey such as lizards and smaller dinosaurs.

Pint-Size Predator

Microraptor zhaoianus, one of the smallest meat-eating dinosaurs, measured just 16 inches (40 cm) tall. With long toe tips for grasping branches, it's thought to be closely related to today's birds.

Super Spines

Known as the "spine lizard," **Spinosaurus** had huge spines sticking out of its back, some taller than a fourth grader! With a snout like a crocodile, it's the first dino known to live in the water.

DINOSAUR MYTHS

CHECK OUT THESE PREHISTORIC PUZZLES.

Some ideas about dinosaurs are just plain wrong, but they still can be hard to get rid of: Have you heard the one about *Stegosaurus* having a brain in its rump? It didn't. Here's another myth about *Stegosaurus*, along with more news about other dinos you may know.

THE MYTH
STEGOSAURUS' BRAIN WAS ONLY THE SIZE OF A WALNUT.

WHERE IT PROBABLY CAME FROM

In 1877, a paleontologist named O. C. Marsh studied the first *Stegosaurus* found. He measured plaster casts of the inside of the tiny braincase and announced it had "the smallest brain of any known land vertebrate." Newspapers began trumpeting the tiny brain. Publishers found they could sell books if they included the not-very-smart *Stegosaurus*, saying it had "a brain no larger than a walnut."

WHAT WE KNOW NOW

More than a century later, Ashley Morhardt of Ohio University's WitmerLab wondered if the walnut story was true. Using computers, she produced a digital cast of *Stegosaurus'* brain cavity. She modeled the brain's odd shapes in a software program and figured out each shape's volume. Then she added them up. The brain was really the size of *two* walnuts! "*Stegosaurus* was still probably pretty dumb, though," Morhardt says.

THE MYTH

DINOSAURS FOUND IN THE "DEATH POSE" DIED IN AGONY.

WHERE IT PROBABLY CAME FROM

Head pulled back upside down over the hips, tail stretched forward. The death pose is common among theropods, which were two-legged, mostly meat-eating dinosaurs. Paleontologists long wondered why. One thought the dinos had died while sleeping. Others believed that they'd been poisoned, suffocated, or died in agony. Or that dead dinos might have become fossilized pretzels as they dried out.

WHAT WE KNOW NOW

What if the dead dinosaurs ended up in a lake or a stream? wondered Alicia Cutler and Brooks Britt of Brigham Young University. To test this idea, they placed dead chickens in buckets of water. The heads swung back almost instantly! In water, the head and neck float. That allows ligaments between the backbones to shorten, pulling the neck into a tight arch. A chicken placed on dry sand didn't take the death pose, even months after drying out.

THE MYTH

ONLY LITTLE DINOSAURS HAD FEATHERS.

WHERE IT PROBABLY CAME FROM

Paleontologists have been finding extremely well-preserved skeletons of small, nonflying feathered dinosaurs in China's Liaoning Province. Scientists think the feathers might have kept them warm or helped attract mates. It seemed only little dinosaurs had feathers. The biggest was *Beipiaosaurus*, which was seven feet (2.1 m) long. Other feathered dinos were pip-squeaks, like *Sinosauropteryx*. But a feathered *Tyrannosaurus rex*? No way!

WHAT WE KNOW NOW

Recently, Chinese and Canadian scientists reported a huge new dinosaur with long feathers covering most of its body. *Yutyrannus* was 30 feet (9.2 m) long and 40 times heavier than *Beipiaosaurus*. And it was a tyrannosaur, three-quarters the length of its ginormous later relative, *T. rex*. So maybe the terrifying Tyrant King was really soft and fluffy.

QUIZ WHIZ

Are you an animal ace? Quiz yourself to check your species smarts!

ANSWERS BELOW

1 **True or false?** Wolverines cover up to 20 miles (32 km) a day.

2 What do you call baby puffins?
- **a.** chicks
- **b.** puff balls
- **c.** tweeters
- **d.** pufflings

3 Per Chinese tradition, giant panda cubs aren't named until they're _____ days old.
- **a.** 10
- **b.** 1,000
- **c.** 100
- **d.** 200

4 If your pet dog play-bows to you, what is she likely trying to communicate?
- **a.** "Let's play!"
- **b.** "You're the boss."
- **c.** "I'm scared."
- **d.** "I'm tired."

5 *Quetzalcoatlus* had a wing span the length of a _____.
- **a.** guitar
- **b.** bus
- **c.** 10-year-old
- **d.** teaspoon

Not **STUMPED** yet? Check out the *NATIONAL GEOGRAPHIC KIDS QUIZ WHIZ* collection for more crazy **ANIMAL** questions!

ANSWERS: 1. True; 2. d; 3. c; 4. a; 5. b

Wildly Good Animal Reports

beluga whale

Your teacher wants a written report on the beluga whale. Not to worry. Use these organizational tools so you can stay afloat while writing a report.

STEPS TO SUCCESS: Your report will follow the format of a descriptive or expository essay (see p. 35 for "How to Write a Perfect Essay") and should consist of a main idea, followed by supporting details and a conclusion. Use this basic structure for each paragraph as well as the whole report, and you'll be on the right track.

1. Introduction
State your **main idea.**
The beluga whale is a common and important species of whale.

2. Body
Provide **supporting points** for your main idea.
The beluga whale is one of the smallest whale species.
It is also known as the "white whale" because of its distinctive coloring.
These whales are common in the Arctic Ocean's coastal waters.

Then **expand** on those points with further description, explanation, or discussion.
The beluga whale is one of the smallest whale species.
Belugas range in size from 13 to 20 feet (4 to 6.1 m) in length.
It is also known as the "white whale" because of its distinctive coloring.
Belugas are born gray or brown. They fade to white at around five years old.
These whales are common in the Arctic Ocean's coastal waters.
Some Arctic belugas migrate south in large herds when sea ice freezes over.

3. Conclusion
Wrap it up with a **summary** of your whole paper.
Because of its unique coloring and unusual features, belugas are among the most familiar and easily distinguishable of all the whales.

KEY INFORMATION

Here are some things you should consider including in your report:

> What does your animal look like?
> To what other species is it related?
> How does it move?
> Where does it live?
> What does it eat?
> What are its predators?
> How long does it live?
> Is it endangered?
> Why do you find it interesting?

SEPARATE FACT FROM FICTION: Your animal may have been featured in a movie or in myths and legends. Compare and contrast how the animal has been portrayed with how it behaves in reality. For example, penguins can't dance the way they do in *Happy Feet.*

PROOFREAD AND REVISE: As with any great essay, when you're finished, check for misspellings, grammatical mistakes, and punctuation errors. It often helps to have someone else proofread your work, too, as he or she may catch things you have missed. Also, look for ways to make your sentences and paragraphs even better. Add more descriptive language, choosing just the right verbs, adverbs, and adjectives to make your writing come alive.

BE CREATIVE: Use visual aids to make your report come to life. Include an animal photo file with interesting images found in magazines or printed from websites. Or draw your own! You can also build a miniature animal habitat diorama. Use creativity to help communicate your passion for the subject.

THE FINAL RESULT: Put it all together in one final, polished draft. Make it neat and clean, and remember to cite your references.

Super Science

Almanac Explorer!

I'll live to be about 30 years old in the wild.

This is clue #4!
Collect them all and unscramble the letters to find the secret animal. Enter the animal name at kids.nationalgeographic.com/almanac-2016!

COOL inventions

SIDE VIEW

MOTORIZED SKATES

It'd be awesome to cruise along on roller skates without ever pushing off. With spnKiX (pronounced "spin kicks"), you can do just that. These accelerating accessories are like small motorized vehicles you strap to your shoes. Each spnKiX skate has a tiny electric motor that can propel the skater up to ten miles an hour (16 km/h)—about as fast as a swift jogger—for about six miles (9.6 km) on one battery charge. The rider controls the speed with a wireless handheld remote and skids to a stop using heel brakes. But just because the skates are motorized doesn't mean you get a free ride. "You need to use muscles to balance and steer," spnKiX inventor Peter Treadway says. "You'll still sweat."

ORU KAYAK

THIS TURNS INTO THIS!

BOAT IN A BOX

This will totally float your boat. The Oru Kayak is a 12-foot (3.7-m)-long vessel that folds down into a carrying case not much bigger than a pizza box. What makes it so portable? The kayak's thin plastic frame contains several creases that allow you to bend it into a compact shape in about five minutes. The boat's seat cushion and footrest fit snugly into the Oru when it's in carrying-case mode. At just 25 pounds (11.3 kg), it's probably the only boat you can bring inside the car!

FACE-MASK
CAMERA

Every undersea explorer needs a waterproof camera. Here's one that's impossible to forget onshore—because it's built into the snorkeling mask. Set right above the eyes, the lens on the Liquid Image Scuba Series HD mask snaps photos and records more than an hour of high-definition video. An easy-to-reach shutter button above the right eye activates the camera, while crosshairs on the goggles' glass make it easy to line up the perfect shot. Just point your head and shoot, then download all your pics of photogenic fish once you're back on land.

CLICK!

WANNA GO TO THE ZOO NEXT?

I'M READY TO ROLL!

ROBOT TAKES YOU PLACES

Wish you could attend a concert or catch a movie—from the comfort of your bed? Call on the Double. This roving robot will serve as your eyes and ears in distant places. The android consists of an iPad tablet or iPhone attached to an adjustable stand that's mounted on motorized wheels. Make a video call to the bot from your own tablet. Once you're connected, the Double will stream live video of its surroundings to you. Your own face pops up on the Double's screen. You can move the Double around with controls on your tablet and interact with anyone you meet. So next time you hit up a museum to see its cool new exhibit, it could be in your pj's!

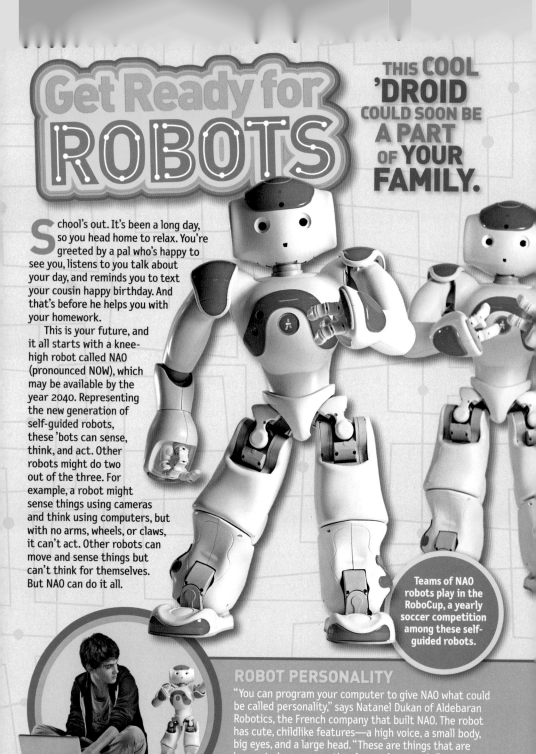

Get Ready for ROBOTS

School's out. It's been a long day, so you head home to relax. You're greeted by a pal who's happy to see you, listens to you talk about your day, and reminds you to text your cousin happy birthday. And that's before he helps you with your homework.

This is your future, and it all starts with a knee-high robot called NAO (pronounced NOW), which may be available by the year 2040. Representing the new generation of self-guided robots, these 'bots can sense, think, and act. Other robots might do two out of the three. For example, a robot might sense things using cameras and think using computers, but with no arms, wheels, or claws, it can't act. Other robots can move and sense things but can't think for themselves. But NAO can do it all.

Teams of NAO robots play in the RoboCup, a yearly soccer competition among these self-guided robots.

ROBOT PERSONALITY

"You can program your computer to give NAO what could be called personality," says Natanel Dukan of Aldebaran Robotics, the French company that built NAO. The robot has cute, childlike features—a high voice, a small body, big eyes, and a large head. "These are things that are known to have an emotional appeal to people," robot expert Dan Kara says. NAO's friendly design helps in one of NAO's main functions—to teach people how useful personal robots can be. Someday one may help you ace a test!

ACCIDENTS Happen

BUT SOMETIMES THEY RESULT IN AMAZING DISCOVERIES.

Hey, they happen. Sometimes accidents are totally embarrassing. But other times they lead to something awesome. Check out these fortunate mistakes.

THE INVENTION: ARTIFICIAL SWEETENER

THE MOMENT OF "OOPS": Dirty hands

THE DETAILS: In the late 1870s, Constantin Fahlberg was working in his lab when he tipped over a beaker of chemicals, spilling them all over his hands. Without pausing to wash, Fahlberg went on with his work. When he went home to eat, the chemical residue was still on his fingers. After biting into a piece of bread, he noticed that it tasted strangely sweet. It wasn't the bread— it was something on his hands.

Fahlberg rushed back to work and found that the substance in the beaker that had spilled was sweet— much sweeter than sugar. He named his discovery saccharin—the first artificial sweetener.

THE INVENTION: MICROWAVE OVEN

THE MOMENT OF "OOPS": Accidentally melting a chocolate bar in a pocket

THE DETAILS: In the 1940s, Percy Spencer was experimenting with radar— radio waves used to detect objects. When he stepped in front of a magnetron—a device that makes waves called microwaves—the chocolate bar in his pocket melted! Spencer then aimed a beam of microwaves at some kernels of popping corn. They burst. Then he zapped a raw egg, which exploded. This proved that microwaves could heat food superfast, leading to the first microwave oven.

105

THE UNIVERSE BEGAN WITH A BIG BANG

Clear your mind for a minute and try to imagine this: All the things you see in the universe today—all the stars, galaxies, and planets—are not yet out there. Everything that now exists is concentrated in a single, incredibly hot, dense state that scientists call a singularity. Then, suddenly, the basic elements that make up the universe flash into existence. Scientists say that actually happened about 13.8 billion years ago, in the moment we call the big bang.

For centuries scientists, religious scholars, poets, and philosophers have wondered how the universe came to be. Was it always there? Will it always be the same, or will it change? If it had a beginning, will it someday end, or will it go on forever?

These are huge questions. But today, because of recent observations of space and what it's made of, we think we may have some of the answers. Everything we can see or detect around us in the universe began with the big bang. We know the big bang created not only matter but also space itself. And scientists think that in the very distant future, stars will run out of fuel and burn out. Once again the universe will become dark.

POWERFUL PARTICLE

It's just one tiny particle, but without it the world as we know it would not exist. That's what scientists are saying after the recent discovery of the Higgs boson particle, a subatomic speck related to the Higgs field, which is thought to give mass to everything around us. Without the Higgs boson, all the atoms created in the big bang would have zipped around the cosmos too quickly to collect into stars and planets. So you can think of it as a building block of the universe—and of us!

EARLY LIFE ON EARTH

About 3.5 billion years ago Earth was covered by one gigantic reddish ocean. The color came from hydrocarbons.

The first life-forms on Earth were Archaea that could live without oxygen. They released large amounts of methane gas into an atmosphere that would have been poisonous to us.

About 3 billion years ago erupting volcanoes linked together to form larger landmasses. And a new form of life appeared—cyanobacteria, the first living things that used energy from the sun.

Some 2 billion years ago the cyanobacteria algae filled the air with oxygen, killing off the methane-producing Archaea. Colored pools of greenish brown plant life floated on the oceans. The oxygen revolution that would someday make human life possible was now under way.

About 530 million years ago the Cambrian explosion occurred. It's called an explosion because it's the time when most major animal groups first appeared in our fossil records. Back then, Earth was made up of swamps, seas, a few active volcanoes, and oceans teeming with strange life.

More than 450 million years ago life began moving from the oceans onto dry land. About 200 million years later dinosaurs began to appear. They would dominate life on Earth for more than 150 million years.

PLANETS

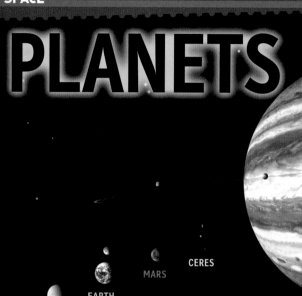

CERES

MARS

EARTH

VENUS

MERCURY

JUPITER

SUN

MERCURY
Average distance from the sun:
   35,980,000 miles (57,900,000 km)
Position from the sun in orbit: first
Equatorial diameter: 3,030 miles (4,878 km)
Length of day: 59 Earth days
Length of year: 88 Earth days
Surface temperatures: -300°F (-184°C)
   to 800°F (427°C)
Known moons: 0
Fun fact: On Mercury, the sun appears to rise
   and set twice a day.

VENUS
Average distance from the sun:
   67,230,000 miles (108,200,000 km)
Position from the sun in orbit: second
Equatorial diameter: 7,520 miles (12,100 km)
Length of day: 243 Earth days
Length of year: 225 Earth days
Average surface temperature: 864°F (462°C)
Known moons: 0
Fun fact: The clouds on Venus rain
   sulfuric acid.

EARTH
Average distance from the sun:
   93,000,000 miles (149,600,000 km)
Position from the sun in orbit: third
Equatorial diameter: 7,900 miles (12,750 km)
Length of day: 24 hours
Length of year: 365 days
Surface temperatures: -126°F (-88°C)
   to 136°F (58°C)
Known moons: 1
Fun fact: Earth moves around the sun at a
   rate 100 times faster than a speeding jet.

MARS
Average distance from the sun:
   141,633,000 miles (227,936,000 km)
Position from the sun in orbit: fourth
Equatorial diameter: 4,221 miles (6,794 km)
Length of day: 25 Earth hours
Length of year: 1.88 Earth years
Surface temperatures: -270°F (-168°C)
   to 80°F (27°C)
Known moons: 2
Fun fact: Some dust storms on Mars
   may last for several months.

This artwork shows the 13 planets and dwarf planets. The relative sizes and positions of the planets are shown but not the relative distances between them.

SATURN

URANUS

NEPTUNE

PLUTO

HAUMEA

MAKEMAKE

ERIS

JUPITER
Average distance from the sun:
   483,682,000 miles (778,412,000 km)
Position from the sun in orbit: sixth
Equatorial diameter: 88,840 miles (142,980 km)
Length of day: 9.9 Earth hours
Length of year: 11.9 Earth years
Average surface temperature: -235°F (-148°C)
Known moons: 67*
Fun fact: There is almost constant volcanic
   activity on Jupiter's Moon Io.

SATURN
Average distance from the sun:
   890,800,000 miles (1,433,500,000 km)
Position from the sun in orbit: seventh
Equatorial diameter: 74,900 miles (120,540 km)
Length of day: 10.7 Earth hours
Length of year: 29.46 Earth years
Average surface temperature: -218°F (-139°C)
Known moons: 62*
Fun fact: A billion Earths could fit into one
   of Saturn's rings.

*Includes provisional moons, which await confirmation
  and naming from the International Astronomical Union.

URANUS
Average distance from the sun:
   1,784,000,000 miles (2,870,970,000 km)
Position from the sun in orbit: eighth
Equatorial diameter: 31,760 miles (51,120 km)
Length of day: 17.2 Earth hours
Length of year: 84 Earth years
Average surface temperature: -323°F (-197°C)
Known moons: 27
Fun fact: Uranus' axis is so tilted, the planet
   appears to be tipped over on its side.

NEPTUNE
Average distance from the sun:
   2,795,000,000 miles (4,498,250,000 km)
Position from the sun in orbit: ninth
Equatorial diameter: 30,775 miles (49,528 km)
Length of day: 16 Earth hours
Length of year: 164.8 Earth years
Average surface temperature: -353°F (-214°C)
Known moons: 14*
Fun fact: Neptune may have oceans of
   liquid diamond.

For information about dwarf planets—Ceres,
Pluto, Haumea, Makemake, and Eris—see p. 110.

DWARF PLANETS

Haumea

Eris

Thanks to advanced technology, astronomers have been spotting many never-before-seen celestial bodies with their telescopes. One new discovery? A population of icy objects orbiting the sun beyond Pluto. The largest, like Pluto itself, are classified as dwarf planets. Smaller than the moon but still massive enough to pull themselves into a ball, dwarf planets nevertheless lack the gravitational "oomph" to clear their neighborhood of other sizable objects. So, while larger, more massive planets pretty much have their orbits to themselves, dwarf planets orbit the sun in swarms that include other dwarf planets as well as smaller chunks of rock or ice.

So far, astronomers have identified five dwarf planets: Ceres (which circles the sun in the asteroid belt between Mars and Jupiter), Pluto, Haumea, Makemake, and Eris. Astronomers are studying hundreds of newly found objects in the frigid outer solar system, trying to figure out just how big they are. As time and technology advance, the family of known dwarf planets will surely continue to grow.

CERES
Position from the sun in orbit: fifth
Length of day: 9.1 Earth hours
Length of year: 4.6 Earth years
Known moons: 0

PLUTO
Position from the sun in orbit: tenth
Length of day: 6.4 Earth days
Length of year: 248 Earth years
Known moons: 5

HAUMEA
Position from the sun in orbit: eleventh
Length of day: 3.9 Earth hours
Length of year: 282 Earth years
Known moons: 2

MAKEMAKE
Position from the sun in orbit: twelfth
Length of day: 22.5 Earth hours
Length of year: 305 Earth years
Known moons: 0

ERIS
Position from the sun in orbit: thirteenth
Length of day: 25.9 Earth hours
Length of year: 561 Earth years
Known moons: 1

SUPER SUN!

E ven from 93 million miles (150 million km) away, the sun's rays are powerful enough to provide the energy needed for life to flourish on Earth. This 4.6-billion-year-old star is the anchor of our solar system and accounts for 99 percent of the matter in the solar system. What else makes the sun so special? For starters, it's larger than one million Earths and is the biggest object in our solar system. The sun also converts about four million tons (3,628,739 MT) of matter to energy every second, helping to make life possible here on Earth. Now that's *sun*-sational!

IF YOU COULD DRIVE TO THE SUN, IT WOULD TAKE ABOUT 190 YEARS TO GET THERE.

The SUN'S surface is 9,932°F! (5,500°C)

Some sunspots — magnetic fields on the sun — are bigger than Earth.

Storms on the Sun!

Solar flares are ten million times more powerful than a volcanic eruption on Earth.

With the help of specialized equipment, scientists have observed solar flares—bursts of magnetic energy that explode from the sun's surface as a result of storms on the sun. Solar storms occur on a cycle of about 11 years, with 2014 being the most recent active year for these types of events. And while most solar storms will not impact the Earth, the fiercer the flare, the more we may potentially feel its effects, as it could disrupt power grids or interfere with GPS navigation systems. Solar storms can also trigger stronger-than-usual auroras, light shows that can be seen on Earth.

Some solar storms travel at speeds of THREE MILLION MILES AN HOUR (4.8 million km/h).

Solar storm

Sky Calendar
2016

Jupiter

Leonid meteor shower

Partial solar eclipse

January 3–4 Quadrantids Meteor Shower Peak. A nearly full moon will affect visibility this year, but several bright meteors can still be spotted.

March 8 Jupiter at Opposition. The giant planet is at its closest approach to Earth.

March 9 Total Solar Eclipse. Visible in parts of Indonesia and the Pacific Ocean. A partial solar eclipse will be visible in northern Australia and Southeast Asia.

March 23 Lunar Eclipse. Visible in eastern Asia, eastern Australia, the Pacific Ocean, and the west coast of North America.

May 9 Transit of Mercury Across the Sun. A rare event. Positioned directly between Earth and the sun, Mercury will appear as a dark disk crossing the sun when viewed with solar filters or telescopes.

May 22 Mars at Opposition. The red planet makes its closest approach to Earth.

June 3 Saturn at Opposition. The best time to view the ringed planet. It makes its closest approach to Earth.

August 11–12 Perseid Meteor Shower Peak. One of the best! Up to 60 meteors per hour. Best viewing is in the direction of the constellation Perseus.

September 2 Neptune at Opposition. The blue planet will be at its closest approach to Earth. Because Neptune is so far away, binoculars or a telescope are necessary for viewing. Unless you have a very powerful telescope, Neptune will appear as a small blue dot.

October 20–21 Orionid Meteor Shower Peak. View up to 20 meteors per hour. Look toward the constellation Orion for the best show.

November 16–17 Leonid Meteor Shower Peak. View up to 15 meteors per hour.

December 12–13 Geminid Meteor Shower Peak. A spectacular show! Up to 120 multi-colored meteors per hour.

Various dates throughout 2016
View the International Space Station. Visit spotthestation.nasa.gov to find out when the ISS will be flying over your neighborhood.

Dates may vary slightly depending on your location. Check with a local planetarium for the best viewing time in your area.

SOLAR AND LUNAR ECLIPSES

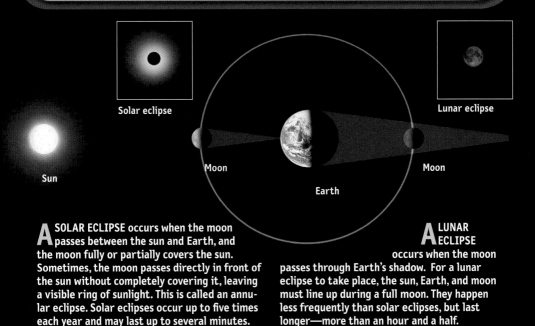

Solar eclipse

Lunar eclipse

Sun

Moon

Moon

Earth

A SOLAR ECLIPSE occurs when the moon passes between the sun and Earth, and the moon fully or partially covers the sun. Sometimes, the moon passes directly in front of the sun without completely covering it, leaving a visible ring of sunlight. This is called an annular eclipse. Solar eclipses occur up to five times each year and may last up to several minutes.

A LUNAR ECLIPSE occurs when the moon passes through Earth's shadow. For a lunar eclipse to take place, the sun, Earth, and moon must line up during a full moon. They happen less frequently than solar eclipses, but last longer—more than an hour and a half.

The Big Dipper, also called the Plough, is part of the constellation commonly known as the Great Bear.

SKY DREAMS

L ONG AGO, people looking at the sky noticed that some stars made shapes and patterns. By playing connect-the-dots, they imagined people and animals in the sky. Their legendary heroes and monsters were pictured in the stars.

Today, we call the star patterns identified by the ancient Greeks and Romans "constellations." There are 88 constellations in all. Some are visible only when you're north of the Equator, and some only when you're south of it.

In the 16th-century age of exploration, European ocean voyagers began visiting southern lands, and they named the constellations

that are visible in the Southern Hemisphere, such as the Southern Cross. Astronomers used the star observations of these navigators to fill in the blank spots on their celestial maps.

Constellations aren't fixed in the sky. The star arrangement that makes up each one would look different from another location in the universe. Constellations also change over time because every star we see is moving through space. Over thousands of years, the stars in the Big Dipper, which is part of the larger constellation Ursa Major (the Great Bear), will move so far apart that the dipper pattern will disappear.

ASTEROID STRIKE!

5 WAYS TO STOP SPACE ROCKS HEADED TOWARD EARTH

ASTEROIDS are rocks in space. When an asteroid hits Earth's atmosphere, it's called a meteor. If it reaches Earth's surface, it's a meteorite.

MOST METEORITES ARE SMALL.

Our planet is pummeled by space rocks all the time. Fifty thousand tons (45,359 MT) of material hit us every day—enough to fill 5,000 dump trucks. Most of these space rocks are too small to do any damage, but a really big rock could be a really big problem. To prevent a disaster, scientists are coming up with some game plans in case they spot a dangerous space rock headed for a collision with Earth. Here are five of them.

A METEOR STREAKS THROUGH THE SKY OVER THE CITY OF CHELYABINSK. ITS SHOCK WAVE DAMAGED MANY OF THE CITY'S BUILDINGS.

1 SHOVE IT

If done early enough, ramming an asteroid with a spacecraft would be enough to change its orbit and speed. "If you can change its speed by just that of a crawling baby, in 20 years it will pass by Earth instead of hitting us," says David Morrison, who studies asteroid impacts at the SETI Institute.

2 TOW IT

A SPACECRAFT APPROACHES AN ASTEROID.

If you fly a spacecraft right next to the asteroid, the spacecraft's gravity will pull the asteroid just enough to change its speed. But this is a tricky approach: Even a light bump could blow a fragile asteroid apart and create smaller but just-as-dangerous space rocks.

PAINT IT 3

Some scientists think that painting an asteroid white would reflect sunlight—and cause the sun's rays to bounce off the surface, giving the space rock a slight push. You'd have to start centuries in advance, but this could be enough to save the planet from a collision.

EAT IT

CONTROLLED BY HOVERING SPACECRAFT, ROBOTS CHEW UP AN ASTEROID.

4

Hungry robots would land on the side of the asteroid and chew up the rock surface. Then they'd blow the rubble into space. The force from all the blowing would rocket the asteroid ahead to avoid a collision course.

BLAST IT

The "Laser Bees" project calls for small spacecraft to swarm around the asteroid. Each spacecraft would focus a laser beam onto a well-chosen spot on the asteroid's surface. The lasers would vaporize the rock into superheated rocketlike gas plumes, changing the asteroid's speed and path.

5

Continents on the Move

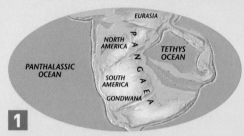

1

PANGAEA About 240 million years ago, Earth's landmasses were joined together in one super-continent that extended from Pole to Pole.

2

BREAKUP By 94 million years ago, Pangaea had broken apart into landmasses that would become today's continents. Dinosaurs roamed Earth during a period of warmer climates.

3

EXTINCTION About 65 million years ago, an asteroid smashed into Earth, creating the Gulf of Mexico. Scientists think this impact resulted in the extinction of half the world's species, including the dinosaurs. This was one of several mass extinctions.

4

ICE AGE By 18,000 years ago, the continents had drifted close to their present positions, but most far northern and far southern lands were buried beneath huge glaciers.

A LOOK INSIDE

The distance from Earth's surface to its center is 3,963 miles (6,378 km) at the Equator. There are four layers: a thin, rigid crust; the rocky mantle; the outer core, which is a layer of molten iron; and finally the inner core, which is believed to be solid iron.

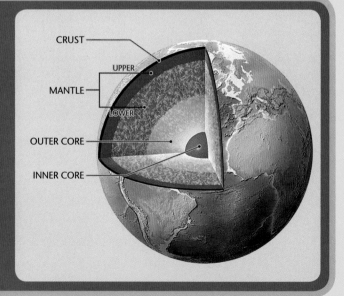

CRUST

UPPER

MANTLE

LOWER

OUTER CORE

INNER CORE

ROCK STARS

The world is full of rocks—some big, some small, some formed deep beneath the Earth, and some formed at the surface. While they may look similar, not all rocks are created equal. Look closely, and you'll see differences between every boulder, stone, and pebble. Here's more about the three top varieties of rocks.

Igneous

Named for the Greek word meaning "from fire," igneous rocks form when hot, molten liquid called magma cools. Pools of magma form deep underground and slowly work their way to the Earth's surface. If they make it all the way, the liquid rock erupts and is called lava. As the layers of lava build up they form a mountain called a volcano. Typical igneous rocks include obsidian, basalt, and pumice, which is so chock-full of gas bubbles that it actually floats in water.

OBSIDIAN   PUMICE

Metamorphic

Metamorphic rocks are the masters of change! These rocks were once igneous or sedimentary, but thanks to intense heat and pressure deep within the Earth, they have undergone a total transformation from their original form. These rocks never truly melt; instead, the heat twists and bends them until their shapes substantially change. Metamorphic rocks include slate as well as marble, which is used for buildings, monuments, and sculptures.

MARBLE   SLATE

Sedimentary

When wind, water, and ice constantly wear away and weather rocks, smaller pieces called sediment are left behind. These are sedimentary rocks, also known as gravel, sand, silt, and clay. As water flows downhill it carries the sedimentary grains into lakes and oceans, where they get deposited. As the loose sediment piles up, the grains eventually get compacted or cemented back together again. The result is new sedimentary rock. Sandstone, gypsum, limestone, and shale are sedimentary rocks that have formed this way.

SANDSTONE   GYPSUM

Name That ROCK

Whether you're kicking one down the road or climbing on top of one at the park, rocks are all around you. But what kind of rocks are they? Can you identify the variety of rocks on this page?

Answers are at the bottom of page 119.

A

This is the stuff of hopscotch and tic-tac-toe. It was formed with the skeletons of microorganisms.

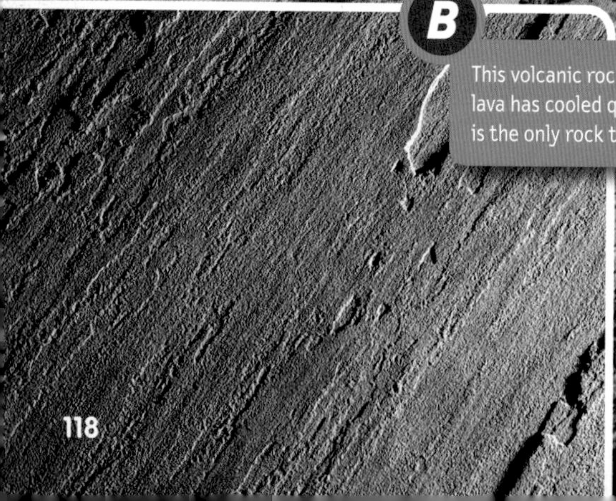

B

This volcanic rock forms after lava has cooled quickly, and it is the only rock that floats!

CHECK OUT THE BOOK!

GET OUTSIDE GUIDE

C This rock formed in a similar way to granite, but you can see large crystals in it.

D This rock is so soft it can break up in water.

fun fact

Diamonds are the hardest rocks on Earth. They come in a variety of colors, including yellow, red, and even green.

E Some of the oldest fossils found on Earth are preserved in this soft sedimentary rock.

F The most common volcanic rock on Earth, it formed by cooling quickly, but it has fine grains on the surface.

G A seated Abraham Lincoln and Michelangelo's "David" were both carved out of this white, sedimentary rock.

A. Chalk; B. Pumice; C. Gabbro; D. Mudstone; E. Shale; F. Basalt; G. Marble

Volcano!

Fiery hot lava flows down a Hawaiian mountainside like dark, thick syrup. **When it reaches the sea, it hisses and explodes** in scalding jets of steam.

> Lava flowing from a volcano can be hotter than **2100°F** (1149°C).

Farther up the slope, volcanologist Ken Hon picks his way slowly across the rough surface. The hot lava is slippery to walk on. "It's like walking on ice," Hon says. "But the bottom part of your boots starts to melt a little. If you fall, you'll get burned."

Hon plants his feet carefully and slowly. He is collecting data on the lava flowing out of Kīlauea (kee-luh-WAY-uh, shown here), a volcano that has been erupting since 1983. Knowing the lava's movements can save lives on the slopes below. But Hon must be careful. New waves of lava are flowing down toward him. Every few minutes he looks up to see where the streams are and makes sure the moving lava hasn't cut off his escape route.

"It's searing hot out there—like the heat from an oven," Hon says. "Up close, you have to wear firefighters' gear so the clothes you're wearing don't catch on fire or melt."

SLOW FLOW

Earth's interior is so hot that rock softens and flows. Volcanoes form at certain places where liquid rock, or magma, pushes through cracks to the Earth's surface. The cracks eject lava, which is what magma is called when it reaches the surface. Ash that forms volcanic mountains also explodes from the crater. Some volcanoes, such as Kīlauea, typically erupt gently. But they can pour out rivers of lava that engulf everything in their path.

LAVA ON ROAD

"Back in 1990, lava entered the town of Kalapana," Hon says. "We had to evacuate people from about 150 homes. The lava inched forward and consumed all of the houses." Everyone escaped. But today Kalapana is buried under 30 feet (9.1 m) of lava.

In 2014, about 20 families in Pahoa, Hawaii, were evacuated as Kilauea's lava once again threatened homes.

Volcanoes aren't scary to Hon. They're fascinating and exciting. Still, Hon knows how to keep safe—and knows when the lava is too close. But the danger is worth it, because the more Hon and other scientists can learn about volcanoes, the safer they can keep the people who live around these powerful forces of nature.

Hawaii's Mauna Loa is the world's largest active volcano.

More than **1,500** volcanoes on Earth are active.

DOOMED HOUSE

LAVA LAMPS

FOUR WAYS VOLCANOES ERUPT

1. FIERY FLOW
Lava sprays through cracks in the Earth and flows down the slopes.

2. SHORT BURST
The pressure in the gas inside stickier magma increases, causing small but frequent bursts of lava.

3. ROCKY RUSH
Stickier magma forms a dome in the volcano's opening. The dome collapses and then explodes, sending ash and rock down the volcano's sides.

4. HUGE *KABOOM!*
The stickiest magma traps large amounts of gas and produces great pressure in the magma chamber. The gas blows the magma into pieces, shooting ash and rock miles into the air.

Get Out of the Way!

As magma moves upward inside a volcano, the volcano becomes more likely to erupt. Here are signs that it might be happening.

- Many small or moderate earthquakes
- Bulges and other deformations in the volcano's surface
- Major changes in the release of gases from cracks and other openings

Kaboom!

How demolition **experts** bring down **buildings**

1 BEFORE

TEXAS STADIUM

2 EXPLODING!

3 AFTER

Deafening explosions and fiery flashes raced in waves around Texas Stadium. Concrete supports fell like trees, and the steel beams across the top of the building crashed to the ground. Soon a large dust cloud hovered over the rubble. The football arena was gone.

For nearly 40 years, the Dallas Cowboys played home football games at Texas Stadium in Irving. But after the team moved to the new Cowboys Stadium in 2009, the old stadium was no longer needed. So city officials planned to demolish it.

When a structure isn't useful anymore, sometimes the best way to bring it down is also dramatic to watch. Teams of experts can use carefully timed explosions to make a building, bridge, or other structure collapse in a matter of seconds. Let's take a look behind the scenes of the stadium's spectacular demolition.

CONTROLLED DESTRUCTION

The first step to figuring out the most efficient way to demolish Texas Stadium was to study its original plans. Demolition experts take advantage of gravity as much as possible, using the weight of the building to help it collapse. An initial team took out parts of the structure such as walls and ramps so that the whole building perched only on its basic supports, particularly at the lower level of the structure.

EXPLOSIVE SITUATION

Texas Stadium had 12 concrete support structures, called abutments, which circled the outside of the building and held up the roof's six steel beams, called trusses. The team planning the explosion did test blasts to figure out how much dynamite was needed to bring these supports down in the safest way possible. The demolition crew then drilled 3,300 holes into the concrete supports, where they placed sticks of dynamite. Special explosives called linear-shaped charges, equipped with a fast-burning, fuse-like cord, cut through the steel in the roof trusses. The charges were linked together so that the concrete supports holding up each of the six trusses exploded at exactly the same time. If they hadn't, the roof trusses might not have fallen to the ground.

SO LONG, STADIUM

After six months of planning, it was time for the explosion. Police and firefighters stopped traffic on highways surrounding Texas Stadium. People gathered at a safe distance to watch. After a countdown, the press of a button set off the series of explosions that, in 60 seconds, left nothing but a massive pile of rubble.

DEMOLITION IN CHINA

1 BEFORE

A BRIDGE IN CHINA WAS DEMOLISHED IN MUCH THE SAME WAY AS TEXAS STADIUM.

2 EXPLODING!

3 AFTER

CRASH AND BURN

PREP TIME FOR TEXAS STADIUM DEMOLITION	NUMBER OF HOLES FOR EXPLOSIVES	TIME TO LOAD EXPLOSIVES	POUNDS OF EXPLOSIVES	TIME TO BRING DOWN TEXAS STADIUM	COST OF DEMOLITION
6 months	3,300	5 days	more than 2,000 (907 kg)	60 seconds	$6 million

WHAT IS LIFE?

This seems like such an easy question to answer. Everybody knows that singing birds are alive and rocks are not. But when we start studying bacteria and other microscopic creatures, things get more complicated.

SO WHAT EXACTLY IS LIFE?

Most scientists agree that something is alive if it can do the following: reproduce; grow in size to become more complex in structure; take in nutrients to survive; give off waste products; and respond to external stimuli, such as increased sunlight or changes in temperature.

KINDS OF LIFE

Biologists classify living organisms by how they get their energy. Organisms such as algae, green plants, and some bacteria use sunlight as an energy source. Animals (like humans), fungi, and some Archaea use chemicals to provide energy. When we eat food, chemical reactions within our digestive system turn our food into fuel.

Living things inhabit land, sea, and air. In fact, life also thrives deep beneath the oceans, embedded in rocks miles below the Earth's crust, in ice, and in other extreme environments. The life-forms that thrive in these challenging environments are called extremophiles. Some of these draw directly upon the chemicals surrounding them for energy. Since these are very different forms of life than what we're used to, we may not think of them as alive, but they are.

HOW IT ALL WORKS

To try and understand how a living organism works, it helps to look at one example of its simplest form—the single-celled bacterium called *Streptococcus*. There are many kinds of these tiny organisms, and some are responsible for human illnesses. What makes us sick or uncomfortable are the toxins the bacteria give off in our bodies.

A single *Streptococcus* bacterium is so small that at least 500 of them could fit on the dot above the letter *i*. These bacteria are some of the simplest forms of life we know. They have no moving parts, no lungs, no brain, no heart, no liver, and no leaves or fruit. Yet this life-form reproduces. It grows in size by producing long chain structures, takes in nutrients, and gives off waste products. This tiny life-form is alive, just as you are alive.

What makes something alive is a question scientists grapple with when they study viruses, such as the ones that cause the common cold and smallpox. They can grow and reproduce within host cells, such as those that make up your body. Because viruses lack cells and cannot metabolize nutrients for energy or reproduce without a host, scientists ask if they are indeed alive. And don't go looking for them without a strong microscope— viruses are a hundred times smaller than bacteria.

Scientists think life began on Earth some 3.9 to 4.1 billion years ago, but no fossils exist from that time. The earliest fossils ever found are from the primitive life that existed 3.6 billion years ago. Other life-forms, some of which are shown below, soon followed. Scientists continue to study how life evolved on Earth and whether it is possible that life exists on other planets.

MICROSCOPIC ORGANISMS*

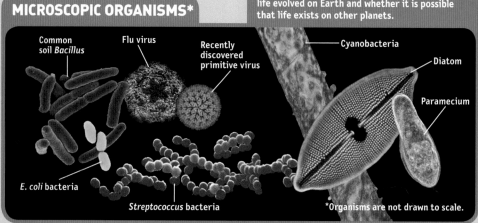

Common soil *Bacillus*

Flu virus

Recently discovered primitive virus

Cyanobacteria

Diatom

Paramecium

E. coli bacteria

Streptococcus bacteria

*Organisms are not drawn to scale.

The Three Domains of Life

Biologists divide all living organisms into three domains: Bacteria, Archaea, and Eukarya. Archaean and Bacterial cells do not have nuclei; they are so different from each other that they belong to different domains. Since human cells have a nucleus, humans belong to the Eukarya domain.

1 BACTERIA

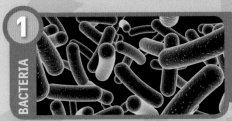

Domain Bacteria: These single-celled microorganisms are found almost everywhere in the world. Bacteria are small and do not have nuclei. They can be shaped like rods, spirals, or spheres. Some of them are helpful to humans, and some are harmful.

2 ARCHAEA

Domain Archaea: These single-celled microorganisms are often found in extremely hostile environments. Like Bacteria, Archaea do not have nuclei, but they have some genes in common with Eukarya. For this reason, scientists think the Archaea living today most closely resemble the earliest forms of life on Earth.

3 EUKARYA

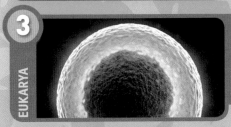

Domain Eukarya: This diverse group of life-forms is more complicated than Bacteria and Archaea, as Eukarya have one or more cells with nuclei. These are the tiny cells that make up your whole body. Eukarya are divided into four groups: fungi, protists, plants, and animals.

What is a domain? Scientifically speaking, a domain is a major taxonomic division into which natural objects are classified (see p. 60 for "What Is Taxonomy?").

FYI

FUNGI

Kingdom Fungi (about 100,000 species): Mainly multicellular organisms, fungi cannot make their own food. Mushrooms and yeast are fungi.

PROTISTS

Protists (about 250,000 species): Once considered a kingdom, this group is a "grab bag" that includes unicellular and multicellular organisms of great variety.

PLANTS

Kingdom Plantae (about 300,000 species): Plants are multicellular, and many can make their own food using photosynthesis (see p. 140 for "Photosynthesis").

ANIMALS

Kingdom Animalia (about 1,000,000 species): Most animals, which are multicellular, have their own organ systems. Animals do not make their own food.

Your Amazing Body!

The human body is a complicated mass of systems— nine systems, to be exact. Each system has a unique and critical purpose in the body, and we wouldn't be able to survive without all of them.

The **NERVOUS** system controls the body.

The **MUSCULAR** system makes movement possible.

The **SKELETAL** system supports the body.

The **CIRCULATORY** system moves blood throughout the body.

The **RESPIRATORY** system provides the body with oxygen.

The **DIGESTIVE** system breaks down food into nutrients and gets rid of waste.

The **IMMUNE** system protects the body against disease and infection.

The **ENDOCRINE** system regulates the body's functions.

The **REPRODUCTIVE** system enables people to produce offspring.

Weird but true

YOUR **BRAIN** CAN HOLD **100 TIMES** MORE INFORMATION THAN AN AVERAGE **COMPUTER.**

A speck of **blood** contains about **5 million red** blood cells.

Your hands and wrists contain 26 percent of the bones in your body.

Your Amazing
eyes

Discover the magic of your body's built-in cameras.

Y ou carry around a pair of cameras in your head so incredible they can work in bright sunshine or at night. Only about an inch (2.5 cm) in diameter, they can bring you the image of a tiny ant or a twinkling star trillions of miles (km) away. They can change focus almost instantly and stay focused even when you're shaking your head or jumping up and down. These cameras are your eyes.

A CRUCIAL PART OF YOUR EYE IS AS FLIMSY AS A WET TISSUE.

A dragonfly darts toward your head! Light bounces off the insect, enters your eye, passes through your pupil (the black circle in the middle of your iris), and goes to the lens. The lens focuses the light onto your retina—a thin lining on the back of your eye that is vital but is as flimsy as a wet tissue. Your retina acts like film in a camera, capturing the picture of this dragonfly. The picture is sent to your brain, which instantly sends you a single command—*duck!*

YOU BLINK MORE THAN 10,000 TIMES A DAY.

Your body has many ways to protect and care for your eyes. Each eye sits on a cushion of fat, almost completely surrounded by protective bone. Your eyebrows help prevent sweat from dripping into your eyes. Your eyelashes help keep dust and other small particles out. Your eyelids act as built-in windshield wipers, spreading tear fluid with every blink to keep your eyes moist and wash away bacteria and other particles. And if anything ever gets too close to your eyes, your eyelids slam shut with incredible speed—in two-fifths of a second—to protect them!

YOUR EYES SEE EVERYTHING UPSIDE DOWN AND BACKWARD!

As amazing as your eyes are, the images they send your brain are a little quirky: They're upside down, backward, and two-dimensional! Your brain automatically flips the images from your retinas right side up and combines the images from each eye into a three-dimensional picture. There is a small area of each retina, called a blind spot, that can't record what you're seeing. Luckily your brain makes adjustments for this, too.

YOUR PUPILS CHANGE SIZE WHENEVER THE LIGHT CHANGES.

Your black pupils may be small, but they have an important job—they grow or shrink to allow just the right amount of light to enter your eyes to let you see.

THE EYEBALL'S TOUGH OUTER LAYERS, THE **CORNEA (1)** AND **SCLERA (2)**, GIVE IT STRENGTH.

THE COLORED **IRIS** ABSORBS BRIGHT LIGHT.

THE **PUPIL** EXPANDS AND CONTRACTS TO LET IN THE AMOUNT OF LIGHT NEEDED TO SEE.

THE **LENS**, WITH THE CORNEA, FOCUSES LIGHT.

COLORLESS, JELLYLIKE **VITREOUS HUMOR** FILLS THE EYEBALL, HELPING IT TO KEEP ITS SHAPE.

A MILLION FIBERS IN THE **OPTIC NERVE** CONNECT THE EYE TO THE BRAIN.

THE **RETINA** CHANGES LIGHT RAYS INTO ELECTRICAL SIGNALS SENT TO THE BRAIN.

Your Amazing
brain

Inside your body's supercomputer

You carry around a three-pound (1.4-kg) mass of wrinkly material in your head that controls every single thing you will ever do. From enabling you to think, learn, create, and feel emotions to controlling every blink, breath, and heartbeat—this fantastic control center is your brain. It is a structure so amazing that a famous scientist once called it the "most complex thing we have yet discovered in our universe."

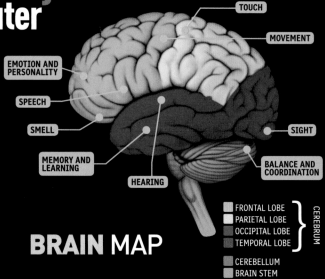

TOUCH

MOVEMENT

EMOTION AND PERSONALITY

SPEECH

SMELL

MEMORY AND LEARNING

HEARING

SIGHT

BALANCE AND COORDINATION

BRAIN MAP

FRONTAL LOBE
PARIETAL LOBE
OCCIPITAL LOBE
TEMPORAL LOBE
} CEREBRUM

CEREBELLUM
BRAIN STEM

THE BIG QUESTION

WHAT TAKES UP TWO-THIRDS OF YOUR BRAIN'S WEIGHT AND ALLOWS YOU TO SWIM, EAT, AND SPEAK?

Answer: The huge hunk of your brain called the cerebrum. It's definitely the biggest part of the brain. The four lobes of the cerebrum house the centers for memory, the senses, movement, and emotion, among other things.

The cerebrum is made up of two hemispheres—the right and the left. Each side controls the muscles of the opposite side of the body.

How to Decode Your Dreams

YOUR BRAIN MAY BE TELLING YOU SOMETHING.

How many times have you told someone, "I had the craziest dream last night"? Lots of times, huh? You can have up to six dreams a night. Some of them are sure to be wild!

Dreams are created by the part of your brain that stores memories, emotions, and thoughts. At night your brain blends what's stored in your mind with what you've been thinking about lately.

Dreams hardly ever become reality, but they may contain hints about what's going on in your life. "Dreams help us get in touch with our deeper feelings," says dream researcher Alan Siegel. "They can tell us a lot about ourselves and may even help us figure out problems."

Scientists have discovered that many dreams contain common themes that have meaning. Here are eight types of dreams that may tell you a lot about yourself and what's happening in your life!

THE THEME Being chased

WHAT IT MEANS The scary thing that's chasing you is probably a symbol of a real-life problem you don't want to deal with. But this dream is telling you it's time to stop running from the problem and start facing it.

THE THEME Showing up in pajamas

WHAT IT MEANS Your brain may be helping you recover from a real-life embarrassing moment. If no one's making a big deal about the pj's, chances are your friends think you're cool no matter what. If they *are* laughing? It may be time for some new friends.

THE THEME Flying

WHAT IT MEANS It's likely you're flying high in real life as well. Maybe your friends see you as a leader or your parents have given you more freedom.

THE THEME Being lost

WHAT IT MEANS You're probably feeling a little lost in life. Are you currently facing a tough decision? You might be afraid of making the wrong choice. Think carefully about your options to find your way out of this dilemma.

THE THEME Falling

WHAT IT MEANS You might have too much going on. It's time to slow down and take a break from whatever is stressing you out. And the soft landing? A sign that you'll soon get over this tough time.

THE THEME Not being able to move

WHAT IT MEANS You're probably feeling "stuck" in life. (Maybe your parents just grounded you.) You need to think about how you got into this sticky situation and then try to make smarter choices in the future.

THE THEME Losing something

WHAT IT MEANS You may be looking for an ego boost. Perhaps you want to try out a new sport or hobby, and you're not sure if you can do it. Search deep inside yourself for that confidence. It's there—you just have to find it!

THE THEME Being unprepared or late

WHAT IT MEANS You're worrying big-time about an upcoming event or project. If you're prepared, it's just a sign that you're nervous. That's normal. But if you've been slacking, take this dream as a hint and get to work!

ZZzz!

A dream usually lasts from 10 to 40 minutes.

Your brain waves can be more active when you're dreaming than when you're awake.

You'll spend about six years of your life dreaming.

1 An adult human heart averages **72 BEATS PER MINUTE;** a beluga whale's heart averages **100 BEATS PER MINUTE,** though it slows to 12 to 20 beats per minute while diving.

2 SEA STARS—COMMONLY CALLED STARFISH—HAVE **NO HEARTBEAT,** BECAUSE THEY HAVE **NO HEART.**

3 THE HUMAN HEART BEATS 100,000 TIMES A DAY, OR **40 MILLION TIMES A YEAR.**

4 **EACH HUMAN HEARTBEAT** fills a four-chambered heart with fresh blood.

5 At some restaurants in Vietnam, you can order up a **STILL-BEATING SNAKE'S HEART.**

16 HEART-

6 The human heart weighs just over **HALF A POUND** (283.5 g) and is shaped like a fist.

7  An elephant's heart weighs as much as **46** pounds (21 kg), about the same as a four-year-old kid.

8 The heart symbol is meant to represent love. The feeling of love actually has **NOTHING TO DO WITH YOUR HEART—** it comes from neurological responses that **PRODUCE CHEMICALS IN YOUR BRAIN.**

9

SNAKE VENOM was used to make TWO DRUGS that PREVENT HEART ATTACKS in humans.

10

EARTHWORMS HAVE 5 HEARTS.

11

A hummingbird heart is about the size of a **CRANBERRY.**

12

A BLUE WHALE'S HEART IS AS LARGE AS A **SMALL CAR.**

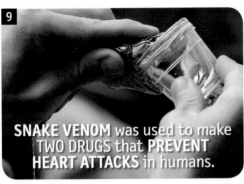

PUMPING FACTS

13

A giraffe's heart is **2 FEET (.6 M) LONG** and weighs **25 POUNDS (11 KG).**

14

A HUMAN HEART **CIRCULATES** NEARLY SIX QUARTS (5.6 L) OF BLOOD THROUGH THE BODY.

16

A DEVELOPING HUMAN HEART FIRST RESEMBLES A **FISH HEART,** THEN A **FROG'S,** THEN A **SNAKE'S,** AND FINALLY A **HUMAN'S.**

15

The human heart pumps blood through a network of blood vessels **60,000 MILES LONG (96,500 KM).**

131

That's GROSS!

WHO NEEDS **SLOBBERING ZOMBIES AND SLIMY MONSTERS** THIS HALLOWEEN? THE BACTERIA LIVING INSIDE YOUR BODY ARE **ICKY ENOUGH.**

Don't panic, but you're outnumbered by alien life-forms. They look like hairy hot dogs, spiky blobs, and oozing spirals, and they're crawling across—and deep inside—your body right this very minute. They're bacteria!

Your body is built of trillions of itty-bitty living blobs, called cells, that work together to do amazing things, such as hold in your organs or help beat your brother at *Clash of Clans*. But for every cell you call your own, about ten foreign bacteria are clustering around or near it. You can't see these hitchhikers, but you sure can smell a lot of them. Like any living thing, bacteria eat, reproduce, die, and create waste. A lot of this waste is the source of your body odor, bad breath, and torturous toots. In other words, some bacteria can make your life stink!

If the thought of being a human-shaped planet for microscopic inhabitants makes you queasy, relax. Most of your body's microbes have been harmlessly hanging out in your body for years and are essential for good health. And just like a fingerprint, your bacteria make you who you are, because no two people host the same mix of microorganisms. But that doesn't make things any less disgusting!

Little Monsters

Meet **four** famous bacteria that **call your body** "home sweet home..."

1 ACTINOMYCES VISCOSUS
When your dentist breaks out the power tools to jackhammer the brownish coat of slime known as plaque from your teeth, she's really attacking these mouth-dwelling bacteria.

4 BREVIBACTERIUM LINENS

This foul-smelling microbe thrives in the sweat simmering in your sneakers, unleashing an awful stink when you kick off your shoes. It's also used to ferment stinky Limburger cheese.

2 METHANOGENS

About half of all people have these supersimple microbes living in their guts. Methanogens produce methane, a greenhouse gas that animals— including humans—pass into the atmosphere when they, um, toot.

3 ESCHERICHIA COLI

This rod-shaped microbe lives deep in your guts, the body's busiest bacterial neighborhood. Helpful *E. coli* strains produce an important vitamin. Harmful ones make you vomit for days.

More Grossness

Your body's bacterial zoo begins when you're born, as you ingest bacteria from your mom's skin and milk. You also consume lots of harmless and helpful bacteria through food and water every day.

Some bacteria are used by scientists to help produce new vaccines and other medicine.

Your body's bacteria eat everything from salt inside your intestines to chemicals in your sweat.

Belly-button lint—a mix of clothing fibers and dead skin cells—is a hot spot for bacteria. Scientists recently found more than 1,400 species of microbes living in people's navels.

QUIZ WHIZ

Are you smart about science? Take this quiz to find out!
ANSWERS BELOW

1 **True or false?** Uranus doesn't have any moons.

2 An elephant's heart weighs as much as_____.
a. a car
b. a four-year-old kid
c. a hummingbird
d. a laptop

3 **Fill in the blank.** Your pupils change _____ whenever the light changes.

4 How do scientists plan to stop a giant asteroid from plunging into the Earth?
a. ramming it with a spacecraft
b. painting it white
c. blasting it with "Laser Bees"
d. all of the above

5 There are more than _____ active volcanoes on Earth.
a. 20
b. 150
c. 1,500
d. 2,000

Not **STUMPED** yet? Check out the *NATIONAL GEOGRAPHIC KIDS QUIZ WHIZ* collection for more crazy **SCIENCE** questions!

ANSWERS:
1. False. Uranus has 27 known moons;
2. b; 3. size; 4. d; 5. c

Research Like a Pro

There is so much information on the Internet. How do you find what you need and make sure it's accurate?

Be Specific
To come up with the most effective key-words—words that describe what you want to know more about—write down what you're looking for in the form of a question, and then circle the most important words in that sentence. Those are the keywords to use in your search. And for best results, use words that are specific rather than general.

Research
Research on the Internet involves "looking up" information using a search engine (see list below). Type one or two keywords, and the search engine will provide a list of websites that contain information related to your topic.

Use Trustworthy Sources
When conducting Internet research, be sure the website you use is reliable and the information it provides can be trusted. Sites produced by well-known, established organizations, companies, publications, educational institutions, or the government are your best bets.

Don't Copy
Avoid Internet plagiarism. Take careful notes and cite the websites you use to conduct research.

HELPFUL AND SAFE SEARCH ENGINES FOR KIDS

Google Safe Search	squirrelnet.com/search/Google_SafeSearch.asp
Yahoo! Kids	kids.yahoo.com
SuperKids	super-kids.com
Ask Kids	askkids.com
Kids Click	kidsclick.org
AOL Kids	kids.aol.com

Wonders of
Nature

Volcanic lightning—a rare phenomenon caused by an eruption plume from a volcano interacting with a passing thunderstorm—lights up the sky above Rabaul, New Britain Island, Papua New Guinea.

Almanac Explorer!

I reach 10 feet (3 m) in length and can weigh over 300 pounds (136 kg).

This is clue #5!
Collect them all and unscramble the letters to find the secret animal. Enter the animal name at kids.nationalgeographic .com/almanac-2016!

Weather and Climate

Weather is the condition of the atmosphere—temperature, precipitation, humidity, and wind—at a given place at a given time. Climate, however, is the average weather for a particular place over a long period of time. Different places on Earth have different climates, but climate is not a random occurrence. It is a pattern that is controlled by factors such as latitude, elevation, prevailing winds, the temperature of ocean currents, and location on land relative to water. Climate is generally constant, but evidence indicates that human activity is causing a change in the patterns of climate.

WEATHER EXTREMES

HEAVIEST HAILSTONE: 2.25 pounds (1.02 kg), discovered during a hailstorm in Gopalganj District, Bangladesh, on April 14, 1986

COLDEST CITIES: Oymyakon, Russia, and Verkhoyansk, Russia, each with the lowest recorded temperature of -90.4°F (-67.8°C)

MOST TIME WITHOUT RAIN: 14.42 years in Arica, Chile

GLOBAL CLIMATE ZONES

Climatologists, people who study climate, have created different systems for classifying climates. One often used system is called the Köppen system, which classifies climate zones according to precipitation, temperature, and vegetation. It has five major categories—Tropical, Dry, Temperate, Cold, and Polar—with a sixth category for locations where high elevations override other factors.

ARCTIC OCEAN
ARCTIC CIRCLE
ATLANTIC OCEAN
TROPIC OF CANCER
PACIFIC OCEAN
EQUATOR
PACIFIC OCEAN
TROPIC OF CAPRICORN
INDIAN OCEAN
ANTARCTIC CIRCLE

Climate
Tropical Dry Humid temperate Humid cold Polar

Bet you didn't know

6 wacky facts about weather

1 **Supercells—** giant thunderstorms made of swirling winds that rise into the sky— can be **50,000 feet tall.** (15,240 m)

2 **Frogs** are said to **croak** louder when **bad weather** is approaching.

3 **Hailstones** can contain pebbles, insects, and **even nuts.**

4 One weather-forecasting tool tests **strands** of human hair to **check humidity.**

5 **Brontophobia** is the fear of thunder.

6 Many **tornadoes** occur between 3 P.M. and 9 P.M.

HOW DOES YOUR GARDEN GROW?

The plant kingdom is more than 300,000 species strong, growing all over the world: on top of mountains, in the sea, in frigid temperatures—everywhere. Without plants, life on Earth would not be able to survive. Plants provide food and oxygen for animals and humans.

Three characteristics make plants distinct:

1. Most have chlorophyll (a green pigment that makes photosynthesis work and turns sunlight into energy), while some are parasitic.

2. They cannot change their location on their own.

3. Their cell walls are made from a stiff material called cellulose.

Photosynthesis

Plants are lucky—they don't have to hunt or shop for food. Most use the sun to produce their own food. In a process called photosynthesis, the plant's chloroplast (the part of the plant where the chemical chlorophyll is located) captures the sun's energy and combines it with carbon dioxide from the air and nutrient-rich water from the ground to produce a sugar called glucose. Plants burn the glucose for energy to help them grow. As a waste product, plants emit oxygen, which humans and other animals need to breathe. When we breathe, we exhale carbon dioxide, which the plants then use for more photosynthesis—it's all a big, finely tuned system. So the next time you pass a lonely houseplant, give it thanks for helping you live.

Plant a BUTTERFLY GARDEN

TAILED JAY

SPICEBUSH SWALLOWTAIL

BUCKEYE

BENEFITS OF BUTTERFLIES

Sure, butterflies are pretty. But they're also pollinators. Like bees, they travel to flowers seeking nectar. In the process, they spread pollen from one area to another, helping other plants grow. That's why "nectar plants" are an important part of your butterfly garden. They help spread the growth of valuable plants to many other places.

MONARCH

SUPPLY LIST
- BUTTERFLY-FRIENDLY PLANTS
- HOST PLANTS TO LAY EGGS ON

EASTERN TIGER SWALLOWTAIL

1 Choose a spot for your garden. Butterflies like lots of sun, so make sure you plant your garden in an area that gets at least six hours of direct sunlight a day.

2 Besides sun, butterflies need protection from wind and rain. Make sure trees or shrubs are part of your butterfly garden.

3 Find out what butterflies you should attract. Look in a field guide or ask a ranger at a local park about which butterfly species are common in your area.

4 Certain butterflies like certain types of plants. Your local nursery can help guide you to the right ones. Many butterflies are attracted to coneflower, lilac, and purple verbena. Try to pick plants that bloom at different times of the year so butterflies are always attracted to your garden.

5 Butterflies will also need some host plants such as milkweed to lay their eggs on. Your nursery can help you select the best ones.

6 Set up some chairs or a bench and watch your garden. Butterflies are less shy than birds and usually don't mind people being around them.

Time: a full afternoon to plant your garden

CARNIVOROUS Plants

Most plants get their nutrients from soil. But many carnivorous plants grow in places where the soil is poor, so they eat insects instead. Here's more about these meat-eaters!

Sarracenia

Sarracenia is a genus of plants that trap bugs with their pitchers, or pitcher-shaped leaves, but that's not all. Some species contain a chemical-laced nectar that dazes their prey. After a few sips, a woozy insect becomes less steady on its feet, leaving it little chance to fend off an inevitable—and untimely—death.

sundew

The "dew" on this plant is inviting to insects. But those droplets—made of a thick, sticky substance attached to the tips of the plant's hairs—are deadly. After landing on the plant's narrow leaves to suck up moisture, the insect gets stuck in the hairs and eventually suffocates or dies from exhaustion. Digestive enzymes in the droplets break down the insect, completing the meal.

cobra lily

This plant picks up its ferocious name from its pitcher, which is formed from a modified leaf that look like a cobra ready to strike. Instead of using fangs to attack its prey, the cobra lily draws insects into its sunny pitcher, thanks to transparent windows on top of its trap that work like a skylight. The insects are drawn to the light, but once they're trapped inside, it's, uh, lights out.

butterwort

The shiny leaves on this plant may look inviting to a thirsty insect, but watch out! Things are not what they seem. The butterwort's leaves are covered with short hairs that are topped with a gluey fluid that acts as a trap. The fluid also contains enzymes that slowly digest the victim.

monkey cup

These plants, native to Southeast Asia, typically trap insects. But they've also been known to eat much bigger species, including small mammals like mice, rats, and occasionally even birds that come to sip at its pitcher. At least the monkeys who are said to drink rainwater out of the plant's pitcher manage to stay out of harm's way!

pitcher plant

Bugs beware! There are many kinds of pitcher plants, but they're all dangerous places to dine. A bug is attracted to the plant's delicious nectar, but if a hungry insect crawls too close to the edge, it slips down the plant's slick insides and becomes trapped at the bottom of the pitcher.

Venus flytrap

No wonder this plant shares a name with a planet—it's truly out of this world! Its leaves are like trapdoors, drawing small insects in with sweet-smelling nectar. If tiny hairs on the surface of the trap are brushed twice in quick succession, the leaves snap shut in the blink of an eye. This sophisticated system ensures that the plant won't waste energy on nonfood items.

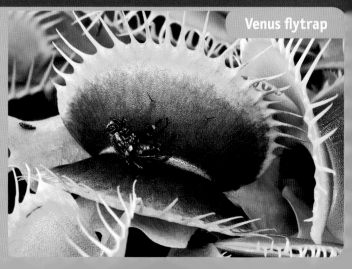

Biomes

A BIOME, OFTEN CALLED A MAJOR LIFE ZONE, is one of the natural world's major communities where plants and animals adapt to their specific surroundings. Biomes are classified depending on the predominant vegetation, climate, and geography of a region. They can be divided into six major types: forest, freshwater, marine, desert, grassland, and tundra. Each biome consists of many ecosystems.

Biomes are extremely important. Balanced ecological relationships among biomes help to maintain the environment and life on Earth as we know it. For example, an increase in one species of plant, such as an invasive one, can cause a ripple effect throughout the whole biome.

Because biomes can be fragile in this way, it is important to protect them from negative human activity, such as deforestation and pollution. We must work to conserve these biomes and the unique organisms that live within them.

FOREST

The forest biomes have been evolving for about 420 million years. Today, forests occupy about one-third of Earth's land area. There are three major types of forests: tropical, temperate, and boreal (taiga). Forests are home to a diversity of plants, some of which may hold medicinal qualities for humans, as well as thousands of animal species, some still undiscovered. Forests can also absorb carbon dioxide, a greenhouse gas, and give off oxygen.

FRESHWATER

Most water on Earth is salty, but freshwater ecosystems—including lakes, ponds, wetlands, rivers, and streams—usually contain water with less than one percent salt concentration. The countless animal and plant species that live in a freshwater biome vary from continent to continent, but they include algae, frogs, turtles, fish, and the larvae of many insects. Throughout the world, people use food, medicine, and other resources from this biome.

MARINE

The marine biome covers almost three-fourths of Earth's surface, making it the largest habitat on our planet. The four oceans make up the majority of the saltwater marine biome. Coral reefs are considered to be the most biodiverse of any of the biome habitats. The marine biome is home to more than one million plant and animal species. Some of the largest animals on Earth, such as the blue whale, live in the marine biome.

DESERT

Covering about one-fifth of Earth's surface, deserts are places where precipitation is less than 10 inches (25 cm) per year. Although most deserts are hot, there are other kinds as well. The four major kinds of deserts in the world are hot, semiarid, coastal, and cold. Far from being barren wastelands, deserts are biologically rich habitats with a vast array of animals and plants that have adapted to the harsh conditions there.

GRASSLAND

Biomes called grasslands are characterized by having grasses instead of large shrubs or trees. Grasslands generally have precipitation for only about half to three-fourths of the year. If it were more, they would become forests. Widespread around the world, grasslands can be divided into two types: tropical (savannas) and temperate. Grasslands are home to some of the largest land animals on Earth, such as elephants, hippopotamuses, rhinoceroses, and lions.

TUNDRA

The coldest of all biomes, a tundra is characterized by an extremely cold climate, simple vegetation, little precipitation, poor nutrients, and a short growing season. There are two types of tundra: arctic and alpine. A very fragile environment, a tundra is home to few kinds of vegetation. Surprisingly, though, there are quite a few animal species that can survive the tundra's extremes, such as wolves, caribou, and even mosquitoes.

Natural Disasters

Every world region has its share of natural disasters—the mix just varies from place to place. And the names of similar storms may vary as well. Take, for example, cyclones, typhoons, and hurricanes. The only difference among these disasters is where in the world they strike. In the Atlantic and the Northeast Pacific, they're hurricanes; in the Northwest Pacific near Asia they're typhoons; and in the South Pacific and Indian Oceans, they're cyclones.

Despite their distinct titles, these natural disasters are each classified by violent winds, massive waves, torrential rain, and floods. The only obvious variation among these storms? They spin in the opposite direction if they're south of the Equator.

TYPHOON!

HURRICANES IN 2016

HELLO, MY NAME IS . . .

Hurricane names come from six official international lists. The names alternate between male and female. When a storm becomes a hurricane, a name from the list is used, in alphabetical order. Each list is reused every six years. A name "retires" if that hurricane caused a lot of damage or many deaths.

Alex
Bonnie
Colin
Danielle
Earl
Fiona
Gaston
Hermine
Ian
Julia
Karl
Lisa
Matthew
Nicole
Otto
Paula
Richard
Shary
Tobias
Virginie
Walter

A monster storm with gusts of 235 miles an hour (380 km/h) barrels down onto a cluster of islands in the heart of the Philippines in November 2013. Howling winds whip debris into the street as palm trees bend nearly in half, and seawater rises as high as a two-story building. This is Super Typhoon Haiyan, and it's about as dangerous as they come.

What classifies a super typhoon? According to the U.S. National Oceanic and Atmospheric Administration (NOAA), winds must sustain speeds of more than 150 miles an hour (240 km/h) for at least a minute. And not only is Haiyan powerful, it's also gigantic: The storm's clouds cover at least two-thirds of the Philippines, which is roughly the size of Arizona, U.S.A.

The word "typhoon" comes from the Greek *typhon*, meaning "whirlwind." These superstrong storms form when tropical winds suck up moisture as they pass over warm water. Increasing in speed and strength as they near the coast, typhoons can topple homes and cause massive flooding once they hit land.

The Philippines endures an average of eight or nine tropical storms every year. But none have been as disastrous as Haiyan. Resulting in over 6,300 casualties, affecting 16 million people, and racking up millions of dollars in damage, the storm was one of the strongest typhoons to ever hit land anywhere in the world.

Scale of Hurricane Intensity

CATEGORY	ONE	TWO	THREE	FOUR	FIVE
DAMAGE	Minimal	Moderate	Extensive	Extreme	Catastrophic
WINDS	74–95 mph (119–153 kph)	96–110 mph (154–177 kph)	111–129 mph (178–208 kph)	130–156 mph (209–251 kph)	157 mph or higher (252+ kph)
(DAMAGE refers to wind and water damage combined.)					

Wildfire!

During the summer of 2014, a lightning strike triggered a fire in a camp area in the Klamath National Forest in northern California, U.S.A. Burning for more than a month, the fire charred more than 100,000 acres (4,047 ha) of land parched by a lengthy drought. In some spots, the fire burned so intensely that it wiped out homes and buildings, leaving nothing but a blackened wasteland in its path.

While this fire was sparked by lightning, others are the result of a careless act by a human, such as leaving a campfire unattended or irresponsibly disposing of a cigarette. Some are ignited by fallen power lines. Others are deliberately set to control dried forest area. However they begin, wildfires can quickly rage out of control.

Highly trained firefighters are equipped and experienced to fight huge forest fires. Some even parachute into a remote area to battle the blaze. In addition to the work of skilled firefighters, a break in the weather can also help in beating a wildfire. For these fires, a little rain goes a long way.

Flood!

In September 2014, five days of heavy rain caused the Jhelum River, which flows from Indian-administered Kashmir into Pakistan, to swell to epic levels. The water burst through embankments, submerging streets and buildings, triggering flash floods and landslides, and ravaging hundreds of towns.

As the rain finally relented, residents waded in neck-deep floodwater to find their belongings, while others sought refuge on top of their homes.

Rescue efforts poured in from around the world, with helicopters flying in food, blankets, and other supplies. Many people were airlifted to safer areas, where camps were set up to help the victims. Still, with countless amounts of damage and thousands of people displaced, the flood is logged in history books as one of the most devastating natural disasters in the area's history.

What is a
tornado?

TORNADOES, ALSO KNOWN AS TWISTERS, are funnels of rapidly rotating air that are created during a thunderstorm. With wind speeds of up to 300 miles an hour (483 km/h), tornadoes have the power to pick up and destroy everything in their path.

Supercell

A massive rotating thunderstorm that generates the most destructive of all tornadoes. A series of supercells in the southern United States caused an outbreak of 92 tornadoes in ten states over a 15-hour period in 2008.

Weather Alert

TORNADOES HAVE OCCURRED IN ALL 50 U.S. STATES AND ON EVERY CONTINENT EXCEPT ANTARCTICA.

Funnel cloud

This rotating funnel of air formed in a cumulus or cumulonimbus cloud becomes a tornado if it touches the ground.

Fire whirls

These tornadoes made of wind and fire occur during a wildfire. Their flaming towers can be five to ten stories tall and can last for more than an hour. They are also called fire devils.

Waterspout

This funnel-shaped column forms over water and is usually weaker than a land tornado.

THE ENHANCED FUJITA SCALE

The Enhanced Fujita (EF) Scale, named after tornado expert T. Theodore Fujita, classifies tornadoes based on wind speed and the intensity of damage that they cause.

EF0
65–85 mph winds
(105–137 kph)
Slight damage

EF1
86–110 mph winds
(138–177 kph)
Moderate damage

EF2
111–135 mph winds
(178–217 kph)
Substantial damage

EF3
136–165 mph winds
(218–266 kph)
Severe damage

EF4
166–200 mph winds
(267–322 kph)
Massive damage

EF5
More than 200 mph winds
(322+ kph)
Catastrophic damage

THE WATER CYCLE

RISING UP

Some of the water and spray from the waterfall in this picture will **evaporate** into the air. Heat from the sun causes some water to evaporate, or turn into water vapor, or gas. This water vapor rises into the air.

RUNNING OFF

Some of the melted snow and rain that runs downhill eventually ends up in large bodies of water. Water that flows over the ground's surface is called **runoff.**

Scientists think that the water we drink, bathe in, and use to grow crops today has been here on Earth since long before the time of the dinosaurs. It has just been moving around and around on, in, and above the Earth in a nearly endless cycle. But there's not much water in the air. In fact, if all of the atmosphere's water rained down at once, it would cover one inch (2.5 cm) of Earth's surface. It's a good thing, then, that we have the water cycle—Earth's original recycling project. Here's how it works:

CHILLING OUT

As water vapor cools in the air, it **condenses.** This means that it changes back into liquid form. You will notice the same kind of thing happening if you pour a cold glass of water on a hot day. Water forms on the outside of the glass. The water vapor in the warm air touches the cold glass and turns to liquid.

FALLING DOWN

After so much water has condensed that the air can't hold it anymore, it falls as **precipitation**—rain, hail, sleet, or snow—into Earth's oceans, lakes, and rivers and onto land.

IGUAZÚ FALLS IN BRAZIL

THE OC

PACIFIC OCEAN

STATS

Surface area
65,436,200 sq mi (169,479,000 sq km)

Portion of Earth's water area
47 percent

Greatest depth
**Challenger Deep
(in the Mariana Trench)
-36,070 ft (-10,994 m)**

Surface temperatures
**Summer high: 90°F (32°C)
Winter low: 28°F (-2°C)**

Tides
**Highest: 30 ft (9 m) near Korean peninsula
Lowest: 1 ft (0.3 m) near Midway Islands**

Cool creatures: giant Pacific octopus,
bottlenose whale, clownfish, great
white shark

ATLANTIC OCEAN

STATS

Surface area
35,338,500 sq mi (91,526,300 sq km)

Portion of Earth's water area
25 percent

Greatest depth
**Puerto Rico Trench
-28,232 ft (-8,605 m)**

Surface temperatures
**Summer high: 90°F (32°C)
Winter low: 28°F (-2°C)**

Tides
**Highest: 52 ft (16 m)
Bay of Fundy, Canada
Lowest: 1.5 ft (0.5 m)
Gulf of Mexico and Mediterranean Sea**

Cool creatures: blue whale, Atlantic spotted
dolphin, sea turtle

GREAT WHITE SHARK

GREEN SEA TURTLE

EANS

INDIAN OCEAN

STATS

Surface area
28,839,800 sq mi (74,694,800 sq km)

Portion of Earth's water area
21 percent

Greatest depth
Java Trench
-23,376 ft (-7,125 m)

Surface temperatures
Summer high: 93°F (34°C)
Winter low: 28°F (-2°C)

Tides
Highest: 36 ft (11 m)
Lowest: 2 ft (0.6 m)
Both along Australia's west coast

Cool creatures: humpback whale, Portuguese man-of-war, dugong (sea cow)

DUGONG

ARCTIC OCEAN

STATS

Surface area
5,390,000 sq mi (13,960,100 sq km)

Portion of Earth's water area
4 percent

Greatest depth
Molloy Deep
-18,599 ft (-5,669 m)

Surface temperatures
Summer high: 41°F (5°C)
Winter low: 28°F (-2°C)

Tides
Less than 1 ft (0.3 m) variation throughout the ocean

Cool creatures: beluga whale, orca, harp seal, narwhal

ORCA

To see the major oceans and bays in relation to landmasses, look at the map on pages 258 and 259.

1 THE BERMUDA ISLANDS AND THE BAHAMAS ARE REALLY ANCIENT CORAL REEFS.

2 FACE MASKS were invented in the 1930s, giving divers a closer look at coral reefs.

3 Two-thirds of warm-water reefs are in DANGER OF DISAPPEARING.

4 A QUARTER OF ALL FISH SPECIES LIVE AROUND CORAL REEFS.

16 COOL FACTS ABOUT

5 Chemicals from coral reefs are USED AS MEDICINE.

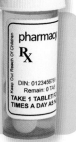

pharmacy
Rx

Keep Out Reach Of Children

DIN: 0123456789
Remain: 0 TAB
TAKE 1 TABLET...
TIMES A DAY AS N...

6 THE OCEAN'S MOST VENOMOUS CREATURE, **THE BOX JELLYFISH,** LIVES ALONG THE GREAT BARRIER REEF.

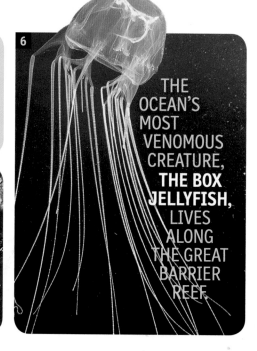

7 Australia's Great Barrier Reef **is so big** it can be seen from space.

8
MANGROVE FORESTS LOCATED ON THE SHORE NEAR REEFS PROVIDE AN IMPORTANT NURSERY FOR YOUNG REEF FISH.

9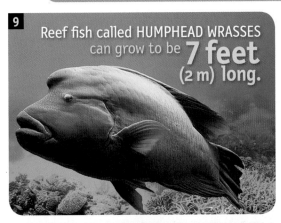
Reef fish called HUMPHEAD WRASSES can grow to be **7 feet (2 m) long.**

10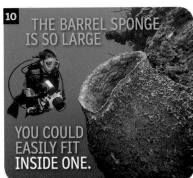
THE BARREL SPONGE IS SO LARGE YOU COULD EASILY FIT INSIDE ONE.

11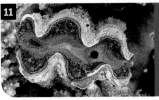
The lips of giant clams contain algae gardens that provide the clams' food.

CORAL REEFS

12
HAWKSBILL TURTLES EAT CORALS.

13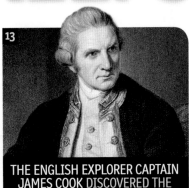
THE ENGLISH EXPLORER CAPTAIN JAMES COOK DISCOVERED THE GREAT BARRIER REEF WHEN HIS SHIP CRASHED INTO IT.

14
WHEN FIRE CORAL TOUCHES SKIN, IT CAUSES A PAINFUL BURNING SENSATION AND A RED RASH.

15
Reefs cover about 100,000 square miles (256,000 sq km) of ocean— that's about twice the size of Greece.

16
Goby fish live on fan corals similar to the way birds live in trees.

155

QUIZ WHIZ

Are you one with nature? Take this quiz to find out how much you know about the great outdoors.

ANSWERS BELOW

(1) **True or false?** Typhoons, hurricanes, and cyclones are all the same type of storm.

(2) Which is the coldest biome?
a. grassland
b. desert
c. tundra
d. forest

(3) Brontophobia is the fear of _____.
a. thunder
b. tornadoes
c. hurricanes
d. dinosaurs

(4) _____ of warm-water reefs are in danger of disappearing.
a. one-quarter
b. one-third
c. one-half
d. two-thirds

(5) Which sea animal does not live in the Atlantic Ocean?
a. blue whale
b. sea turtle
c. spotted dolphin
d. roosterfish

Not **STUMPED** yet? Check out the *NATIONAL GEOGRAPHIC KIDS QUIZ WHIZ* collection for more crazy **NATURE** questions!

ANSWERS:
1. True; 2. c; 3. a; 4. d; 5. d Roosterfish are exclusive to the Pacific Ocean.

SPEAK NATURALLY

Oral Reports Made Easy

Does the thought of public speaking start your stomach churning like a tornado? Would you rather get caught in an avalanche than give a speech?

Giving an oral report does not have to be a natural disaster. The basic format is very similar to that of a written essay. There are two main elements that make up a good oral report—the writing and the presentation. As you write your oral report, remember that your audience will be hearing the information as opposed to reading it. Follow the guidelines below, and there will be clear skies ahead.

TIP: Make sure you practice your presentation a few times. Stand in front of a mirror or have a parent record you so you can see if you need to work on anything, such as eye contact.

Writing Your Material

Follow the steps in the "How to Write a Perfect Essay" section on p. 35, but prepare your report to be spoken rather than written. Try to keep your sentences short and simple. Long, complex sentences are harder to follow. Limit yourself to just a few key points. You don't want to overwhelm your audience with too much information. To be most effective, hit your key points in the introduction, elaborate on them in the body, and then repeat them once again in your conclusion.

An oral report has three basic parts:

- **Introduction**—This is your chance to engage your audience and really capture their interest in the subject you are presenting. Use a funny personal experience or a dramatic story, or start with an intriguing question.

- **Body**—This is the longest part of your report. Here you elaborate on the facts and ideas you want to convey. Give information that supports your main idea, and expand on it with specific examples or details. In other words, structure your oral report in the same way you would a written essay so that your thoughts are presented in a clear and organized manner.

- **Conclusion**—This is the time to summarize the information and emphasize your most important points to the audience one last time.

Preparing Your Delivery

1 Practice makes perfect.
Practice! Practice! Practice! Confidence, enthusiasm, and energy are key to delivering an effective oral report, and they can best be achieved through rehearsal. Ask family and friends to be your practice audience and give you feedback when you're done. Were they able to follow your ideas? Did you seem knowledgeable and confident? Did you speak too slowly or too fast, too softly or too loudly? The more times you practice giving your report, the more you'll master the material. Then you won't have to rely so heavily on your notes or papers, and you will be able to give your report in a relaxed and confident manner.

2 Present with everything you've got.
Be as creative as you can. Incorporate videos, sound clips, slide presentations, charts, diagrams, and photos. Visual aids help stimulate your audience's senses and keep them intrigued and engaged. They can also help to reinforce your key points. And remember that when you're giving an oral report, you're a performer. Take charge of the spotlight and be as animated and entertaining as you can. Have fun with it.

3 Keep your nerves under control.
Everyone gets a little nervous when speaking in front of a group. That's normal. But the more preparation you've done—meaning plenty of researching, organizing, and rehearsing—the more confident you'll be. Preparation is the key. And if you make a mistake or stumble over your words, just regroup and keep going. Nobody's perfect, and nobody expects you to be.

FUN and GAMES

Find the HIDDEN ANIMALS

Animals often blend in with their environments for protection. Find the animals listed below in the photographs. Write the letter of the correct photo next to each animal's name.

ANSWERS ON PAGE 338

1. pygmy seahorses
2. Brazilian long-nosed bats
3. stone grasshopper
4. gray wolf
5. lion
6. European hares

A

B

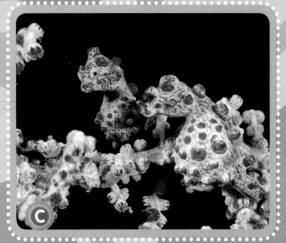

C

D

E

F

HEART-TO-HEART

These photographs show close-up and faraway views of heart-shaped things. Unscramble the letters to identify what's in each picture. **Bonus:** Use the highlighted letters to solve the puzzle below. ANSWERS ON PAGE 338

LUODC
_____

OPER
_____

FALE
_____

LFWEOR
_____

SDILNAS
_____

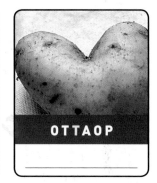

OTTAOP
_____

TEUORMPC EMSUO
_____

VIOALRI
_____

OROD AHLEDN
_____

HINT: How do you interrupt a candy conversation heart?

ANSWER: _Y_ __ __ __ __ __ __ __

Roman Holiday

These tourists are spending the day at the Colosseum in Rome, Italy. Help the traveler at the top left find his tour group while avoiding the other visitors blocking his path.

ANSWER ON PAGE 338

START

END

FUNNY FILL-IN
Gold Rush

Ask a friend to give you words to fill in the blanks in this story without showing it to him or her. Then read it out loud for a laugh.

_____ [friend's name] and I were exploring the bottom of the _____ [body of water] when we found a shipwreck. And not just any shipwreck—the _____ [celebrity], which disappeared in the _____ [historical era]. We swam through the _____ [liquid] to see what we could find. My favorite part was an old ballroom with a(n) _____ [piece of furniture] hanging from the ceiling, lots of old-fashioned _____ [noun, plural], and plenty of _____ [animal, plural] swimming around. Best of all, we found a large wooden _____ [noun]. We struggled to open it, and _____ [something gross] billowed out when we finally lifted off the top. But inside were lots of _____ [color] _____ [noun, plural] and sparkly jewelry. While we were _____ [verb ending in –ing] our discovery we heard a noise. A giant _____ [animal] had _____ [adverb ending in –ly] wrapped its _____ [body part, plural] around the fortune! Uh-oh. Looks like this treasure's already been claimed.

SIGNS
OF THE TIMES

Seeing isn't always believing.
Two of these funny signs are
not real. Can you figure out
which two are fake?

ANSWER ON
PAGE 338

1

ΠΡΟΣΟΧΗ ΚΙΝΔΥΝΟΣ
ΔΡΟΜΟΣ ΟΛΙΣΘΗΡΟΣ
ΕΚ ΣΤΑΦΥΛΟΧΥΜΟΥ
Caution Danger
Road Slippery
With Grape Juice

2

3

COWGIRL
PARKING
ONLY
←→
ALL OTHERS
WILL BE
LASSOED

4

ANT
XING

5

ATTRACTIONS·AHEAD
Myway
Orda
Highway
Visitor Center ?

6

ON THIS SITE
IN 1897 NOTHING
HAPPENED

7

PUSH

Green Scene

You're the newly elected mayor of this busy city. The first order of business? Transform it into the greenest town in the world. Start by finding 15 pieces of litter from the list below. Then locate ten blue recycling bins to toss the trash in.

1. cardboard box
2. crumpled-up paper
3. soda can
4. paper cup
5. phone book
6. cereal box
7. newspapers
8. half-eaten apple
9. egg carton
10. paper bag
11. banana peel
12. glass bottle
13. magazine
14. take-out box
15. milk carton

ANSWERS ON PAGE 338

Grab a parent and **build your own eco-friendly city online** by playing **National Geographic's** Plan It Green.

plan it green
The big switch

nationalgeographic.com/plan-it-green/

What in the World?

PURPLE PIZZAZZ

These photos show close-up views of things that are purple. Unscramble the letters to identify what's in each picture.

Bonus: Use the highlighted letters to solve the puzzle below. ANSWERS ON PAGE 338

I S A Y D

_____

M U L S P

_____

A N R Y

_____

T G R E T I L

_____

E S A R A S T

_____

R S M O M O U H

_____

E I L H Y J S L F

_____

L O T L A U C C R A

_____

H A M T T Y E S

_____

HINT: Why did the grape stop in the middle of the road?

ANSWER: ___ ___ ___ ___ ___ N ___ U ___ O ___ ___ I ___ ___ .

Iguana

Just Joking

KNOCK,
KNOCK.

Who's there?
Turnip.
Turnip who?
**Turnip the heat.
It's freezing in here!**

CUSTOMER: Do you enjoy being a baker?
BAKER: I sure do—it's a piece of cake!

TONGUE TWISTER!

Say this fast three times:

Six thick socks on seven thin sirs.

Q Who **chews on trees and sings?**

A Justin Beaver.

Q **What did the polar bear order for lunch?**

A An iceberg-er.

WANT MORE?

Check out the NG Kids book *Just Joking 4* and the Just Joking app.

NATIONAL GEOGRAPHIC

ANIMAL JAM

Welcome to Jamaa

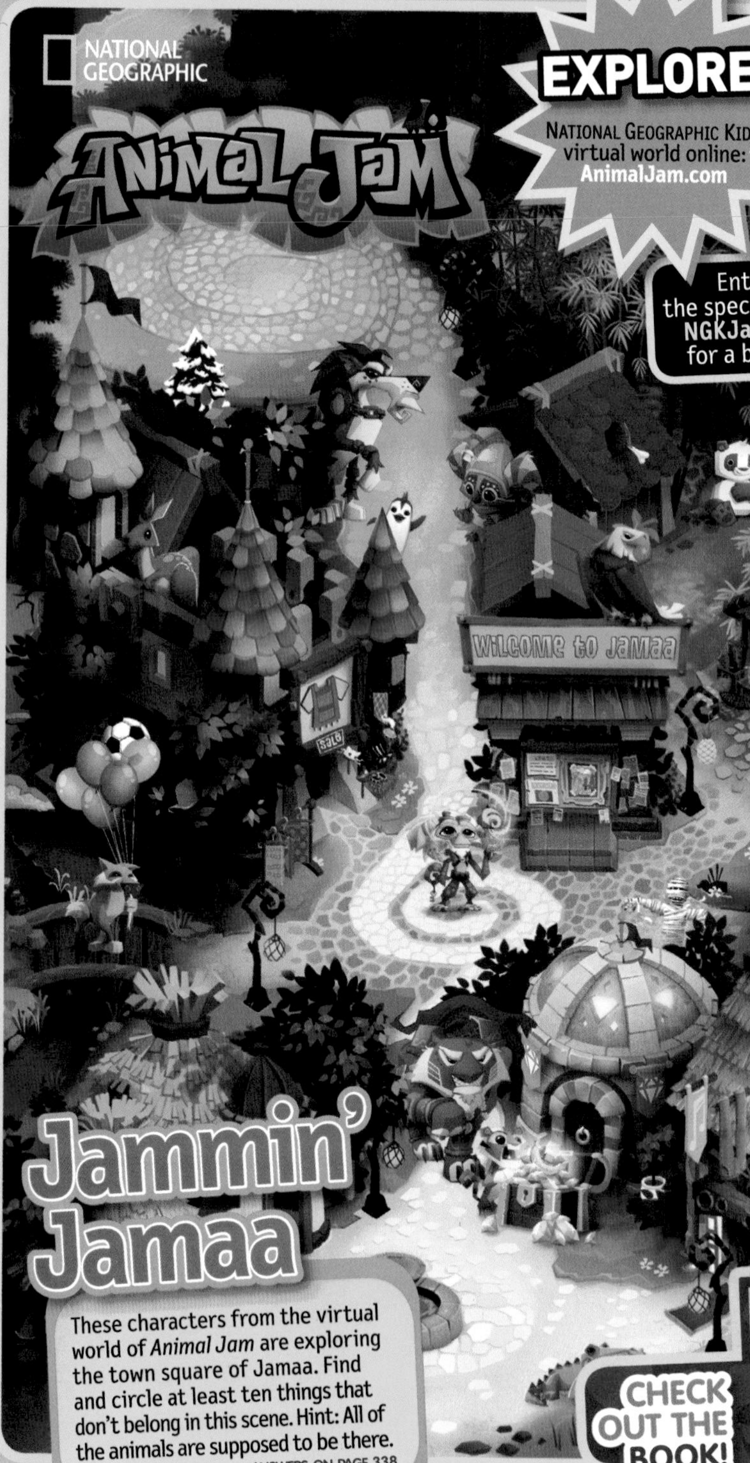

Jammin' Jamaa

These characters from the virtual world of *Animal Jam* are exploring the town square of Jamaa. Find and circle at least ten things that don't belong in this scene. Hint: All of the animals are supposed to be there.

ANSWERS ON PAGE 338

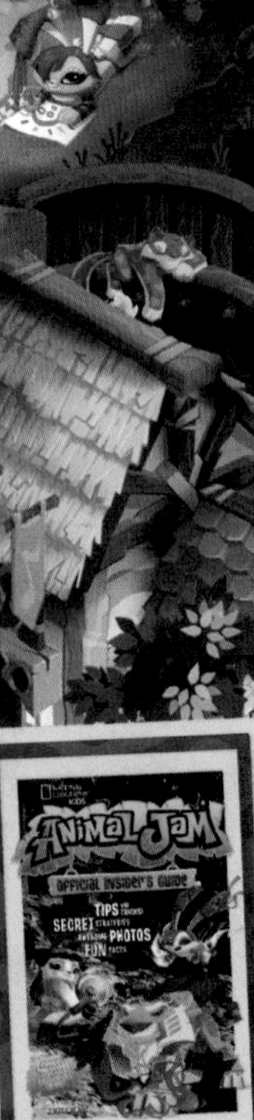

Laugh Out Loud

"IT'S 'BRING YOUR IMAGINARY MONSTER UNDER THE BED TO SCHOOL' DAY!"

"WHAT'S IT LIKE TO GO FOR A WALK AND ACTUALLY *GO* SOMEWHERE?"

"I DON'T CARE WHAT YOU SAY... NEXT YEAR WE MIGRATE EARLIER."

"SO I PUT ON A FEW POUNDS OVER THE HOLIDAYS!"

"IT'S GREAT YOU GOT A JOB AND ALL, BUT YOU DIDN'T TELL ME YOU WENT OVER TO THE DARK SIDE."

Funny FILL-IN

Dining with Dinosaurs

Ask a friend to give you words to fill in the blanks in this story without showing it to him or her. Then read it out loud for a laugh.

Having dinner with dinosaurs is a really *big* deal. _____ and I were invited to
                                                        (friend's name)

eat at the home of a(n) _____ named _____ with her two dinosaur
                         (type of dinosaur)   (female celebrity)

friends. She's much bigger than a(n) _____ and a better cook too. Dinner
                                       (mythical creature)

was a heaping portion of barbecued _____ with a side of steamed
                                      (something gross, plural)

_____ . We sat atop the chef's pet, a(n) _____ . I started to
(type of seafood, plural)   (animal)

take a bite of my meal, but a(n) _____ _____ suddenly
                                   (color)   (same type of seafood)

_____ across the table! Surprised, I jumped back from the food,
(past-tense verb)

_____ _____ everywhere. "_____ !" roared the chef
(verb ending in -ing) (liquid)   (silly expression)

as she dropped the _____ she was holding. Barbecue sauce splashed everywhere—
                     (noun)

including on the pet. I think I'll skip dessert.

Hidden Hike

These hikers are spending St. Patrick's Day exploring Ireland's Cliffs of Moher. But their adventure includes some seriously strange sights. Find and circle at least 15 things that are wrong in the scene. ANSWERS ON PAGE 338

171

Just Joking

Great gray owl

KNOCK, KNOCK.

Who's there?
Who.
Who who?
Hey, that's my line!

JIM: Which circus performers can see in the dark?
NANCY: The acro-bats.

Q What do you get if you cross a pastry with a snake?
A A pie-thon.

TONGUE TWISTER!

Say this fast three times:
Eddie edited it.

You've **got** to be joking...

Q What did the cherries do with the treasure?
A They berried it on a dessert island.

WANT MORE?
Check out the NG Kids book *Just Joking 5* and the Just Joking app.

174

Undersea Stars

This underwater band is jamming onstage, but it looks as if their instruments have disappeared. Or have they? Find the ten instruments listed below hidden in the scene. ANSWERS ON PAGE 338

1. piano
2. drums
3. flute
4. saxophone
5. triangle
6. violin
7. accordion
8. guitar
9. maracas
10. tambourine

CHECK IT OUT!

Check out "Undersea Stars" and other touch-to-play games on the iPad version of NG KIDS. It's **FREE** with your print subscription! Grab a parent and go online. ngm.com/kidsdigital

Just Joking

KNOCK, KNOCK.

Who's there?
Yam.
Yam who?
I yam so happy to see you!

African elephant

Q What did one tornado say to the other tornado?

A See you round!

ADULT: Can I help you?
KID: How much does it cost to adopt a puppy?
ADULT: Ten dollars apiece.
KID: Ten dollars a piece? I wanted one that was already put together.

TONGUE TWISTER!

Say this fast three times:

Randy rode a raft down a rapidly rushing river.

You've **got** to be joking...

Q What do you call a **hippo** that likes **rap music?**

A A hip-hop-o-potamus.

CHECK OUT THE BOOK!

Just Joking 5
300

Funny Fill-In
A Wild Space Walk

Ask a friend to give you words to fill in the blanks in this story without showing it to him or her. Then read it out loud for a laugh.

We're flying through space at _____ miles an hour in our ship. I look outside and see

(large number)

lots of sparkly _____ whizzing by. Suddenly the ship comes to a dead stop.

(noun, plural)

We're stuck in space! I reach into a box labeled "_____" and put on a suit made of

(silly word)

_____ . _____ attaches a(n) _____ to me so I won't drift away.

(favorite food)   (friend's name)   (noun)

I open the door and _____ outside. I see _____ smeared all over the ship.

(verb)   (something sticky)

It must be from when we flew through the cloud of _____ yesterday. I use

(something gross)

_____ to clean it off with my _____ . Just then I see a(n) _____

(liquid)   (body part, plural)   (type of transportation)

in the distance. It's headed right for us. "Need help?" a voice says from inside. It's a(n)

_____ —they do exist! The _____ creature gives us a tow

(mythical creature)   (color)

back to Earth. Who knew extraterrestrials were so friendly?

WANT MORE?

Check out the NG Kids book *Funny Fill-in: My Space Adventure.*

Almanac Explorer!

I am a eptile.

This is clue #7!
Collect them all and
unscramble the letters to
find the secret animal.
Enter the animal name at
kids.nationalgeographic
.com/almanac-2016!

Girls enjoy a Bedouin wedding
on the Sinai Peninsula in Egypt.

Culture
Connection

1 The Beatles' Paul McCartney wrote the song, "Martha My Dear," ABOUT HIS PET DOG.

2 TRADITIONALLY, WEST INDIANS REUSED OIL BARRELS AS STEEL DRUMS.

3 Strings for Spanish acoustic guitars used to be made from SHEEP INTESTINES.

4 **16** DIFFERENT SONGS called "Hold On" have hit Billboard's Top 100 charts—making it the most common song title among popular music.

16 COOL THINGS ABOUT

5 FAMOUS COMPOSER BEETHOVEN WENT COMPLETELY DEAF AT THE HEIGHT OF HIS CAREER.

6 Hip-hop began in the mid-1970s when deejays used TWO TURNTABLES to make music for dancing crowds.

7 Macaque monkeys and chimpanzees will sometimes drum on dead trees.

8 GREECE has one of the longest national anthems in the world, with a total of 158 verses.

9

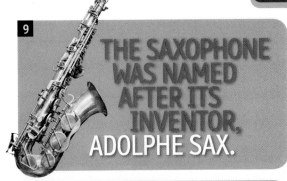

THE SAXOPHONE WAS NAMED AFTER ITS INVENTOR, ADOLPHE SAX.

10

A hymn found on a song tablet in Syria from 1400 B.C. IS THE OLDEST KNOWN WRITTEN SONG.

11

A musician in Paraguay creates instruments MADE ENTIRELY OF TRASH, like tossed forks, oil cans, and wood.

12

A wad of gum chewed by BRITNEY SPEARS sold on eBay for **$14,000.**

MUSIC

14

THERE ARE ABOUT 800 MILLION iTunes ACCOUNTS WORLDWIDE.

13

BEIJING OPERA PERFORMANCES OFTEN INCLUDE MARTIAL ARTS.

15

ROCK 'N' ROLL MARATHONS—held in cities around the world—feature different bands stationed at every mile of the 26.2-mile (42.2-km) race.

16

SOME AMERICAN INDIANS OF THE GREAT PLAINS KEPT THEIR DRUMS IN SPECIAL BUILDINGS CALLED "DRUM HOUSES."

BUTTERFLY

THE ARTIST FIRST OUTLINED

the butterfly's pattern with a makeup pencil. Then he used a brush and nontoxic water-colors to paint the colorful parts. "If I make a mistake, it's very easy to correct or remove," Daniele says.

THE REAL ANIMAL : BUTTERFLIES DON'T HAVE MOUTHS. INSTEAD, THEY SIP MEALS THROUGH A PROBOSCIS, A STRAW-LIKE TUBE FOR FEEDING.

HANDIMALS

WOLF

A YOUNG GIRL'S SMALLER HANDS

and short fingers created just the right pro-portion for the wolf's head and snout. When he's finished, Daniele uses a nontoxic spray to protect the painting. "Then the model can show the handimal to all her friends," he says.

THE REAL ANIMAL

A WOLF'S EYES APPEAR TO GLOW IN THE DARK BECAUSE OF A LIGHT-REFLECTING LAYER OF EYE TISSUE.

PYTHON

THE SNAKE'S COMPOSITION

and texture made this the most challenging handimal to create. Daniele spent two days painting the royal python—one day for each of his son's arms. Then he used computer magic to combine three photos, two of which are the right arm.

THE REAL ANIMAL

SNAKES CAN'T SLITHER ON GLASS.

CHECK OUT THESE **WILD HANDMADE** CREATIONS.

What do you get when you cross a human hand with an animal? A "handimal"! Artist Guido Daniele, who lives in Milan, Italy, positions people's hands into animal shapes and then paints them to create realistic works of art. He paints the animals onto the hands of models—usually his son or daughter. Check out these "handimals" and some of the secrets to Daniele's art. In this case, it's OK to "handle" the animals!

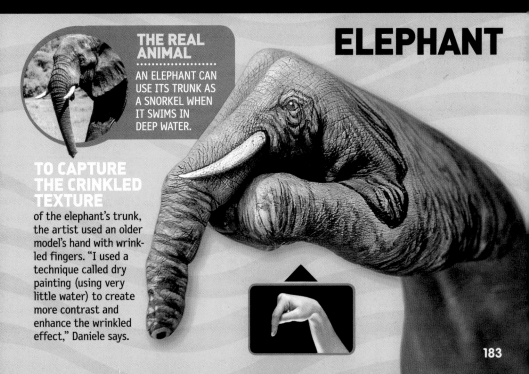

THE REAL ANIMAL

AN ELEPHANT CAN USE ITS TRUNK AS A SNORKEL WHEN IT SWIMS IN DEEP WATER.

ELEPHANT

TO CAPTURE THE CRINKLED TEXTURE

of the elephant's trunk, the artist used an older model's hand with wrinkled fingers. "I used a technique called dry painting (using very little water) to create more contrast and enhance the wrinkled effect," Daniele says.

183

World's Wackiest
HOUSES

Check out these not-so-humble abodes from around the globe.

Your house is a place to kick back and get cozy. But what if it also had 27 floors, a replica of King Tut's burial chamber, or an indoor garden? Make yourself at home in some of the coolest dwellings from around the world.

Nearly 30,000 registered archaeological sites are spread across Mexico.

HOBBIT HOME

Pembrokeshire, Wales

Not all hobbit houses are located in mythical Middle Earth. Simon Dale constructed a family home that looks as if it came straight from *The Lord of the Rings* movies. The grass-covered dwelling was made from scrap wood, twisty tree limbs, and plaster. Inside, floor-to-ceiling tree trunks hold up the roof. Dale built the home in four months with mainly a hammer, chain saw, and chisel—no wizards necessary.

Wales is said to have more castles per square mile than any other European country.

TOWER POWER

Mumbai, India

For a billionaire looking for new digs, the sky's the limit. One wealthy businessman even had a 27-story skyscraper built as a private home for his family of five. The tower—which supposedly cost one billion dollars—boasts a spa, ballroom, movie theater, and yoga studio. Literally living the high life comes at a price, though. The building's first electric bill reportedly totaled $115,000!

Some 447 languages are spoken in India.

Brazil's soccer team has won five World Cups—that's more than any other nation.

ROUND RESIDENCE

São Paulo, Brazil

Sculpted from cement and iron by Eduardo Longo, the 32-foot (9.8-m)-tall house known as the Sphere has three stories and a sleek interior. Instead of a staircase, levels are linked by a winding ramp. For outdoor fun, you can grab onto a rope swing attached to the exterior and go flying around the orb. Longo hopes to create neighborhoods of stacked Sphere houses as a way to save space in his jam-packed city.

CELEBRATIONS

1 CHINESE NEW YEAR
February 8
Also called Lunar New Year, this holiday marks the new year according to the lunar calendar. Families celebrate with parades, feasts, and fireworks. Young people may receive gifts of money in red envelopes.

2 NAURYZ
March 21
This ancient holiday is a major moment on the Kazakhstan calendar. To usher in the start of spring, the people of this Asian country set up tentlike shelters called yurts, play games, go to rock concerts, and feast on rich foods.

3 HOLI
March 23
This festival in India celebrates spring and marks the triumph of good over evil. People cover one another with powdered paint, called *gulal,* and douse one another with buckets of colored water.

4 EASTER
March 27
A Christian holiday that honors the resurrection of Jesus Christ, Easter is celebrated by giving baskets filled with gifts, decorated eggs, or candy to children.

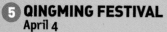

5 QINGMING FESTIVAL
April 4
Also known as "Grave Sweeping Day," this Chinese celebration calls on people to return to the graves of their deceased loved ones. There, they tidy up the grave, as well as light firecrackers, burn fake money, and leave food as an offer to the spirits.

6 VESAK DAY
May 21
Buddhists around the world observe Buddha's Birthday with special rituals including chanting and prayer, candlelight processions, and meditation.

7 BERMUDA DAY
May 24
The first day of the year that Bermudians take a dip in the ocean. It is also traditionally the first day on which Bermuda shorts are worn as business attire. To celebrate the holiday, there is a parade in Hamilton, and a road race from the west end of the island into Hamilton.

8 RAMADAN AND EID AL-FITR
June 5*–July 5**
A Muslim religious holiday, Ramadan is a month long, ending in the Eid Al-Fitr celebration. Observers fast during this month—eating only after sunset. Muslims pray for forgiveness and hope to purify themselves through observance.

9 TANABATA
July 7 or August 7
To commemorate this Star Festival, people in Japan first write wishes on colorful strips of paper. Then, they hang the paper on bamboo branches in their yards and around their homes in the hopes that their wishes will come true.

10 BASTILLE DAY
July 14
The French call this day *La Fête Nationale,* as it is the celebration of the start of the French Revolution in 1789. In Paris, fireworks light up the night skies while dance parties spill into the streets.

*Begins at sundown.
**Dates may vary slightly by location.

186

Around the World

11 NAG PANCHAMI
August 7
In Nepal and India, Hindus worship snakes—and keep evil spirits out of their homes—by sticking images of serpents on their doors and making offerings to the revered reptiles.

12 MELON DAY
August 14
Since 1994, people in the Asian nation Turkmenistan have taken a day—aptly named Melon Day—to celebrate the country's sweet muskmelons.

13 ROSH HASHANAH
October 2*–4
A Jewish religious holiday marking the beginning of a new year on the Hebrew calendar. Celebrations include prayer, ritual foods, and a day of rest.

14 HANUKKAH
December 24*–January 1, 2017
This Jewish holiday is eight days long. It commemorates the rededication of the Temple in Jerusalem. Hanukkah celebrations include the lighting of menorah candles for eight days and the exchange of gifts.

15 CHRISTMAS DAY
December 25

A Christian holiday marking the birth of Jesus Christ, Christmas is usually celebrated by decorating trees, exchanging presents, and having festive gatherings.

2016 CALENDAR

JANUARY
S	M	T	W	T	F	S
					1	2
3	4	5	6	7	8	9
10	11	12	13	14	15	16
17	18	19	20	21	22	23
24	25	26	27	28	29	30
31						

FEBRUARY
S	M	T	W	T	F	S
	1	2	3	4	5	6
7	8	9	10	11	12	13
14	15	16	17	18	19	20
21	22	23	24	25	26	27
28	29					

MARCH
S	M	T	W	T	F	S
		1	2	3	4	5
6	7	8	9	10	11	12
13	14	15	16	17	18	19
20	21	22	23	24	25	26
27	28	29	30	31		

APRIL
S	M	T	W	T	F	S
					1	2
3	4	5	6	7	8	9
10	11	12	13	14	15	16
17	18	19	20	21	22	23
24	25	26	27	28	29	30

MAY
S	M	T	W	T	F	S
1	2	3	4	5	6	7
8	9	10	11	12	13	14
15	16	17	18	19	20	21
22	23	24	25	26	27	28
29	30	31				

JUNE
S	M	T	W	T	F	S
			1	2	3	4
5	6	7	8	9	10	11
12	13	14	15	16	17	18
19	20	21	22	23	24	25
26	27	28	29	30		

JULY
S	M	T	W	T	F	S
					1	2
3	4	5	6	7	8	9
10	11	12	13	14	15	16
17	18	19	20	21	22	23
24	25	26	27	28	29	30
31						

AUGUST
S	M	T	W	T	F	S
	1	2	3	4	5	6
7	8	9	10	11	12	13
14	15	16	17	18	19	20
21	22	23	24	25	26	27
28	29	30	31			

SEPTEMBER
S	M	T	W	T	F	S
				1	2	3
4	5	6	7	8	9	10
11	12	13	14	15	16	17
18	19	20	21	22	23	24
25	26	27	28	29	30	

OCTOBER
S	M	T	W	T	F	S
						1
2	3	4	5	6	7	8
9	10	11	12	13	14	15
16	17	18	19	20	21	22
23	24	25	26	27	28	29
30	31					

NOVEMBER
S	M	T	W	T	F	S
		1	2	3	4	5
6	7	8	9	10	11	12
13	14	15	16	17	18	19
20	21	22	23	24	25	26
27	28	29	30			

DECEMBER
S	M	T	W	T	F	S
				1	2	3
4	5	6	7	8	9	10
11	12	13	14	15	16	17
18	19	20	21	22	23	24
25	26	27	28	29	30	31

Bet you didn't know

8
New Year's Celebrations
Across the Globe

1 IN THAILAND, giant water fights ring in the New Year in early spring.

2 IN IRAN, festivities kick off with the arrival of spring and last 13 days.

3 IN BELGIUM, kids write letters to their parents and godparents, and read them aloud on New Year's Day.

4 IN LONDON, New Year's revelers have been showered with edible banana confetti and peach-flavored snow at midnight.

5 IN SCOTLAND, residents open their front doors before midnight on New Year's Eve to let the old year out and the new year in.

6 IN ETHIOPIA, New Year's comes in September, which is the end of the rainy season.

7 IN CANADA, more than 2,000 people take an icy plunge at Vancouver's Polar Bear Swim each New Year's Day.

8 IN OKLAHOMA, the Muscogee Indians' new year starts in midsummer, after the corn ripens.

new year's party

Sparkling Cider

The highlight of every New Year's party is toasting the arrival of midnight. Start things off right by making this fun and fancy drink. It's super-easy and sure to impress! Any sparkling juice will do, but I like apple cider best. The flavors really come alive when spruced up with the jazzy aromas of cinnamon and citrus.

Prep: 5 minutes / Serves: 1

- 5 ounces (148 ml) sparkling apple cider
- 1 strip lemon zest (peel)
- 1 strip orange zest (peel)
- 1 cinnamon stick

① Pour the cider slowly into a fun glass so that it doesn't foam up.

② Using a vegetable peeler remove a strip of the peel from an orange and another strip from a lemon. You want to get one long strip, about 2 inches (5 cm) long, so go slowly and don't press too hard or you will get too much of the bitter white skin, known as the pith. Take the citrus peels and wrap them around the cinnamon stick.

③ Place the cinnamon stick on the rim of the glass and serve immediately. Before you take a sip, dunk the cinnamon stick into the glass and give it a quick stir to combine the flavors. Enjoy!

—Barton Seaver

WANT MORE? Check out the NG Kids book *Cookbook A Year-Round Fun Food Adventure.*

RINGING IN THE NEW YEAR is a tradition all on its own. The holiday can be traced all the way back to more than 3,000 years ago! Today, everyone celebrates differently. Some people light fireworks, some dine on special foods or beverages, and some give gifts. Many cultures even toast the New Year on completely different dates.

What's Your Chinese Horoscope?
Locate your birth year to find out.

In Chinese astrology the zodiac runs on a 12-year cycle, based on the lunar calendar. Each year corresponds to one of 12 animals, each representing one of 12 personality types. Read on to find out which animal year you were born in and what that might say about you.

RAT
1972, '84, '96, 2008
Say cheese! You're attractive, charming, and creative. When you get mad, you can have really sharp teeth!

HORSE
1966, '78, '90, 2002, '14
Being happy is your "mane" goal. And while you're smart and hardworking, your teacher may ride you for talking too much.

OX
1973, '85, '97, 2009
You're smart, patient, and as strong as an ... well, you know what. Though you're a leader, you never brag.

SHEEP
1967, '79, '91, 2003, '15
Gentle as a lamb, you're also artistic, compassionate, and wise. You're often shy.

TIGER
1974, '86, '98, 2010
You may be a nice person, but no one should ever enter your room without asking—you might attack!

MONKEY
1968, '80, '92, 2004, '16
No "monkey see, monkey do" for you. You're a clever problem-solver with an excellent memory.

RABBIT
1975, '87, '99, 2011
Your ambition and talent make you jump at opportunity. You also keep your ears open for gossip.

ROOSTER
1969, '81, '93, 2005, '17
You crow about your adventures, but inside you're really shy. You're thoughtful, capable, brave, and talented.

DRAGON
1976, '88, 2000, '12
You're on fire! Health, energy, honesty, and bravery make you a living legend.

DOG
1970, '82, '94, 2006
Often the leader of the pack, you're loyal and honest. You can also keep a secret.

SNAKE
1977, '89, 2001, '13
You may not speak often, but you're very smart. You always seem to have a stash of cash.

PIG
1971, '83, '95, 2007
Even though you're courageous, honest, and kind, you never hog all the attention.

Make a 3-D Valentine!

Be sweet to your loved ones and the Earth this Valentine's Day by turning everyday items around your house into something heartfelt. Show how much you care about the environment by creating recycled cards for your family and friends.

YOU WILL NEED

Old newspaper or leftover tissue paper

Heart-shaped cookie cutter

A clean plate

Bowl of water

Paintbrush

Glue wash (equal parts glue and water)

An old greeting card

WHAT TO DO

1 Tear newspaper or tissue paper into small pieces. Place the cookie cutter on the plate. Making sure each piece overlaps, position a few pieces of the paper inside the cookie cutter to create a thin layer. Dip your finger into the bowl of water and then press it gently on the paper layer, making the paper damp. Continue layering, dipping, and pressing until the cookie cutter is about half full. Let it dry for at least a day.

2 When the paper mold is completely dry, gently press down on the mold and carefully lift off the cookie cutter. Using a clean paintbrush, apply a light coat of glue wash to the mold. As it dries, move on to Step 3.

3 Cover an old greeting card with things from around the house—such as construction paper, magazines, newspapers, or doilies. Write a poem or message inside the card and then glue the 3-D heart to the front. Now you're ready to give this Earth-friendly valentine to someone you love!

MONEY Around the World!

ONE KING CELEBRATED A HORSE-RACING VICTORY IN **356** B.C. BY MINTING A COIN WITH AN IMAGE OF **HIS HORSE AND ITS RIDER.**

A CAMBODIAN LEADER **ONCE ABOLISHED THE USE OF MONEY.**

THE SOUTHERN CROSS CONSTELLATION APPEARS ON **BRAZILIAN COINS.**

IN ARGENTINA, **"MANGO"** IS SLANG FOR **"PESO."**

THIS WILL BUY YOU A LOT OF DOG TREATS.

BELGIUM ISSUED A COIN FEATURING THE CARTOON **HERO TINTIN** AND HIS DOG, **SNOWY.**

© HERGE/ML

SINCE 1929 75

IN THE NETHERLANDS IN 1636, **TULIPS** WERE SO VALUABLE THAT SOME COST AS MUCH AS **A HOUSE.**

The INCA called gold **"THE SWEAT OF THE SUN"** and silver **"THE TEARS OF THE MOON."**

A nearly
**220-YEAR-OLD
PENNY**
recently sold for
$1.38 MILLION.

I KNEW I SHOULD'VE TRIED A FAKE ATM INSTEAD.

IN 2002, A MAN OPENED A FAKE BANK AND TOOK IN
$650,000
BEFORE HE WAS CAUGHT.

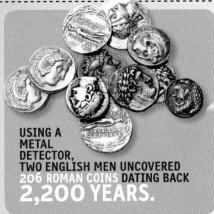

USING A METAL DETECTOR, TWO ENGLISH MEN UNCOVERED 206 ROMAN COINS DATING BACK **2,200 YEARS.**

THE PHRASE **"BRING HOME THE BACON"** STARTED AFTER A 12TH-CENTURY PRIEST REWARDED A MARRIED COUPLE WITH A SIDE OF BACON.

BRICKS OF COMPRESSED TEA LEAVES WERE ONCE USED AS CURRENCY IN SIBERIA, MONGOLIA, AND CHINA.

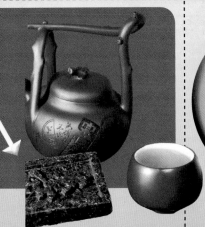

MONEY TIP!
ANYTIME YOU BUY SOMETHING **ON SALE,** PUT WHAT YOU SAVED IN YOUR PIGGY BANK.

CHEW ON THIS

QUESADILLAS!

The quesadilla you order at a restaurant can be filled with lots of things, but the traditional treat from Mexico is almost sure to have one ingredient: cheese. Think of a quesadilla—or, roughly translated, "little cheesy thing" in Spanish—as a twist on a grilled cheese sandwich that you can add other ingredients to.

Astronauts take **TORTILLAS** into space because they produce fewer crumbs than bread.

ZUCCHINI gets its name from the Italian word for squash.

Eating **MONTEREY JACK CHEESE** may help prevent cavities.

The spicy flavor of a **JALAPEÑO** is concentrated near its seeds.

One ear of **CORN** produces about 600 kernels.

MAKE YOUR OWN QUESADILLAS

Get a parent's help to heat up this cheesy dish.

1 Preheat the oven to 400°F (200°C). In a skillet, heat 3 tablespoons (45 ml) of olive oil over medium heat.

2 Cut 1 zucchini in half lengthwise and thinly slice the halves crosswise.

3 Add zucchini and 1 cup (240 ml) of frozen corn kernels to the skillet. Cook, stirring occasionally, for 6 minutes.

4 Brush one side of 4 tortillas with olive oil. Lay 2 of the tortillas, oiled side down, on a baking sheet.

5 Place half of the vegetable filling on each tortilla, and sprinkle each with 1 cup (240 ml) of grated Monterey Jack cheese.

6 Place the remaining 2 tortillas on top, with their oiled side up.

7 Bake for 5 minutes, then flip. Continue baking until cheese has melted, for about 5 more minutes.

8 Cut each quesadilla into wedges and top with a handful of sliced jalapeños.

CANDY APPLES!

Legend says that the store owner just wanted to sell more cinnamon-flavored candies. Instead, he sparked a candy apple craze! After dipping some apples into the melted red sweets, the man displayed the fruit in his window. He then discovered that customers didn't want just the cinnamon candy—they wanted the whole treat, apple and all. Soon he was selling thousands of candy apples a year.

COCONUTS were once so valued that their shells were sometimes mounted and painted in gold.

One **PISTACHIO** tree can produce about 50,000 nuts every two years.

CARAMEL, butterscotch, and toffee share most of the same ingredients but are cooked at different temperatures.

Pilgrims on the *Mayflower* brought **APPLE** seeds from England to the United States.

CANDY CORN was sold as a summertime treat in the 1950s.

MAKE YOUR OWN CARAMEL APPLES

Get a parent's help to create some fun fruit.

1 Wash and dry 6 apples and remove the stems. Stick a wooden skewer in the stem end of each apple. (You can also use ice pop sticks.)

2 Unwrap and place 40 individual caramels in a microwave-safe bowl with 2 tablespoons (30 ml) of milk.

3 Microwave the mixture for 2 minutes, stirring once. Allow the caramel to cool.

4 Roll each apple in the caramel, twirling to make sure the apple is completely coated.

5 Place the apples on a baking sheet covered with parchment paper. Sprinkle the apples with your favorite topping— such as pistachios or candy corn—and allow them to set.

12 Ways to Say Happy Birthday

1. **ARABIC** Eid milaad sa'eed
2. **FRENCH (CANADA)** Bonne Fête
3. **GERMAN** Alles Gute zum Geburtstag
4. **GREEK** Hronia polla
5. **HAWAIIAN** Hau'oli La Hanau
6. **HEBREW** Yom Huledet Sameakh
7. **HINDI** Janmadin mubarak ho
8. **MANDARIN** Shengrì kuàilè
9. **RUSSIAN** S dniom rojdeniya
10. **SPANISH** ¡Feliz cumpleaños!
11. **SWAHILI** Nakutakia mema kwa siku yako ya kuzaliwa!
12. **TURKISH** Dogum günün kutlu olsun

LANGUAGES IN PERIL

TODAY, there are more than 7,000 languages spoken on Earth. But by 2100, more than half of those may disappear. In fact, experts say one language dies every two weeks, due to the increasing dominance of larger languages, such as English, Spanish, and Mandarin. So what can be done to keep dialects from disappearing? Efforts like National Geographic's Enduring Voices Project are now tracking down and documenting the world's most threatened indigenous languages, such as Tofa, spoken only by people in Siberia, and Magati Ke, from Aboriginal Australia. The hope is to preserve these languages—and the cultures they belong to.

10 LEADING LANGUAGES

Approximate population of first-language speakers (in millions)

Language	Speakers
1. Chinese*	1,197
2. Spanish	414
3. English	335
4. Hindi	260
5. Arabic	237
6. Portuguese	203
7. Bengali	193
8. Russian	167
9. Japanese	122
10. Javanese	83

Some languages have only a few hundred speakers, while Chinese has nearly one billion two hundred million native speakers worldwide. That's about triple the next largest group of language speakers. Colonial expansion, trade, and migration account for the spread of the other most widely spoken languages. With growing use of the Internet, English is becoming the language of the technology age.

*Includes all forms of the language.

Bet you didn't know

6 epic facts about mythology

1 One **cyclops** from Greek mythology **liked to snack** on **humans.**

2 To live **forever,** gods in ancient Chinese myths **ate** peaches from a **magic tree.**

3 An Irish folklore **hero** carried a **spear** made of **sea monster bones.**

4 The spirits of **old umbrellas** appear in some **Japanese myths.**

5 Certain African tales feature a **snake** that **belches out rainbows.**

6 According to **Viking** lore, the god Odin rode an **eight-legged horse.**

197

MYTHOLOGY

GREEK

EGYPTIAN

The ancient Greeks believed that many gods and goddesses ruled the universe. According to this mythology, the Olympians lived high atop Greece's Mount Olympus. Each of these 12 principal gods and goddesses had a unique personality that corresponded to particular aspects of life, such as love or death.

THE OLYMPIANS

Aphrodite was the goddess of love and beauty.

Apollo, Zeus's son, was the god of the sun, music, and healing. Artemis was his twin.

Ares, Zeus's son, was the god of war.

Artemis, Zeus's daughter and Apollo's twin, was the goddess of the hunt and of childbirth.

Athena, born from the forehead of Zeus, was the goddess of wisdom and crafts.

Demeter was the goddess of fertility and nature.

Hades, Zeus's brother, was the god of the under-world and the dead.

Hephaestus, the son of Hera, was the god of fire.

Hera, the wife and older sister of Zeus, was the goddess of women and marriage.

Hermes, Zeus's son, was the messenger of the gods.

Poseidon, the brother of Zeus, was the god of the sea and earthquakes.

Zeus was the most powerful of the gods and the top Olympian. He wielded a thunderbolt and was the god of the sky and thunder.

Egyptian mythology is based on a creation myth that tells of an egg that appeared on the ocean. When the egg hatched, out came Ra, the sun god. As a result, ancient Egyptians became worshippers of the sun and of the nine original deities, most of whom were the children and grandchildren of Ra.

THE NINE DEITIES

Geb, son of Shu and Tefnut, was the god of the Earth.

Isis (Ast), daughter of Geb and Nut, was the goddess of fertility and motherhood.

Nephthys (Nebet-Hut), daughter of Geb and Nut, was protector of the dead.

Nut, daughter of Shu and Tefnut, was the goddess of the sky.

Osiris (Usir), son of Geb and Nut, was the god of the afterlife.

Ra (Re), the sun god, is generally viewed as the creator. He represents life and health.

Seth (Set), son of Geb and Nut, was the god of the desert and chaos.

Shu, son of Ra, was the god of air.

Tefnut, daughter of Ra, was the goddess of rain.

All cultures around the world have unique legends and traditions that have been passed down over generations. Many myths refer to gods or supernatural heroes who are responsible for occurrences in the world. For example, Norse mythology tells of the red-bearded Thor, the god of thunder, who is responsible for creating lightning and thunderstorms. And many creation myths, especially those from some of North America's native cultures, tell of an earth-diver represented as an animal that brings a piece of sand or mud up from the deep sea. From this tiny piece of earth, the entire world takes shape.

NORSE

ROMAN

Norse mythology originated in Scandinavia, in northern Europe. It was complete with gods and goddesses who lived in a heavenly place called Asgard that could be reached only by crossing a rainbow bridge.

While Norse mythology is lesser known, we use it every day. Most days of the week are named after Norse gods, including some of these major deities.

NORSE GODS

Balder was the god of light and beauty.

Freya was the goddess of love, beauty, and fertility.

Frigg, for whom Friday was named, was the queen of Asgard. She was the goddess of marriage, motherhood, and the home.

Heimdall was the watchman of the rainbow bridge and the guardian of the gods.

Hel, the daughter of Loki, was the goddess of death.

Loki, a shape-shifter, was a trickster who helped the gods—and caused them problems.

Skadi was the goddess of winter and of the hunt. She is often represented as "The Snow Queen."

Thor, for whom Thursday was named, was the god of thunder and lightning.

Tyr, for whom Tuesday was named, was the god of the sky and war.

Wodan, for whom Wednesday was named, was the god of war, wisdom, death, and magic.

Much of Roman mythology was adopted from Greek mythology, but the Romans also developed a lot of original myths as well. The gods of Roman mythology lived everywhere, and each had a role to play. There were thousands of Roman gods, but here are a few of the stars of Roman myths.

ANCIENT ROMAN GODS

Ceres was the goddess of the harvest and motherly love.

Diana, daughter of Jupiter, was the goddess of hunting and the moon.

Juno, Jupiter's wife, was the goddess of women and fertility.

Jupiter, the patron of Rome and master of the gods, was the god of the sky.

Mars, the son of Jupiter and Juno, was the god of war.

Mercury, the son of Jupiter, was the messenger of the gods and the god of travelers.

Minerva was the goddess of wisdom, learning, and the arts and crafts.

Neptune, the brother of Jupiter, was the god of the sea.

Venus was the goddess of love and beauty.

Vesta was the goddess of fire and the hearth. She was one of the most important of the Roman deities.

World Religions

Around the world, religion takes many forms. Some belief systems, such as Christianity, Islam, and Judaism, are monotheistic, meaning that followers believe in just one supreme being. Others, like Hinduism, Shintoism, and most native belief systems, are polytheistic, meaning that many of their followers believe in multiple gods.

All of the major religions have their origins in Asia, but they have spread around the world. Christianity, with the largest number of followers, has three divisions—Roman Catholic, Eastern Orthodox, and Protestant. Islam, with about one-fifth of all believers, has two main divisions—Sunni and Shiite. Hinduism and Buddhism account for almost another one-fifth of believers. Judaism, dating back some 4,000 years, has more than 13 million followers, less than one percent of all believers.

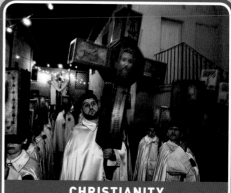

CHRISTIANITY

Based on the teachings of Jesus Christ, a Jew born some 2,000 years ago in the area of modern-day Israel, Christianity has spread worldwide and actively seeks converts. Followers in Switzerland (above) participate in an Easter season procession with lanterns and crosses.

BUDDHISM

Founded about 2,400 years ago in northern India by the Hindu prince Gautama Buddha, Buddhism spread throughout East and Southeast Asia. Buddhist temples have statues, such as the Mihintale Buddha (above) in Sri Lanka.

HINDUISM

Dating back more than 4,000 years, Hinduism is practiced mainly in India. Hindus follow sacred texts known as the Vedas and believe in reincarnation. During the festival of Navratri, which honors the goddess Durga, the Garba dance is performed (above).

CLOSE-UP

Now that's a BIG crowd!

It has been 1,200 years since the bishop of Rome became known as the pope. Today, the pope is still the head of the Roman Catholic Church. Every Easter Sunday about 100,000 people gather in St. Peter's Square in Vatican City to receive his blessing.

ISLAM

Muslims believe that the Koran, Islam's sacred book, records the words of Allah (God) as revealed to the Prophet Muhammad beginning around A.D. 610. Believers (above) circle the Kaaba in the Haram Mosque in Mecca, Saudi Arabia, the spiritual center of the faith.

JUDAISM

The traditions, laws, and beliefs of Judaism date back to Abraham (the Patriarch) and the Torah (the first five books of the Old Testament). Followers pray before the Western Wall (above), which stands below Islam's Dome of the Rock in Jerusalem.

QUIZ WHIZ

Are you a culture connoisseur? Take this quiz to find out if you know what's up with what's happening around the world.

ANSWERS BELOW

1 What were Spanish acoustic guitar strings once made of?
a. cat whiskers
b. sheep intestines
c. fishing line
d. jellyfish tentacles

2 **True or false?** In the Netherlands, some tulips were once as expensive as a house.

3 *Hronia polla* means _____ in Greek.

4 In which country is Hinduism mainly practiced?
a. Ireland
b. Indonesia
c. India
d. Iceland

5 Poseidon, the brother of Zeus, was the god of the _____?

ZEUS

Not **STUMPED** yet? Check out the *NATIONAL GEOGRAPHIC KIDS QUIZ WHIZ* collection for more crazy **CULTURE** questions!

HOMEWORK HELP

Explore a New Culture

INDIAN STAMP

5-RUPEE COIN

INDIAN FLAG

You're a student, but you're also a citizen of the world. Writing a report on a foreign nation or your own country is a great way to better understand and appreciate how people in other parts of the world live. Pick the country of your ancestors, one that's been in the news, or one that you'd like to visit someday.

Passport to Success
A country report follows the format of an expository essay because you're "exposing" information about the country you choose.

Simple Steps

1. RESEARCH Gathering information is the most important step in writing a good country report. Look to Internet sources, encyclopedias, books, magazine and newspaper articles, and other sources to find important and interesting details about your subject.

2. ORGANIZE YOUR NOTES Put the information you gathered into a rough outline. For example, sort everything you found about the country's system of government, climate, etc.

3. WRITE IT UP Follow the basic structure of good writing: introduction, body, and conclusion. Remember that each paragraph should have a topic sentence that is then supported by facts and details. Incorporate the information from your notes, but make sure it's in your own words. And make your writing flow with good transitions and descriptive language.

4. ADD VISUALS Include maps, diagrams, photos, and other visual aids.

5. PROOFREAD AND REVISE Correct any mistakes, and polish your language. Do your best!

6. CITE YOUR SOURCES Be sure to keep a record of your sources.

Almanac Explorer!

I can run up to 11 mph (18 kph) in short bursts.

This is clue #8! Collect them all and unscramble the letters to find the secret animal. Enter the animal name at kids.nationalgeographic .com/almanac-2016!

Bicycles are a popular—and green—way to travel in Amsterdam, Netherlands, where bikes outnumber cars four to one.

Going
Green

GREEN Extremes

THESE OVER-THE-TOP IDEAS TAKE ECO-FRIENDLY TO A WHOLE NEW LEVEL. FIND OUT HOW FAR SOME PEOPLE WILL GO TO REUSE AND RECYCLE.

Recycled Art

This may look like a regular portrait, but look closely and you'll see it's actually made of discarded pieces of junk. Artist Zac Freeman collects objects like buttons, bike chains, and safety pins, and then glues them to a wooden canvas to create giant works of eco-friendly art.

Energy **Boost**

At a hotel in Denmark, guests can eat a free meal if they ride a stationary bike for 15 minutes, producing 10 watts of energy to help power the building.

Powerful Steps

This lightweight insole in your shoe lets you charge your smartphone's battery with energy produced while you walk.

Great Goats

A pair of goats roam the greens on a golf course in Ontario, Canada, eating weeds, eliminating the need for environmentally unfriendly pesticides.

No-Waste Home

This house is made completely out of recycled products and trash, including 4,000 VHS tapes, 500 bike tires, and 20,000 toothbrushes.

Habitat

WHERE HAVE THE ANIMALS GONE?

All around the world, animals face threats to their habitat, many of which are caused by humans. Read on about two animals and their fight for survival.

SPIDER MONKEY WITH BABY

TWO ADULT SPIDER MONKEYS

BROWN SPIDER MONKEY

A farmer living in South America, deep in one of Colombia's rain forests, has spotted a rare species of spider monkey once thought to be extinct in the region.

Spider monkeys spend most of their lives high in tree branches. They travel in social groups called troops. A spider monkey swings from branch to branch as easily as you walk from your living room to the kitchen. Its tail has a grip strong enough to support the animal's entire weight, leaving the other four long limbs free to pick tasty nuts, fruits, and leaves.

Hunting and habitat loss have threatened all species of spider monkeys. Some are critically endangered, although those living in national parks are safe from hunters and habitat loss.

High in the trees in a protected area, a few dark shapes swing from the highest branches—brown spider monkeys! "This is the only population found within a national protected area," says Néstor Roncancio, a Wildlife Conservation Society researcher. "It's one of the largest fragments of forest left with good habitat for the species."

Destruction

MANATEE RESCUE!

DRINK UP!

Swimming along a river in western Florida, U.S.A., a female manatee floats just beneath the water's surface. Dark in color and moving slowly, the manatee is hard to spot. Above the surface, a boat is heading straight toward her. The people on the boat don't see the manatee just below the surface. Suddenly, the boat collides with the manatee.

Luckily, this manatee, named Della, is rescued and treated at a rehabilitation center. Caretakers determine that she's just weeks away from having a baby. Soon, Della gives birth to a calf, named Pal. She also becomes an adoptive mom to Kee, a rescued orphaned calf. Della regains strength as she spends her days with the two calves, gliding around the water with them, and even napping with them at the bottom of their pool.

Five months later, it's time to release the trio back into the wild. Once submerged in their new stream, the manatee family happily paddles away.

Della, Pal, and Kee are lucky. They were rescued, treated, and given a new home. But that's not always the case. People are living in manatees' habitats. They are driving boats, fishing, and swimming in the water. That puts manatees at risk. Learning to share space with animals is important. Driving boats slowly and carefully in manatee habitats can help save these gentle giants.

When resting, manatees can stay submerged for up to 20 minutes.

Average adult manatees are about 10 feet (3 m) long and weigh 1,000 pounds (454 kg).

Manatees breathe only through their nostrils.

GLOBAL WARMING

Climate Change, Explained

Fact: The world is getting warmer. The summer of 2014 was the warmest summer since records began in 1880. Summer 2013 temperatures were 1.28°F (.71°C) higher than the average summer temperature in the 20th century. This is the direct effect of climate change, which refers not only to the increase in the Earth's average temperature (known as global warming), but also to the long-term effects on winds, rain, and ocean currents. Global warming is the reason glaciers and polar ice sheets are melting—resulting in rising sea levels and shrinking habitats. This makes survival for some animals a big challenge. Warming also means more flooding along the coasts and drought for inland areas.

Why are temperatures climbing?

Some of the recent climate changes can be tied to natural causes—such as changes in the sun's intensity, the unusually warm ocean currents of El Niño, and volcanic activity—but human activities are a major factor as well.

Everyday activities that require burning fossil fuels, such as driving gasoline-powered cars, contribute to global warming. These activities produce greenhouse gases, which enter the atmosphere and trap heat. At the current rate, Earth's global average temperature is projected to rise from 2 to 11.5°F (1 to 6.4°C) by the year 2100, and it will get even warmer after that. And as the climate continues to warm, it will unfortunately continue to affect the environment and our society in many ways.

Polar bear on a piece of melting iceberg

Greenland's Giant Canyon

Think the Grand Canyon in Arizona, U.S.A., is huge? Well, imagine a canyon nearly twice as long! That's just what sits under Greenland's ice sheet, a thick layer of frozen water that covers an area about a quarter of the size of the continental United States.

The recently discovered canyon, which runs as deep as a half a mile (800 m) and as long as 466 miles (750 km), was likely part of a massive river system before an ice sheet covered it millions of years ago. Scientists think that water once flowed in the canyon from the interior of Greenland and that the canyon may one day play a major role in transporting meltwater below the ice into the Arctic Ocean.

Rising sea levels

Global warming is taking a toll on Greenland. In 2009, record-high temperatures caused changes in the ice sheet, like the 150-foot (46-m)-deep Birthday Canyon, carved by meltwater. And although the chances of Greenland's entire ice sheet melting are remote, there is enough frozen freshwater there to raise sea levels by about 20 feet (6 m), which would impact coastlines around the world. It's very important for scientists to have a better understanding of what lies beneath the ice so they can predict how water will flow if— or when—things start to melt.

A massive canyon rests below Greenland's ice sheet.

Scientists are concerned that Greenland's ice sheet has begun to melt in summer. Birthday Canyon, shown here, was carved by meltwater.

Pollution
Cleaning Up Our Act

So what's the big deal about a little dirt on the planet? Pollution can affect animals, plants, and people. In fact, some studies show that more people die every year from diseases linked to air pollution than from car accidents. And right now nearly one billion of the world's people don't have access to clean drinking water.

A LITTLE POLLUTION = BIG PROBLEMS

You can probably clean your room in a couple of hours. (At least we hope you can!) But you can't shove air and water pollution under your bed or cram them into the closet. Once released into the environment, pollution—whether it's oil leaking from a boat or chemicals spewing from a factory's smokestack—can have a lasting environmental impact.

KEEP IT CLEAN

It's easy to blame things like big factories for pollution problems. But some of the mess comes from everyday activities. Exhaust fumes from cars and garbage in landfills can seriously trash the Earth's health. We all need to pitch in and do some house-cleaning. It may mean bicycling more and riding in cars less. Or not dumping water-polluting oil or household cleaners down the drain. Look at it this way: Just as with your room, it's always better not to let Earth get messed up in the first place.

Seeing the Light

Here's the dark truth: Most people see only a few dozen stars on an average night instead of the thousands that are actually up there. Why? Blame light pollution—the result of brightly lit cities and towns dimming our views of the night sky. Worse, though, it also may be disrupting entire ecosystems. For example, sea turtle hatchlings need the light from stars and the moon to guide them from their nests to the water. When light pollution blocks the natural light, the hatchlings become disoriented and don't know which way to go. So, what can you do about light pollution? For starters, turn off any lights in your house that you're not using—especially outdoor lighting. It's one of many simple ways we can pull the plug on light pollution for good.

Declining Biodiversity

Saving All Creatures Great and Small

Earth is home to a huge mix of plants and animals—perhaps 100 million species—and scientists have officially identified and named only about 1.9 million so far! Scientists call this healthy mix biodiversity.

THE BALANCING ACT

The bad news is that half of the planet's plant and animal species may be on the path to extinction, mainly because of human activity. People cut down trees, build roads and houses, pollute rivers, overfish and overhunt. The good news is that many people care. Scientists and volunteers race against the clock every day, working to save wildlife before time runs out. By building birdhouses, planting trees, and following the rules for hunting and fishing, you can be a positive force for preserving biodiversity, too. Every time you do something to help a species survive, you help our planet to thrive.

Green sea turtle

Habitats Threatened

Living on the Edge

Even though tropical rain forests cover only about 7 percent of the planet's total land surface, they are home to half of all known species of plants and animals. Because people cut down so many trees for lumber and firewood and clear so much land for farms, hundreds of thousands of acres of rain forest disappear every year.

SHARING THE LAND

Wetlands are also important feeding and breeding grounds. People have drained many wetlands, turning them into farm fields or sites for industries. More than half the world's wetlands have disappeared within the past century, squeezing wildlife out. Balancing the needs of humans and animals is the key to lessening habitat destruction.

Toucan

213

1 A CAVE BENEATH MEXICO'S YUCATÁN RAIN FOREST HAS A WATER-FILLED SINKHOLE WHERE YOU CAN GO SWIMMING.

2 A PRICK FROM THE TOXIC GYMPIE-GYMPIE PLANT IN AUSTRALIAN AND INDONESIAN RAIN FORESTS CAN STING FOR MONTHS.

3 GOLIATH BEETLES from Africa's rain forests CAN WEIGH nearly as much as a STICK OF BUTTER.

4 In Central American forests, rival STRAWBERRY POISON DART FROGS might WRESTLE for up to 20 MINUTES.

16 FACTS ABOUT THE

5 The wingspan of the blue morpho butterfly from Central and South American rain forests is six inches (15.2 cm) wide.

6 THE AMAZON RAIN FOREST IN SOUTH AMERICA IS NEARLY AS BIG AS THE CONTIGUOUS UNITED STATES.

7 IT CAN TAKE TEN MINUTES FOR A FALLING RAINDROP TO TRAVEL FROM A RAIN FOREST'S THICK CANOPY TO ITS FLOOR.

8 WHEN PANGOLINS——SCALY MAMMALS FROM AFRICAN AND ASIAN RAIN FORESTS——CURL UP, THEY RESEMBLE PINECONES.

9 A LAKE inside a rain forest on the Caribbean island of Dominica SIZZLES AT AROUND 190°F (88°C).

10

CLOUDED LEOPARD

India's Jeypore-Dehing forest is home to **seven wild cat species**, the most ever recorded in a single area.

11

KINKAJOUS, WHICH LIVE IN CENTRAL AND SOUTH AMERICAN RAIN FORESTS, LIKE TO LICK HONEY FROM BEEHIVES.

12

Latin American forests are home to black howler monkeys, whose calls can be heard three miles (4.8 km) away.

RAIN FOREST

13

FOUND IN AUSTRALIAN RAIN FORESTS, THE RED-LEGGED PADEMELON RESTS ITS HEAD ON ITS TAIL WHILE SLEEPING.

16

THE RHINOCEROS HORNBILL BIRD FROM SOUTHEAST ASIAN FORESTS HAS A HORNLIKE STRUCTURE ON ITS HEAD THAT LOOKS LIKE AN EXTRA BEAK.

14

One ritual of the Sateré-Mawé tribe in the Amazon rain forest involves pulling on gloves filled with stinging ants.

15

Tropical rain forests have **RED SOIL** because of high levels of **IRON** and **ALUMINUM.**

FOOD FOR THOUGHT

It may seem as if the world's oceans are so vast that nothing could hurt them. Unfortunately, that's not true. The oceans suffer from people dumping stuff in them that they don't want (pollution) and taking too much from them that they do want (overfishing). You can help turn this problem around.

BE AN OCEAN HERO!

You can be part of the solution if you carefully choose what fish to eat. Some are okay to eat; others you should avoid because they're overfished or caught in ways that harm the ocean. Check out the list below to help guide your seafood choices. To get the most up-to-date info, check out our Seafood Decision Guide at *www.natgeoseafood.com*. Ask your parents to consult it when they buy fish at the market or order it at a restaurant. Ask the grocer or chef where and how the fish was caught. Saving marine life is hard, but if everyone helps, it will make a difference.

BEST CHOICES

abalone (farmed)
catfish (U.S.)
clams (farmed)
clams, softshell
crab, Dungeness
crab, stone
crawfish (U.S.)
halibut, Pacific
lobster, spiny
 (Australia, Baja, U.S.)

mackerel, Atlantic
mahimahi (U.S. troll)
mullet (U.S.)
mussels (farmed)
oysters (farmed)
pollock, Alaska
sablefish/black cod
 (Alaska, Canada)
salmon (Alaska wild)
salmon, canned pink/sockeye

sardines (U.S.)
scallops, bay (farmed)
shrimp, pink (Oregon)
shrimp (U.S. farmed)
squid, longfin (U.S.)
striped bass (farmed)
tilapia (U.S.)
trout, rainbow (farmed)
tuna, albacore (Canada, U.S.)
tuna, yellowfin (U.S. troll)

WORST CHOICES

cod, Atlantic
crab, king (imported)
crawfish (China)
flounder/sole (Atlantic)
grouper
haddock (trawl)

halibut, Atlantic
mahimahi (imported longline)
orange roughy
salmon (farmed or Atlantic)
shark
shrimp/prawns (imported)

swordfish (imported)
tilapia (Asia)
tuna, bigeye (longline)
tuna, bluefin
tuna, yellowfin
 (imported longline)

Try this delicious ocean-friendly recipe from master chef and National Geographic Fellow Barton Seaver.

Salmon Salad Sandwich

Before you go running for the hills after reading the name of this dish, consider this: You've eaten tuna salad, right? Most types of salmon are very sustainable, which means what we take from the oceans is plentiful and doesn't impact the environment in harmful ways A fun challenge is to try a salmon sandwich right next to a tuna sandwich and see if you taste a big difference. Me? I actually prefer the salmon.

Prep: 20 minutes / Serves: 4

1 can (15 ounces) boneless, skinless pink or red salmon

2 tablespoons (30 ml) mayonnaise

½ tablespoon (7.5 ml) onion powder

1 tablespoon (15 ml) pickle relish (or chopped dill pickle)

juice of ½ lemon

1 teaspoon (5 ml) celery salt

8 slices whole wheat bread, toasted

1. Open and drain the can of salmon. Mix the mayonnaise, onion powder, relish, lemon juice, and celery salt in a bowl. Whisk to combine.

2. Add the salmon to the mayonnaise mixture and, using two forks, gently mix until well combined, taking care not to break up the chunks of salmon too much.

3. When it is well incorporated, scoop the salmon onto the bread and spread it flat. Garnish with your favorite ingredients, such as thinly sliced cucumber, lettuce, and tomato, and, if you're like me, slather it with hot sauce!

WANT MORE? Check out the NG Kids *COOKBOOK: A Year-Round Fun Food Adventure* by Barton Seaver

FIGHTING FOOD WASTE

About one-third of the world's food is wasted. And National Geographic Emerging Explorer Tristram Stuart wants to do something about that. To feed some of the one billion hungry people in the world, Stuart has started a global movement against food waste. This includes the campaign Feeding the 5,000, which offers free feasts featuring foods salvaged from farm waste piles, like surplus veggies, imperfect apples, and dinged-up tomatoes. With these types of events, Stuart hopes that everyone around the world will become just as fed up as he is about food waste.

TRISTRAM STUART

8 FUN WAYS to Get Outside

Staying inside all day? Snooze! It's time to step outside and explore the world around you. Here's a roundup of eight activities that will get you outdoors and keep you energized.

1 TAKE A HIKE!

Immerse yourself in the great outdoors by hiking. Organize your family and friends for a walk in your local park, or hit some mountain trails for a challenging and scenic route. Don't forget to pack snacks and water to stay fueled while you walk.

2 PICK IT UP

Grab some gloves and a trash bag, then hit your local park creek to pick up trash. You'll get some fresh air and exercise—and help the environment, too.

3 DESIGN YOUR OWN HEADLAMP

Color-coordinate your camping gear by going online and designing your own headlamp. The company Princeton Tec lets you choose your own look for everything from the headlamp's body to the battery door.

Check out the Get Outside Guide for more ideas!

4 STARGAZING!

On a clear night you can really see, well, forever! Take an evening stroll in your neighborhood to explore the starry skies. Enhance your view with a smartphone app offering a 3-D map of the stars, constellations, and galaxies.

5 THE AMAZING RACE

Get into the competitive spirit by organizing an obstacle race with your neighborhood pals. Set up a series of silly—but safe—stunts (Think: jumping rope, crossing the monkey bars, and hula-hooping), then see who can get through it the fastest. Ready? Go!

6 LIGHT UP THE SOCCER FIELD

Have an electrifying game of soccer—literally! By kicking the SOCCKET ball you can create enough energy to light an LED lamp for several hours.

7 INDOOR PICNIC

Bring the outdoors inside with the PicNYC Table. Its aluminum tabletop frame forms a deep area for growing a lush lawn where you can picnic. You can even sprout an herb garden instead of grass!

Rainy Day Fun

8 GET GROWING

You don't need a huge patch of land to grow a garden. Select a small square of backyard or even a flowerpot on your balcony, plant some seeds, water them daily, then watch your blooms blossom!

QUIZ WHIZ

How much do you know about protecting the planet? Take this quiz to find out!

ANSWERS BELOW

① How can people help protect manatees?
- a. ignore them
- b. put them in zoos
- c. drive boats slowly and carefully
- d. feed them in the wild

② **True or false?** About one-third of the world's food is wasted.

③ **The Amazon Rain Forest in South America is nearly as big as _____.**
- a. the United States
- b. France
- c. India
- d. Antarctica

④ What is not one of the causes of climate change?
- a. the burning of fossil fuels
- b. volcanic activities
- c. changes in the sun's intensity
- d. an increase in forest fires

⑤ What is a group of spider monkeys called?
- a. a herd
- b. a barrel
- c. a troop
- d. a bunch

Not **STUMPED** yet? Check out the *NATIONAL GEOGRAPHIC KIDS QUIZ WHIZ* collection for more crazy **ENVIRONMENT** questions!

ANSWERS:
1. c; 2. True; 3. a; 4. d; 5. c

Write a Letter That Gets Results

Knowing how to write a good letter is a useful skill. It will come in handy anytime you want to persuade someone to understand your point of view. Whether you're emailing your congressperson or writing a letter for a school project or to your grandma, a great letter will help you get your message across. Most important, a well-written letter leaves a good impression.

Check out the example below for the elements of a good letter.

Your address

Date

Salutation
Always use "Dear" followed by the person's name; use Mr., Mrs., Ms., or Dr. as appropriate.

Introductory paragraph
Give the reason you're writing the letter.

Body
The longest part of the letter, which provides evidence that supports your position. Be persuasive!

Closing paragraph
Sum up your argument.

Complimentary closing
Sign off with "Sincerely" or "Thank you."

Your signature

Abby Jones
1204 Green Street
Los Angeles, CA 90045

March 31, 2016

Dear Mr. School Superintendent,

I am writing to you about how much excess energy our school uses and to offer a solution.

Every day, we leave the computers on in the classroom, the TVs are plugged in all the time, and the lights are on all day. All of this adds up to a lot of wasted energy, which is not only harmful for the Earth, as it increases the amount of harmful greenhouse gas emissions into the environment, but is also costly to the school. In fact, I read that schools spend more on energy bills than on computers and textbooks combined!

I am suggesting that we start an Energy Patrol to monitor the use of lighting, air-conditioning, heating, and other energy systems within our school. My idea is to have a group of students dedicated to figuring out ways we can cut back on our energy use in the school. We can do room checks, provide reminders to students and teachers to turn off lights and computers, replace old lightbulbs with energy-efficient products, and even reward the classrooms that do the most to save energy.

Above all, I think our school could help the environment tremendously by cutting back on how much energy we use. Let's see an Energy Patrol at our school soon. Thank you.

Sincerely,

Abby Jones

Abby Jones

COMPLIMENTARY CLOSINGS

Sincerely, Sincerely yours, Thank you, Regards, Best wishes, Respectfully,

Built to protect ancient China from invaders from the north, the Great Wall of China once spanned more than 13,000 miles (21,000 km).

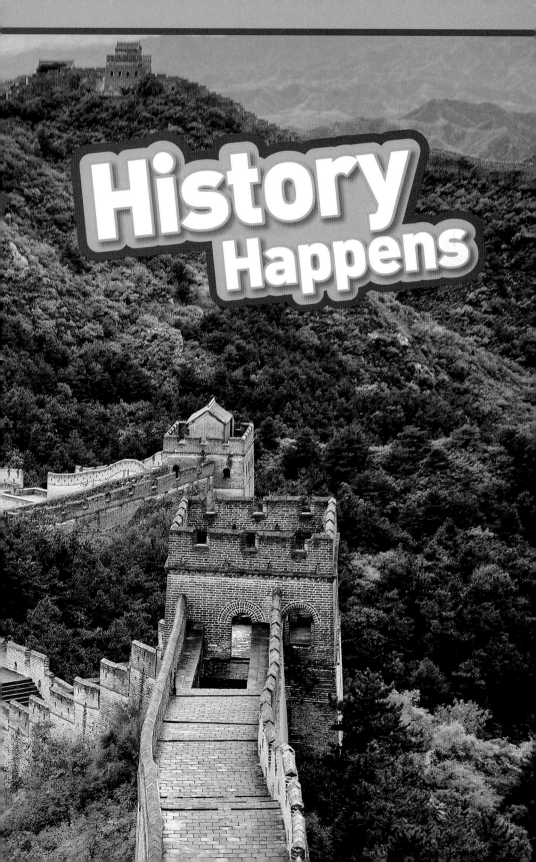

PACKING FOR THE AFTERLIFE

BOATS

Egyptians believed the sun god traveled to the afterlife each night by boat. Model boats—and even full-size versions— were buried with the dead for that same voyage.

IMAGINE HOW YOU'D

FEEL IF YOU BOARDED A PLANE FOR A LONG TRIP

and realized you forgot to pack. To the ancient Egyptians, who viewed death as the start of a great journey, passing into the afterlife unprepared was equally unsettling. That's why family and friends filled the tombs of their dearly departed with everything they would need in the hereafter.

Graves of poor Egyptians were packed with just the essentials: food, cosmetics, and clothes. The ornate burial chambers of pharaohs overflowed with treasures and art. Browse these grave goodies recovered from ancient Egyptian tombs.

FOOD

Family members left food offerings outside a tomb to nourish their loved one's spirit. Paintings of feasts on tomb walls or sculptures of food trays were thought to provide magical bottomless buffets.

GAMES

Board games like Senet provided eternal entertainment.

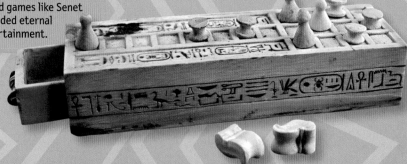

CLOTHES

Most tombs were stocked with chests of clothes, fine linens, sandals, and other attire. It would be unseemly to spend eternity naked, after all.

COFFINS

Coffins were carved in the likeness of the deceased so that spirits could recognize their own bodies.

SERVANTS

Summoned to life by a spell, carved figures known as shabtis served as laborers in the afterlife. One pharaoh's tomb contained nearly a thousand of these ancient action figures.

JEWELRY

The adage "You can't take it with you" would have horrified wealthy Egyptians, who packed their tombs with their favorite jewelry.

225

Ancient World ADVENTURE

KOURION

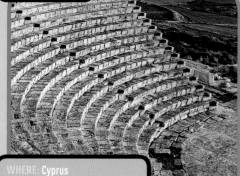

WHERE: Cyprus
BUILT: 13th century B.C.

COOL FACT: Kourion's 3,500-seat amphitheater survived an earthquake in A.D. 364 that leveled the rest of the city. It's still used for performances today.

AYUTTHAYA

WHERE: Thailand
BUILT: About A.D. 1350

COOL FACT: Home to hundreds of thousands of people at the end of the 17th century, this former capital of the Siamese Kingdom was one of the world's largest cities.

FORBIDDEN CITY

WHERE: China
BUILT: Between A.D. 1406 and A.D. 1420

COOL FACT: The 180-acre (73-ha) imperial compound in Beijing is rumored to have more than 9,999 rooms and was home to 24 Chinese emperors over a nearly 500-year span.

*E*ver wonder what it was like on Earth thousands of years ago? *Check out these amazing ancient sites. Visiting them is like taking a time machine into the past!*

PAMUKKALE

WHERE: Turkey
BUILT: About 200 B.C.

COOL FACT: People flocked to this ancient spa town to bathe in its hot springs, which are said to have healing powers. Today, tourists still visit, floating above submerged ruins of ancient columns.

PALENQUE

WHERE: Mexico
BUILT: About A.D. 500

COOL FACT: This ancient Maya city-state's buildings, including temples and tombs, were built without the use of metal tools, pack animals, or even the wheel.

TIMBUKTU

WHERE: Mali
BUILT: About A.D. 1100

COOL FACT: Once known as the fabled "City of Gold," Africa's Timbuktu was a center of learning and culture in the 15th and 16th centuries and is home to a still standing university.

227

Knight Life

Protector of the Castle

It started with a childhood full of boring chores and ended at age 21 with a ceremonial smack to the head that knocked some men on their tails. The road to knighthood was long and rough, but the journey was often worth the trouble. Successful knights found fortune and glory.

In times of war and peace, knights led a dangerous life. These professional warriors were charged with protecting the lord's land from invaders, leading the castle's men-at-arms during sieges, and fighting on behalf of the church. Between battles, they competed in deadly games called tournaments to sharpen their skills.

In exchange for military service, knights were granted their own land along with peasants to farm it—and noble titles. The mightiest knights r to rival lords in power and property. Ulrich von Liechtenstein, one of the century's most famous knights, own three castles.

Not just anyone could become a kr Armor, weapons, and warhorses cost than a typical peasant might earn in lifetime, so knights often hailed from noble families. They started their tra early in life—at the age most kids to begin first grade.

Lord Lore

England's royal family still grants knighthood to actors, scientists, and othe accomplished citizens.

How to Become a Knight

1. Serve as a Page

A boy destined for knighthood left home at age seven to become a servant in a great lord's castle. The page learned courtly manners, received a basic education, and played rough with other pages.

2. Squire for a Knight

Once he turned 14, a page became a squire for a knight. He learned about armor by cleaning his master's suit and helping him dress for battle. He practiced fighting with swords, shields, and other weaponry. Most important of all, he learned to attack from the saddle of a huge warhorse—the type of mounted combat knights were famous for.

3. Get Dubbed

By age 21, a squire was ready for his dubbing ceremony. He knelt before his lord or lady and received a hard slap to help him remember his oath. (This brutal blow later evolved into a friendlier sword tap on the shoulders.) The newly dubbed knight was given the title "sir" and could seek service at a lord's castle.

Knightly Num

55 pounds (25 kg) of a weighed down a kr the battlefield.

45 years was the life expectancy of the average knight.

45 days per year was t typical term of serv knight owed his lord

Good knights acted chivalrously, which meant they protected the weak, treated women with respect, served the church, and were generous and humble.

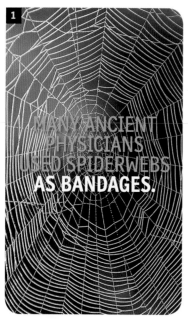

1 MANY ANCIENT PHYSICIANS USED SPIDERWEBS **AS BANDAGES.**

2 Archaeologists discovered a 4,000-year-old bowl of noodles in China.

3 Since the 19th century, Switzerland has been **neutral in all wars.**

16 COOL THINGS ABOUT

4 If you caught a fever in Ancient China, your doctor would have prescribed **HOT EARTHWORM SOUP.**

5 Dormouse was considered a delicacy in ancient Rome.

6 IN ANCIENT EGYPT, ONLY ROYALTY WERE ALLOWED TO EAT MUSHROOMS.

7 The British author who created the character JAMES BOND was a spy himself during World War II.

8 CATHERINE THE GREAT LED RUSSIA FOR 30 YEARS, BUT SHE WAS ACTUALLY GERMAN AND HER BIRTH NAME WAS SOPHIE.

9 Prehistoric humans chewed tree resin as chewing gum.

10 In the 18th century, King Kamehameha of Hawaii was hidden in a cave as a boy so he wouldn't be killed.

11 THE POPULATION OF AUSTRALIA NEARLY DOUBLED IN LESS THAN EIGHT YEARS AFTER GOLD WAS FOUND IN 1851.

HISTORY

12 Princess Diana of Britain had two wedding dresses, in case the first one was revealed before her wedding to Prince Charles.

13 THE CAPITAL CITY OF IRELAND, DUBLIN, WASN'T FOUNDED BY THE CELTS— IT WAS FOUNDED BY VIKINGS.

14 THE YEAR 1752 **WAS SHORTENED BY 11 DAYS** WHEN BRITAIN CHANGED FROM AN OLD STYLE CALENDAR TO THE ONE WE USE TODAY.

15 Ethiopia is the only African country that was never a colony of another country.

16 It took about **2.6 million** people to build Japan's Todaiji Temple in the eighth century A.D.

231

MYSTERY OF THE STONE GIANTS

DID ALIENS PLACE THE STATUES ON EASTER ISLAND? SCIENTISTS WEIGH IN.

MOAI HEAD

A strange army of jumbo-size stones carved to look like humans have "guarded" the coast of Easter Island in the Pacific Ocean for centuries. But not even the island's inhabitants are sure how they got there.

Scientists think islanders began creating the *moai*—which can weigh more than 90 tons (81,647 kg) and stand as tall as a three-story building—some 800 years ago to honor their ancestors. Inland, archaeologists unearthed ancient tools used to carve figures from volcanic rock. But that was about 11 miles (18 km) from where most of the statues now stand. And back then, the islanders didn't have wheels, cranes, or animals to move the rock giants.

Wondering if the islanders could have transported the statues upright with just rope and muscle power, one group of archaeologists attempted to move a ten-foot (3-m)-tall moai replica by wrapping three cords around the statue's forehead.

TINY TOURIST!

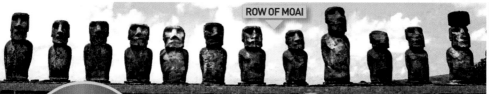

ROW OF MOAI

Easter Island's first inhabitants arrived between 800 and 1,200 years ago. They canoed from other Pacific islands for more than 1,000 miles (1,600 km).

With a team of people pulling each rope they were able to "walk" the moai a short distance by rocking it side to side. Another team laid an actual moai onto a giant log and pulled the log forward. But these techniques might have worked only over short distances and on flat land, or would have damaged the moai. Some researchers suggest the statues were laid on wooden sleds, which were dragged across log tracks. But the truth may never be revealed. Today the only remaining witnesses to the event are the moai themselves. And their stone lips are sealed.

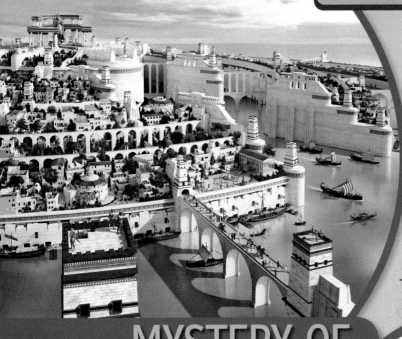

CAN AN ISLAND PARADISE DISAPPEAR IN A DAY? THAT'S WHAT ONE ANCIENT LEGEND SAYS ABOUT THE EMPIRE OF ATLANTIS. TODAY, SCIENTISTS CONTINUE TO TRY TO LOCATE THE LOST ISLAND.

MYSTERY OF
ATLANTIS

Plato, an ancient Greek philosopher, described Atlantis as a wealthy city with palaces, a silver-and-gold temple, abundant fruit trees, and elephants roaming the land. But the good times didn't last. Plato wrote that sudden earthquakes jolted Atlantis and whipped up waves that sank the island within a day.

Was Plato's story true? Recently, researchers in Spain used underground radar in search of buried buildings. Results showed something like a crumbled wall in the soil 40 feet (12.1 m) below, but because there was water beneath the site, a dig seemed improbable.

Other explorers think Atlantis is in the Mediterranean Sea, where images supposedly show remains of canals and walls. Others are skeptical about the story entirely. Such an advanced city, they say, couldn't have been built in the Stone Age, when Plato's story was set.

So, was Atlantis real, fake, or something in between? The search continues.

TREASURE!

Check out these stories of lost treasures found!

SUNKEN GOLD

In the summer of 2013, Rick Schmitt was scuba diving off the coast of eastern Florida when he discovered $300,000 worth of gold chains, coins, and jewelry on the ocean floor. The riches date back to the 1700s, when Spanish ships called galleons often ferried treasure from North and South America to Europe. In July 1715 a hurricane sank 11 galleons near Florida's coast, scattering valuables along the seafloor. Nearly 300 years later, Schmitt found only a portion of this loot. Many more riches still linger at the bottom of the ocean.

MAYA RICHES

During a 2012 expedition to the jungles of northern Guatemala, a team of archaeologists discovered a tomb filled with precious stones and ancient bones dating back to the seventh century. Maya hieroglyphics on a jar in the burial chamber revealed that the bones may have belonged to a warrior queen. The exact worth of the treasure hasn't been calculated—but most people agree that this find is priceless.

PALACE PRIZE

In 2011, workers renovating Hanuman Dhoka, a palace that once housed Nepal's royal family, came upon three safes and a tank filled with gold jewelry, bows with silver arrows, and gold masks. The loot was thought to be at least 500-year-old offerings made to Hindu gods and goddesses, and no one knows for sure why it was placed here. But with the treasure soon on exhibit, the renovated palace museum won't just be spruced up— it'll be blinged out!

THE AMAZING HOUDINI!
Death-Defying Magic Tricks
REVEALED

Throughout history, many magicians have wowed audiences with their amazing illusions. But there has only been one Harry Houdini. Known for his death-defying magic tricks, Houdini, who died in 1926, was one of the most fearless illusionists of all time. Here is the scoop about two of his most legendary stunts.

VANISHING ELEPHANT

The Trick: Houdini promises to make Jenny, a 4,000-pound (1,814-kg) elephant, disappear.

What You See: Houdini coaxes Jenny into an enormous wooden box and closes its front curtain. A moment later, he reopens it and she's gone.

What You Don't See: The box has a secret back door. Houdini closes the curtain and Jenny is lured out the back exit by the smell of her favorite food.

SUSPENDED STRAITJACKET

The Trick: Hanging by his feet from a building while wearing a straitjacket, Houdini vows to free himself—without falling!

What You See: Houdini wriggles against the straps of his straitjacket, freeing one arm at a time. Pulling the jacket over his head, he drops to the ground below.

What You Don't See: Legend has it that Houdini took a deep breath to expand his chest and keep the straitjacket loose. Then he used his flexibility to help him wriggle free.

WAR!

Since the beginning of time, different countries, territories, and cultures have feuded with each other over land, power, and politics. Major military conflicts include the following wars:

1095–1291 THE CRUSADES
Starting late in the 11th century, these wars over religion were fought in the Middle East for nearly 200 years.

1337–1453 HUNDRED YEARS' WAR
France and England battled over rights to land for more than a century before the French eventually drove the English out in 1453.

1754–1763 FRENCH AND INDIAN WAR (part of Europe's Seven Years' War)
A nine-year war between the British and French for control of North America.

1775–1783 AMERICAN REVOLUTION
Thirteen British colonies in America united to reject the rule of the British government and to form the United States of America.

1861–1865 AMERICAN CIVIL WAR
Occurred when the northern states (the Union) went to war with the southern states, which had seceded, or withdrawn, to form the Confederate States of America. Slavery was one of the key issues in the Civil War.

1910–1920 MEXICAN REVOLUTION
The people of Mexico revolted against the rule of dictator President Porfirio Díaz, leading to his eventual defeat and to a democratic government.

1914–1918 WORLD WAR I
The assassination of Austria's Archduke Ferdinand by a Serbian nationalist sparked this wide-spreading war. The U.S. entered after Germany sunk the British ship *Lusitania*, killing more than 120 Americans.

1918–1920 RUSSIAN CIVIL WAR
Following the 1917 Russian Revolution, this conflict pitted the Communist Red Army against the foreign-backed White Army. The Red Army won, leading to the establishment of the Union of Soviet Socialist Republics (U.S.S.R.) in 1922.

1936–1939 SPANISH CIVIL WAR
Aid from Italy and Germany helped the Nationalists gain victory over the Communist-supported Republicans. The war resulted in the loss of more than 300,000 lives and increased tension in Europe leading up to World War II.

1939–1945 WORLD WAR II
This massive conflict in Europe, Asia, and North Africa involved many countries that aligned with the two sides: the Allies and the Axis. After the bombing of Pearl Harbor in Hawaii in 1941, the U.S. entered the war on the side of the Allies. More than 50 million people died during the war.

1946–1949 CHINESE CIVIL WAR
Also known as the "War of Liberation," this pitted the Communist and Nationalist parties in China against each other. The Communists won.

1950–1953 KOREAN WAR
Kicked off when the Communist forces of North Korea, with backing from the Soviet Union, invaded their democratic neighbor to the south. A coalition of 16 countries from the United Nations stepped in to support South Korea.

1950s–1975 VIETNAM WAR
Fought between the Communist North, supported by allies including China, and the government of South Vietnam, supported by the United States and other anticommunist nations.

1967 SIX-DAY WAR
A battle for land between Israel and the states of Egypt, Jordan, and Syria. The outcome resulted in Israel's gaining control of coveted territory, including the Gaza Strip and the West Bank.

1991–PRESENT SOMALI CIVIL WAR
Began when Somalia's last president, a dictator named Mohamed Siad Barre, was overthrown. The war has led to years of fighting and anarchy.

2001–2014 WAR IN AFGHANISTAN
After attacks in the U.S. by the terrorist group al Qaeda, a coalition that eventually included more than 40 countries invaded Afghanistan to find Osama bin Laden and other al Qaeda members and to dismantle the Taliban. Bin Laden was killed in a U.S. covert operation in 2011. The North Atlantic Treaty Organization (NATO) took control of the coalition's combat mission in 2003. That combat mission officially ended in 2014.

2003–2011 WAR IN IRAQ
A coalition led by the U.S., and including Britain, Australia, and Spain, invaded Iraq over suspicions that Iraq had weapons of mass destruction.

SPY TREES

Picture this: You're tossed onto the front lines of World War I. Up ahead, you spot a tree towering over the barren countryside. Ravaged by bullets and bombs and stripped of its leaves, the tree has certainly seen better days. But look closely and you just may see that it's not a real tree, but a replica made of iron and steel.

On the battlefield, it's not uncommon to use extreme tactics to gain an advantage on the enemy. Even constructing fake trees to use as the ultimate observation post for sneaky spies.

That's just what both the British and Germans did during World War I to spy on one another. After measuring, sketching, and photographing real trees on the battlefield, artists would then create lifelike, hollow towers using painted steel and iron. Then, in the middle of the night, troops would cut down the actual tree and replace it with the fake one. By the next morning, a soldier would be hidden inside the camouflaged tower. Offering a perfect vantage point to observe any movement on the enemy's front, these spy trees no doubt elevated the war to a new level.

The Constitution & the Bill of Rights

The United States Constitution was written in 1787 by a group of political leaders from the 13 states that made up the U.S. at the time. Thirty-nine men, including Benjamin Franklin and James Madison, signed the document to create a national government. While some feared the creation of a strong federal government, all 13 states eventually ratified, or approved, the Constitution, making it the law of the land. The Constitution has three major parts: the preamble, the articles, and the amendments.

Here's a summary of what topics are covered in each part of the Constitution. Check out the Constitution online or at your local library for the full text.

THE PREAMBLE outlines the basic purposes of the government: *We the People of the United States, in order to form a more perfect Union, establish justice, insure domestic tranquility, provide for the common defense, promote the general welfare, and secure the blessings of liberty to ourselves and our posterity, do ordain and establish this Constitution for the United States of America.*

SEVEN ARTICLES outline the powers of Congress, the president, and the court system:

Article I outlines the legislative branch—the Senate and the House of Representatives—and its powers and responsibilities.

Article II outlines the executive branch—the Presidency—and its powers and responsibilities.

Article III outlines the judicial branch—the court system—and its powers and responsibilities.

Article IV describes the individual states' rights and powers.

Article V outlines the amendment process.

Article VI establishes the Constitution as the law of the land.

Article VII gives the requirements for the Constitution to be approved.

THE AMENDMENTS, or additions to the Constitution, were put in later as needed. In 1791, the first ten amendments, known as the **Bill of Rights**, were added. Since then another seventeen amendments have been added. This is the Bill of Rights:

1st Amendment: guarantees freedom of religion, speech, and the press, and the right to assemble and petition. The U.S. may not have a national religion.

2nd Amendment: discusses the militia and the right of people to bear arms

3rd Amendment: prohibits the military or troops from using private homes without consent

4th Amendment: protects people and their homes from search, arrest, or seizure without probable cause or a warrant

5th Amendment: grants people the right to have a trial and prevents punishment before prosecution; protects private property from being taken without compensation

6th Amendment: guarantees the right to a speedy and public trial

7th Amendment: guarantees a trial by jury in certain cases

8th Amendment: forbids "cruel and unusual punishments"

9th Amendment: states that the Constitution is not all-encompassing and does not deny people other, unspecified rights

10th Amendment: grants the powers not covered by the Constitution to the states and the people

Read the full text version of the United States Constitution at http://constitutioncenter.org/constitution/full-text

Branches of Government

The **UNITED STATES GOVERNMENT** is divided into three branches: **executive, legislative**, and **judicial**. The system of checks and balances is a way to control power and to make sure one branch can't take the reins of government. For example, most of the president's actions require the approval of Congress. Likewise, the laws passed in Congress must be signed by the president before they can take effect.

White House

Executive Branch

The Constitution lists the central powers of the president: to serve as Commander in Chief of the armed forces; make treaties with other nations; grant pardons; inform Congress on the state of the union; and appoint ambassadors, officials, and judges. The executive branch includes the president and the 15 governmental departments.

Legislative Branch

This branch is made up of Congress—the Senate and the House of Representatives. The Constitution grants Congress the power to make laws. Congress is made up of elected representatives from each state. Each state has two representatives in the Senate, while the number of representatives in the House is determined by the size of the state's population. Washington, D.C., and the territories elect nonvoting representatives to the House of Representatives. The Founding Fathers set up this system as a compromise between big states—which wanted representation based on population—and small states—which wanted all states to have equal representation rights.

The U.S. Capitol in Washington, D.C.

Judicial Branch

The judicial branch is composed of the federal court system— the U.S. Supreme Court, the courts of appeals, and the district courts. The Supreme Court is the most powerful court. Its motto is "Equal Justice Under Law." This influential court is responsible for interpreting the Constitution and applying it to the cases that it hears. The decisions of the Supreme Court are absolute—they are the final word on any legal question.

There are nine justices on the Supreme Court. They are appointed by the president of the United States and confirmed by the Senate.

The U.S. Supreme Court Building in Washington, D.C.

GEORGE WASHINGTON'S
RULES
TO LIVE BY

REAL-LIFE ADVICE FROM THE FIRST U.S. PRESIDENT

Starting as a boy, George Washington followed a set of 110 dos and don'ts on everything from public tooth picking to freaking out friends. Check out three of G.W.'s polite practices.

Rules have not been edited; this is how George actually wrote them.

RULE 2

"In visiting the Sick, do not Presently play the Physicion if you be not Knowing therein."

MODERN-DAY MEANING: You probably don't want to give your friends advice on medicine. Best leave that to the doc and your pals' parents.

WAY BACK FACT: One 18th-century recipe for homemade cold medicine included the tips of crab claws and the "jelly" of vipers.

RULE 3

"Shew Nothing to your Freind that may affright him."

MODERN-DAY MEANING: Scaring a friend is a no-no and yelling "Boo!" may get *you* booed. So don't jump out of a dark hallway in front of your little brother or put a fake snake under your friend's pillow.

WAY BACK FACT: As a general in the Revolutionary War, George Washington tried not to "affright" troops by telling them how bad things were. But in 1775, the war's first year, he was very worried about keeping the army calm and finding food for his thousands of soldiers.

RULE 1

"Cleanse not your teeth with the Table Cloth Napkin Fork or Knife but if Others do it let it be done wt. a Pick Tooth."

MODERN-DAY MEANING: Gross! Who wants to watch somebody rub their teeth clean with table linens or pick at them with silverware? But back in Washington's day, this was OK as long as everybody else was doing the same. According to the rule, you should just trade in the utensils and table linens for toothpicks when spiffing up your pearly whites.

WAY BACK FACT: By his first inauguration in 1789, George Washington had only one real tooth left. So a dentist made him a set of dentures with a hole for that tooth.

George Washington's **Rules** TO LIVE BY

CHECK OUT THE BOOK!

The Indian Experience

Some American Indians used porcupine quills to decorate their clothing and moccasins.

In winter, Lakota children traditionally played with sleds made from buffalo rib bones.

A Lakota woman in traditional costume, Black Hills, South Dakota, U.S.A.

American Indians are indigenous to North and South America—they are the people who were here before Columbus and other European explorers came to these lands. They lived in nations, tribes, and bands across both continents. For decades following the arrival of Europeans in 1492, American Indians clashed with the newcomers who had ruptured the Indians' way of living.

Tribal Land

During the 19th century, both United States legislation and military action restricted the movement of American Indians, forcing them to live on reservations and attempting to dismantle tribal structures. For centuries Indians were displaced or killed, or became assimilated into the general U.S. population. In 1924 the Indian Citizenship Act granted citizenship to all American Indians. Unfortunately, this was not enough to end the social discrimination and mistreatment that many Indians have faced. Today, American Indians living in the U.S. still face many challenges.

Healing the Past

Many members of the 560-plus recognized tribes in the United States live primarily on reservations. Some tribes have more than one reservation, while others have none. Together these reservations make up less than 3 percent of the nation's land area. The tribal governments on reservations have the right to form their own governments and to enforce laws, similar to individual states. Many feel that this sovereignty is still not enough to right the wrongs of the past: They hope for a change in the U.S. government's relationship with American Indians.

The president of the United States is the chief of the executive branch, the Commander in Chief of the U.S. armed forces, and head of the federal government. Elected every four years, the president is the highest policy-maker in the nation. The 22nd Amendment (1951) says that no person may be elected to the office of president more than twice. There have been 44 presidencies and 43 presidents.

JAMES MONROE
5th President of the United States ★ 1817–1825

BORN April 28, 1758, in Westmoreland County, VA
POLITICAL PARTY Democratic-Republican
NO. OF TERMS two
VICE PRESIDENT Daniel D. Tompkins
DIED July 4, 1831, in New York, NY

GEORGE WASHINGTON
1st President of the United States ★ 1789–1797

BORN Feb. 22, 1732, in Pope's Creek, Westmoreland County, VA
POLITICAL PARTY Federalist
NO. OF TERMS two
VICE PRESIDENT John Adams
DIED Dec. 14, 1799, at Mount Vernon, VA

MONROVIA, the capital of the African country Liberia, is named after JAMES MONROE.

JOHN ADAMS
2nd President of the United States ★ 1797–1801

BORN Oct. 30, 1735, in Braintree (now Quincy), MA
POLITICAL PARTY Federalist
NO. OF TERMS one
VICE PRESIDENT Thomas Jefferson
DIED July 4, 1826, in Quincy, MA

JOHN QUINCY ADAMS
6th President of the United States ★ 1825–1829

BORN July 11, 1767, in Braintree (now Quincy), MA
POLITICAL PARTY Democratic-Republican
NO. OF TERMS one
VICE PRESIDENT John Caldwell Calhoun
DIED Feb. 23, 1848, at the U.S. Capitol, Washington, DC

THOMAS JEFFERSON
3rd President of the United States ★ 1801–1809

BORN April 13, 1743, at Shadwell, Goochland (now Albemarle) County, VA
POLITICAL PARTY Democratic-Republican
NO. OF TERMS two
VICE PRESIDENTS 1st term: Aaron Burr
2nd term: George Clinton
DIED July 4, 1826, at Monticello, Charlottesville, VA

ANDREW JACKSON
7th President of the United States ★ 1829–1837

BORN March 15, 1767, in the Waxhaw region, NC and SC
POLITICAL PARTY Democrat
NO. OF TERMS two
VICE PRESIDENTS 1st term: John Caldwell Calhoun
2nd term: Martin Van Buren
DIED June 8, 1845, in Nashville, TN

JAMES MADISON
4th President of the United States ★ 1809–1817

BORN March 16, 1751, at Belle Grove, Port Conway, VA
POLITICAL PARTY Democratic-Republican
NO. OF TERMS two
VICE PRESIDENTS 1st term: George Clinton
2nd term: Elbridge Gerry
DIED June 28, 1836, at Montpelier, Orange County, VA

MARTIN VAN BUREN
8th President of the United States ★ 1837–1841

BORN Dec. 5, 1782, in Kinderhook, NY
POLITICAL PARTY Democrat
NO. OF TERMS one
VICE PRESIDENT Richard M. Johnson
DIED July 24, 1862, in Kinderhook, NY

WILLIAM HENRY HARRISON

9th President of the United States ★ *1841*

BORN Feb. 9, 1773, in Charles City County, VA

POLITICAL PARTY Whig

NO. OF TERMS one (cut short by death)

VICE PRESIDENT John Tyler

DIED April 4, 1841, in the White House, Washington, DC

JOHN TYLER

10th President of the United States ★ *1841–1845*

BORN March 29, 1790, in Charles City County, VA

POLITICAL PARTY Whig

NO. OF TERMS one (partial)

VICE PRESIDENT none

DIED Jan. 18, 1862, in Richmond, VA

JAMES K. POLK

11th President of the United States ★ *1845–1849*

BORN Nov. 2, 1795, near Pineville, Mecklenburg County, NC

POLITICAL PARTY Democrat

NO. OF TERMS one

VICE PRESIDENT George Mifflin Dallas

DIED June 15, 1849, in Nashville, TN

ZACHARY TAYLOR

12th President of the United States ★ *1849–1850*

BORN Nov. 24, 1784, in Orange County, VA

POLITICAL PARTY Whig

NO. OF TERMS one (cut short by death)

VICE PRESIDENT Millard Fillmore

DIED July 9, 1850, in the White House, Washington, DC

MILLARD FILLMORE

13th President of the United States ★ *1850–1853*

BORN Jan. 7, 1800, in Cayuga County, NY

POLITICAL PARTY Whig

NO. OF TERMS one (partial)

VICE PRESIDENT none

DIED March 8, 1874, in Buffalo, NY

FRANKLIN PIERCE

14th President of the United States ★ *1853–1857*

BORN Nov. 23, 1804, in Hillsborough (now Hillsboro), NH

POLITICAL PARTY Democrat

NO. OF TERMS one

VICE PRESIDENT William Rufus De Vane King

DIED Oct. 8, 1869, in Concord, NH

JAMES BUCHANAN

15th President of the United States ★ *1857–1861*

BORN April 23, 1791, in Cove Gap, PA

POLITICAL PARTY Democrat

NO. OF TERMS one

VICE PRESIDENT John Cabell Breckinridge

DIED June 1, 1868, in Lancaster, PA

ABRAHAM LINCOLN

16th President of the United States ★ *1861–1865*

BORN Feb. 12, 1809, near Hodgenville, KY

POLITICAL PARTY Republican (formerly Whig)

NO. OF TERMS two (assassinated)

VICE PRESIDENTS 1st term: Hannibal Hamlin
2nd term: Andrew Johnson

DIED April 15, 1865, in Washington, DC

ABRAHAM LINCOLN KEPT LETTERS IN HIS STOVEPIPE HAT.

ANDREW JOHNSON

17th President of the United States ★ *1865–1869*

BORN Dec. 29, 1808, in Raleigh, NC

POLITICAL PARTY Democrat

NO. OF TERMS one (partial)

VICE PRESIDENT none

DIED July 31, 1875, in Carter's Station, TN

ULYSSES S. GRANT

18th President of the United States ★ *1869–1877*

BORN April 27, 1822,
in Point Pleasant, OH

POLITICAL PARTY Republican

NO. OF TERMS two

VICE PRESIDENTS 1st term: Schuyler Colfax
2nd term: Henry Wilson

DIED July 23, 1885, in Mount McGregor, NY

RUTHERFORD B. HAYES

19th President of the United States ★ *1877–1881*

BORN Oct. 4, 1822,
in Delaware, OH

POLITICAL PARTY Republican

NO. OF TERMS one

VICE PRESIDENT William Almon Wheeler

DIED Jan. 17, 1893, in Fremont, OH

JAMES A. GARFIELD

20th President of the United States ★ *1881*

BORN Nov. 19, 1831, near Orange, OH

POLITICAL PARTY Republican

NO. OF TERMS one (assassinated)

VICE PRESIDENT Chester A. Arthur

DIED Sept. 19, 1881, in Elberon, NJ

CHESTER A. ARTHUR

21st President of the United States ★ *1881–1885*

BORN Oct. 5, 1829, in Fairfield, VT

POLITICAL PARTY Republican

NO. OF TERMS one (partial)

VICE PRESIDENT none

DIED Nov. 18, 1886, in New York, NY

GROVER CLEVELAND

22nd and 24th President of the United States
1885–1889 ★ *1893–1897*

BORN March 18, 1837, in Caldwell, NJ

POLITICAL PARTY Democrat

NO. OF TERMS two (nonconsecutive)

VICE PRESIDENTS 1st administration:
Thomas Andrews Hendricks
2nd administration:
Adlai Ewing Stevenson

DIED June 24, 1908, in Princeton, NJ

BENJAMIN HARRISON

23rd President of the United States ★ *1889–1893*

BORN Aug. 20, 1833,
in North Bend, OH

POLITICAL PARTY Republican

NO. OF TERMS one

VICE PRESIDENT Levi Parsons Morton

DIED March 13, 1901, in Indianapolis, IN

WILLIAM MCKINLEY

25th President of the United States ★ *1897–1901*

BORN Jan. 29, 1843, in Niles, OH

POLITICAL PARTY Republican

NO. OF TERMS two (assassinated)

VICE PRESIDENTS 1st term:
Garret Augustus Hobart
2nd term:
Theodore Roosevelt

DIED Sept. 14, 1901, in Buffalo, NY

THEODORE ROOSEVELT

26th President of the United States ★ *1901–1909*

BORN Oct. 27, 1858, in New York, NY

POLITICAL PARTY Republican

NO. OF TERMS one, plus balance of
McKinley's term

VICE PRESIDENTS 1st term: none
2nd term: Charles
Warren Fairbanks

DIED Jan. 6, 1919, in Oyster Bay, NY

WILLIAM HOWARD TAFT

27th President of the United States ★ *1909–1913*

BORN Sept. 15, 1857, in Cincinnati, OH

POLITICAL PARTY Republican

NO. OF TERMS one

VICE PRESIDENT James Schoolcraft
Sherman

DIED March 8, 1930, in Washington, DC

WOODROW WILSON

28th President of the United States ★ *1913–1921*

BORN Dec. 29, 1856,
in Staunton, VA

POLITICAL PARTY Democrat

NO. OF TERMS two

VICE PRESIDENT Thomas Riley Marshall

DIED Feb. 3, 1924, in Washington, DC

WARREN G. HARDING

29th President of the United States ★ 1921–1923

BORN Nov. 2, 1865, in Caledonia
(now Blooming Grove), OH
POLITICAL PARTY Republican
NO. OF TERMS one (died while in office)
VICE PRESIDENT Calvin Coolidge
DIED Aug. 2, 1923, in San Francisco, CA

HARRY S. TRUMAN

33rd President of the United States ★ 1945–1953

BORN May 8, 1884, in Lamar, MO
POLITICAL PARTY Democrat
NO. OF TERMS one, plus balance of
Franklin D. Roosevelt's term
VICE PRESIDENTS 1st term: none
2nd term:
Alben William Barkley
DIED Dec. 26, 1972, in Independence, MO

CALVIN COOLIDGE

30th President of the United States ★ 1923–1929

BORN July 4, 1872, in Plymouth, VT
POLITICAL PARTY Republican
NO. OF TERMS one, plus balance of
Harding's term
VICE PRESIDENTS 1st term: none
2nd term:
Charles Gates Dawes
DIED Jan. 5, 1933, in Northampton, MA

DWIGHT D. EISENHOWER

34th President of the United States ★ 1953–1961

BORN Oct. 14, 1890, in Denison, TX
POLITICAL PARTY Republican
NO. OF TERMS two
VICE PRESIDENT Richard M. Nixon
DIED March 28, 1969,
in Washington, DC

HERBERT HOOVER

31st President of the United States ★ 1929–1933

BORN Aug. 10, 1874,
in West Branch, IA
POLITICAL PARTY Republican
NO. OF TERMS one
VICE PRESIDENT Charles Curtis
DIED Oct. 20, 1964, in New York, NY

JOHN F. KENNEDY

35th President of the United States ★ 1961–1963

BORN May 29, 1917, in Brookline, MA
POLITICAL PARTY Democrat
NO. OF TERMS one (assassinated)
VICE PRESIDENT Lyndon B. Johnson
DIED Nov. 22, 1963,
in Dallas, TX

FRANKLIN D. ROOSEVELT

32nd President of the United States ★ 1933–1945

BORN Jan. 30, 1882, in Hyde Park, NY
POLITICAL PARTY Democrat
NO. OF TERMS four (died while in office)
VICE PRESIDENTS 1st & 2nd terms: John
Nance Garner; 3rd term:
Henry Agard Wallace;
4th term: Harry S. Truman
DIED April 12, 1945,
in Warm Springs, GA

LYNDON B. JOHNSON

36th President of the United States ★ 1963–1969

BORN Aug. 27, 1908,
near Stonewall, TX
POLITICAL PARTY Democrat
NO. OF TERMS one, plus balance of
Kennedy's term
VICE PRESIDENTS 1st term: none
2nd term: Hubert
Horatio Humphrey
DIED Jan. 22, 1973, near San Antonio, TX

Most of
Franklin D. Roosevelt's
collection of more than
1 million stamps
sold for **$228,000**
after his death.

RICHARD NIXON

37th President of the United States ★ *1969–1974*
BORN Jan. 9, 1913, in Yorba Linda, CA
POLITICAL PARTY Republican
NO. OF TERMS two (resigned)
VICE PRESIDENTS 1st term & 2nd term (partial): Spiro Theodore Agnew; 2nd term (balance): Gerald R. Ford
DIED April 22, 1994, in New York, NY

RICHARD NIXON HAD HIS YOGURT FLOWN FROM CALIFORNIA TO THE WHITE HOUSE EACH DAY.

GERALD R. FORD

38th President of the United States ★ *1974–1977*
BORN July 14, 1913, in Omaha, NE
POLITICAL PARTY Republican
NO. OF TERMS one (partial)
VICE PRESIDENT Nelson Aldrich Rockefeller
DIED Dec. 26, 2006, in Rancho Mirage, CA

JIMMY CARTER

39th President of the United States ★ *1977–1981*
BORN Oct. 1, 1924, in Plains, GA
POLITICAL PARTY Democrat
NO. OF TERMS one
VICE PRESIDENT Walter Frederick (Fritz) Mondale

JIMMY CARTER WAS A PEANUT FARMER BEFORE HE WAS PRESIDENT.

RONALD REAGAN

40th President of the United States ★ *1981–1989*
BORN Feb. 6, 1911, in Tampico, IL
POLITICAL PARTY Republican
NO. OF TERMS two
VICE PRESIDENT George H. W. Bush
DIED June 5, 2004, in Los Angeles, CA

GEORGE H.W. BUSH

41st President of the United States ★ *1989–1993*
BORN June 12, 1924, in Milton, MA
POLITICAL PARTY Republican
NO. OF TERMS one
VICE PRESIDENT James Danforth (Dan) Quayle III

AS A PILOT IN WORLD WAR II, GEORGE H.W. BUSH SURVIVED 2 PLANE CRASHES.

WILLIAM J. CLINTON

42nd President of the United States ★ *1993–2001*
BORN Aug. 19, 1946, in Hope, AR
POLITICAL PARTY Democrat
NO. OF TERMS two
VICE PRESIDENT Albert Gore, Jr.

GEORGE W. BUSH

43rd President of the United States ★ *2001–2009*
BORN July 6, 1946, in New Haven, CT
POLITICAL PARTY Republican
NO. OF TERMS two
VICE PRESIDENT Richard Bruce Cheney

BARACK OBAMA

44th President of the United States ★ *2009–present*
BORN Aug. 4, 1961, in Honolulu, HI
POLITICAL PARTY Democrat
NO. OF TERMS two
VICE PRESIDENT Joseph Biden

On the Money Quiz!

In 1869, George Washington became the first president to be featured on U.S. currency, seven years after the first dollar bill was put into print. In 1909, Teddy Roosevelt commissioned the penny featuring Abraham Lincoln to celebrate the popular president's 100th birthday. Today, more than 30 presidents and other prominent historical figures are featured on various bills and coins. So, do you know which president's face appears on each bill—or coin? See if you can match the president to the correct currency.

A **B** **C**

D **E** **F**

1. Thomas Jefferson
2. George Washington
3. Andrew Jackson
4. Alexander Hamilton
5. Franklin D. Roosevelt
6. Ulysses S. Grant

A. quarter
B. dime
C. $20 bill
D. $10 bill
E. $2 bill
F. $50 bill

ANSWERS: 1. E; 2. A; 3. C; 4. D; 5. B; 6. F

247

CIVIL RIGHTS

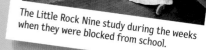

The Little Rock Nine study during the weeks when they were blocked from school.

Although the Constitution protects the civil rights of American citizens, it has not always been able to protect all Americans from persecution or discrimination. During the first half of the 20th century, many Americans, particularly African Americans, were subjected to widespread discrimination and racism. By the mid-1950s, many people were eager to end the bonds of racism and bring freedom to all men and women.

The civil rights movement of the 1950s and 1960s sought to end the racial discrimination against African Americans, especially in the southern states. The movement wanted to restore the fundamentals of economic and social equality to those who had been oppressed.

The Little Rock Nine

September 4, 1957, marked the first day of school at Little Rock Central High in Little Rock, Arkansas. But this was no ordinary back-to-school scene: Armed soldiers surrounded the entrance, awaiting the arrival of Central's first ever African-American students. The welcome was not warm, however, as the students—now known as the Little Rock Nine—were refused entry into the school by the soldiers and a group of protesters, angry about the potential integration. This did not deter the students, who gained the support of President Dwight D. Eisenhower to eventually earn their right to go to an integrated school. Today, the Little Rock Nine are still considered civil rights icons for challenging a racist system—and winning!

Key Events in the Civil Rights Movement

1954	The Supreme Court case *Brown* v. *Board of Education* declares school segregation illegal.
1955	Rosa Parks refuses to give up her bus seat to a white passenger and spurs a bus boycott.
1957	The Little Rock Nine help to integrate schools.
1960	Four black college students begin sit-ins at a restaurant in Greensboro, North Carolina.
1961	Freedom Rides to southern states begin as a way to protest segregation in transportation.
1963	Martin Luther King, Jr., leads the famous March on Washington.
1964	The Civil Rights Act, signed by President Lyndon B. Johnson, prohibits discrimination based on race, color, religion, sex, and national origin.
1967	Thurgood Marshall becomes the first African American to be named to the Supreme Court.
1968	President Lyndon B. Johnson signs the Civil Rights Act of 1968, which prohibits discrimination in the sale, rental, and financing of housing.

STONE OF HOPE:
THE LEGACY OF MARTIN LUTHER KING, JR.

Dr. Martin Luther King, Jr., born in Atlanta, Georgia, in 1929, never backed down in his stand against racism. He dedicated his life to achieving equality and justice for Americans of all colors. King experienced racial prejudice early in life. As an adult fighting for civil rights, his speeches, marches, and mere presence motivated people to fight for justice for all. His March on Washington in 1963 was one of the largest activist gatherings in our nation's history.

Sadly, King was assassinated by James Earl Ray on April 4, 1968. But his spirit lives on through a memorial on the National Mall in Washington, D.C. Built in 2011, 48 years after Dr. King's famous "I Have a Dream" speech, the memorial features a 30-foot (9-m) statue of Dr. King carved into a granite boulder named the "Stone of Hope."

Each year, thousands of visitors pay tribute to this inspirational figure, who will forever be remembered as one of the most prominent leaders of the civil rights movement.

EQUAL in '63 RIGHTS

"The time is always right to do what is right."

Martin Luther King, Jr. Memorial in Washington, D.C.

In 1964, at the age of 35, Martin Luther King, Jr., became the youngest person ever to win the Nobel Peace Prize.

Dr. King's "I Have a Dream" speech drew 250,000 people to the National Mall in Washington, D.C., in 1963.

8 Daring Women in U.S. History!

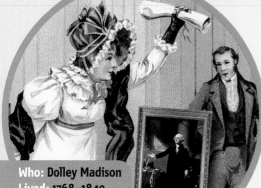

Who: Dolley Madison
Lived: 1768–1849
Why she's daring: As the nation's First Lady from 1809 to 1817, she single-handedly saved a famous—and valuable—portrait of George Washington when it faced almost certain destruction during the War of 1812. As British troops approached the White House, Madison refused to leave until the painting was taken to safety.

Who: Nellie Tayloe Ross
Lived: 1876–1977
Why she's daring: In 1925, Ross became the nation's first woman governor after boldly campaigning for the Wyoming seat left vacant when her husband suddenly passed away. She went on to run the U.S. Mint from 1933 to 1953.

Who: Bessie Coleman
Lived: 1892–1926
Why she's daring: When U.S. flight schools denied her entry, Coleman traveled to France to earn her pilot's license and became the first African-American female aviator. Later, her high-flying, daredevil stunts in air shows earned her the nickname "Queen Bess."

Who: Sacagawea
Lived: c. 1788–1812
Why she's daring: As the only woman to accompany Lewis and Clark into the American West, Sacagawea's calm presence and smarts saved the expedition many times. She served as a Shoshone interpreter for the explorers, found edible plants to feed the crew, and even saved important documents and supplies from a capsizing boat.

Who: Sojourner Truth
Lived: c. 1797–1883
Why she's daring: At age nine, Truth was sold as a slave at auction along with a flock of sheep for $100. Twenty years later, she escaped to freedom and became one of the most prominent and courageous women's rights activists of her time, even meeting with Abraham Lincoln at the White House in 1864.

Who: Danica Patrick
Lived: 1982–
Why she's daring: Arguably the most successful female race car driver in the world, Patrick broke the mold in her sport by becoming the first woman to win a prestigious IndyCar race in 2008 and later winning the time trials at the Daytona 500 in 2013. At just 5'2", Patrick continues to hold her own in a sport dominated by men.

Who: Dolores Huerta
Lived: 1930–
Why she's daring: As a teacher who saw many of her students living in poverty, Huerta rallied to raise awareness for the poor, especially among farmworkers, immigrants, and women. Later, she encouraged Hispanic women to enter politics, helping to increase in the number of women holding offices at the local, state, and federal levels. She received the Presidential Medal of Freedom in 2012.

Who: Lucille Ball
Lived: 1911–1989
Why she's daring: Famous for playing an iconic funny girl in the hit show *I Love Lucy*, Ball worked even more magic behind the screen. A pioneer in the entertainment industry, Ball was the first woman to head a major television studio. At the same time, she made a total of 72 movies, cementing her position as one of the most legendary actresses and comediennes in the world.

QUIZ WHIZ

Are you a history whiz or do you get lost in the past? Take this quiz to find out!
ANSWERS BELOW

1 What is the ancient town of Pamukkale in Turkey best known for?

a. healing hot springs
b. white sandy beaches
c. world famous falafel
d. tall monuments

2 **True or false?** Moai are 800-year-old giant stone statues found in Samoa.

3 Where did a scuba diver recently find $300,000 worth of treasure at the bottom of the ocean?

a. Polynesia
b. Mexico
c. Florida, U.S.A.
d. Hawaii, U.S.A.

4 How many days of service did a knight owe his lord each year?

a. 45
b. 77
c. 180
d. 365

5 In Ancient Egypt, what food was considered a delicacy reserved for royals only?

a. caviar
b. mushrooms
c. chicken wings
d. oatmeal

Not **STUMPED** yet? Check out the *NATIONAL GEOGRAPHIC KIDS QUIZ WHIZ* collection for more crazy **HISTORY** questions!

ANSWERS:
1. a; 2. False. Moai are found on Easter Island. 3. c; 4. a; 5. b

Brilliant Biographies

A biography is the story of a person's life. It can be a brief summary or a long book. Biographers—those who write biographies—use many different sources to learn about their subjects. You can write your own biography of a famous person whom you find inspiring.

How to Get Started

Choose a subject you find interesting. If you think Cleopatra is cool, you have a good chance of getting your reader interested, too. If you're bored by ancient Egypt, your reader will be snoring after your first paragraph.

Your subject can be almost anyone: an author, an inventor, a celebrity, a politician, or a member of your family. To find someone to write about, ask yourself these simple questions:

1. Whom do I want to know more about?
2. What did this person do that was special?
3. How did this person change the world?

Do Your Research

- Find out as much about your subject as possible. Read books, news articles, and encyclopedia entries. Watch video clips and movies, and search the Internet. Conduct interviews, if possible.
- Take notes, writing down important facts and interesting stories about your subject.

Write the Biography

- Come up with a title. Include the person's name.
- Write an introduction. Consider asking a probing question about your subject.
- Include information about the person's childhood. When was this person born? Where did he or she grow up? Whom did he or she admire?
- Highlight the person's talents, accomplishments, and personal attributes.
- Describe the specific events that helped to shape this person's life. Did this person ever have a problem and overcome it?
- Write a conclusion. Include your thoughts about why it is important to learn about this person.
- Once you have finished your first draft, revise and then proofread your work.

Author
Rick Riordan

Here's a SAMPLE BIOGRAPHY of Rick Riordan, best-selling author of the two series Percy Jackson and the Olympians and The 39 Clues. Of course, there is so much more for you to discover, and write about on your own!

Rick Riordan—Author

Rick Riordan was born on June 5, 1964, in San Antonio, Texas, U.S.A. Born into a creative family—his mom was a musician and artist and his dad was a ceramicist—Riordan began writing in middle school, and he published his first short stories while attending college.

After graduating from University of Texas at Austin, Riordan went on to teach English to middle schoolers, spending his summers as a music director at a summer camp. Writing adult mysteries on the side, Riordan soon discovered his knack for writing for younger readers and published *The Lightning Thief*, the first book in the Percy Jackson series, in 2005. *The Sea of Monsters* soon followed. Before long, Riordan quit his teaching job to become a full-time writer.

Today Riordan has penned more than 35 books, firmly establishing himself as one of the most accomplished and well-known authors of our time. When he's not writing, Riordan—who lives with his wife, Becky, and their sons Haley and Patrick—likes to read, swim, play guitar, and travel with his family.

Almanac Explorer!

I have a venOmous bite.

This is clue #10!
Collect them all and unscramble the letters to find the secret animal. Enter the animal name at kids.nationalgeographic .com/almanac-2016!

Hikers trek below a stone arch in Arches National Park in Utah, U.S.A.

Geography
Rocks

THE POLITICAL WORLD

Earth's land area is made up of seven continents, but people have divided much of the land into smaller political units called countries. Australia is a continent made up of a single country, and Antarctica is set aside for scientific research. But the other five continents include almost 200 independent countries. The political map shown here depicts boundaries—imaginary lines created by treaties—that separate countries. Some boundaries, such as the one between the United States and Canada, are very stable and have been recognized for many years.

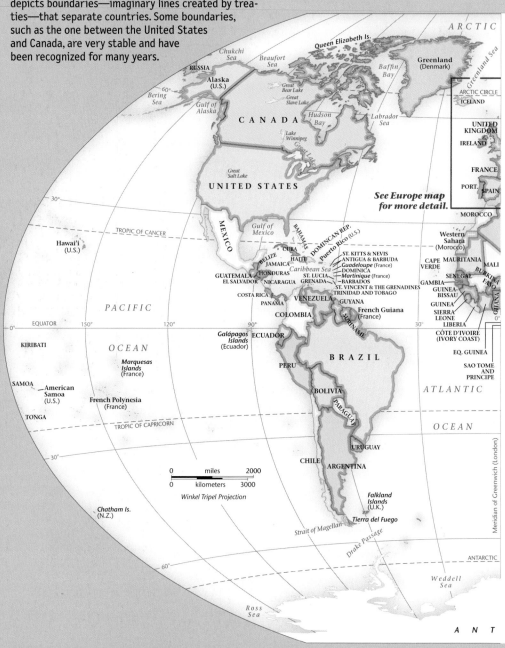

See Europe map for more detail.

Winkel Tripel Projection

Other boundaries, such as the one between Ethiopia and Eritrea in northeast Africa, are relatively new and still disputed. Countries come in all shapes and sizes. Russia and Canada are giants; others, such as El Salvador, are small. Some countries are long and skinny—look at Chile in South America! Still other countries—such as Indonesia and Japan in Asia—are made up of groups of islands. The political map is a clue to the diversity that makes Earth so fascinating.

OCEAN

North Land

New Siberian Islands

East Siberian Sea

Laptev Sea

Barents Sea

Kara Sea

Svalbard (Norway)

Novaya Zemlya

NORWAY

SWEDEN

FINLAND

R U S S I A

60°

Bering Sea

Sea of Okhotsk

DEN.

GERMANY

EST.

LATV.

LITH.

BELARUS

POLAND

UKRAINE

MOLD.

ROMANIA

BULGARIA

GEORGIA

ARM.

AZERB.

TURKMEN.

KAZAKHSTAN

Lake Baikal

MONGOLIA

NORTH KOREA

JAPAN

ITALY

ALBANIA

GREECE

TURKEY

Caspian Sea

UZBEK.

KYRGYZSTAN

TAJIKISTAN

SOUTH KOREA

Mediterranean Sea

CYPRUS

SYRIA

LEBANON

IRAQ

IRAN

AFGHAN.

C H I N A

TAIWAN

30°

The People's Republic of China claims Taiwan as its 23rd province. Taiwan's government (Republic of China) maintains that there are two political entities.

TUNISIA

ISRAEL

JORDAN

KUWAIT

ALGERIA

LIBYA

EGYPT

BAHRAIN

QATAR

SAUDI ARABIA

U.A.E.

OMAN

PAKISTAN

NEPAL

BHUTAN

BANGLADESH

I N D I A

MYANMAR (BURMA)

Taiwan

South China Sea

Philippine Sea

Northern Mariana Islands (U.S.)

PACIFIC

MARSHALL ISLANDS

NIGER

CHAD

SUDAN

ERITREA

YEMEN

DJIBOUTI

Red Sea

Arabian Sea

Bay of Bengal

THAILAND

VIETNAM

LAOS

CAMBODIA

PHILIPPINES

Guam (U.S.)

OCEAN

BENIN

NIGERIA

CAMEROON

C.A.R.

SOUTH SUDAN

ETHIOPIA

SOMALIA

SRI LANKA

MALDIVES

BRUNEI

PALAU

FEDERATED STATES OF MICRONESIA

60°

90°

150°

0°

EQUATOR

KIRIBATI

TOGO

GABON

CONGO

DEM. REP. OF THE CONGO

RWANDA

BURUNDI

UGANDA

KENYA

MALAYSIA

SINGAPORE

I N D O N E S I A

New Guinea

PAPUA NEW GUINEA

SOLOMON ISLANDS

NAURU

TUVALU

Cabinda (Angola)

TANZANIA

SEYCHELLES

I N D I A N

TIMOR-LESTE (EAST TIMOR)

ANGOLA

ZAMBIA

MALAWI

COMOROS

MADAGASCAR

O C E A N

Coral Sea

VANUATU

FIJI

NAMIBIA

ZIMBABWE

BOTSWANA

MOZAMBIQUE

Réunion (France)

MAURITIUS

New Caledonia (France)

SOUTH AFRICA

SWAZILAND

LESOTHO

A U S T R A L I A

30°

Great Australian Bight

North Island

Tasman Sea

Kerguelen Islands (France)

Tasmania

NEW ZEALAND

South Island

CIRCLE

60°

A R C T I C A

Ross Sea

THE PHYSICAL WORLD

Earth is dominated by large landmasses called continents—seven in all—and by an interconnected global ocean that is divided into four parts by the continents. More than 70 percent of Earth's surface is covered by oceans, and the rest is made up of land areas.

Different landforms give variety to the surface of the continents. The Rocky Mountains divide North America, the Andes mark the western edge of South America, and the Himalaya tower above India. The Plateau of Tibet forms the rugged core of Asia, while

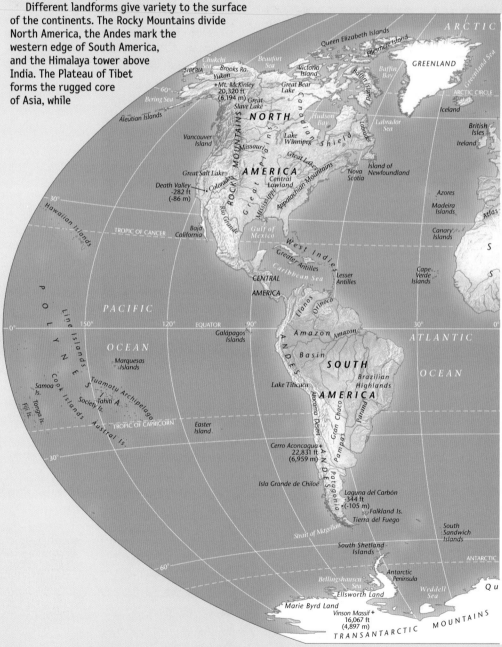

the Northern European Plain extends from the North Sea to the Ural Mountains. Much of Africa is a plateau, and dry plains cover large areas of Australia. Mountains rise more than 16,000 feet (4,877 m) above Antarctica's massive ice sheets. Mountains and trenches make the ocean floors as varied as any continent. A mountain chain called the Mid-Atlantic Ridge runs the length of the Atlantic Ocean. In the western Pacific, trenches drop deep into the ocean floor.

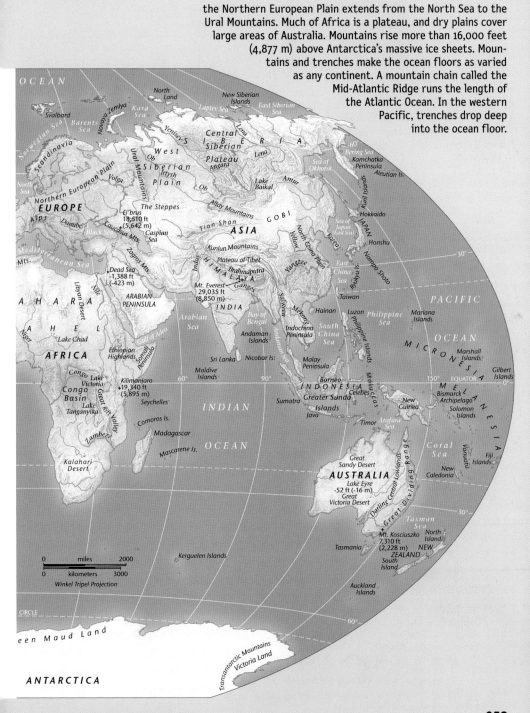

KINDS OF MAPS

Maps are special tools that geographers use to tell a story about Earth. Maps can be used to show just about anything related to places. Some maps show physical features, such as mountains or vegetation. Maps can also show climates or natural hazards and other things we cannot easily see. Other maps illustrate different features on Earth—political boundaries, urban centers, and economic systems.

AN IMPERFECT TOOL

Maps are not perfect. A globe is a scale model of Earth with accurate relative sizes and locations. Because maps are flat, they involve distortions of size, shape, and direction. Also, cartographers—people who create maps— make choices about what information to include. Because of this, it is important to study many different types of maps to learn the complete story of Earth. Three commonly found kinds of maps are shown on this page.

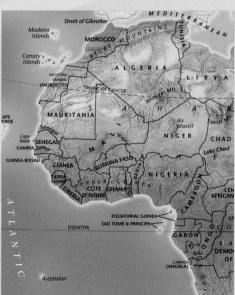

PHYSICAL MAPS. Earth's natural features—landforms, water bodies, and vegetation—are shown on physical maps. The map above uses color and shading to illustrate mountains, lakes, rivers, and deserts of western Africa. Country names and borders are added for reference, but they are not natural features.

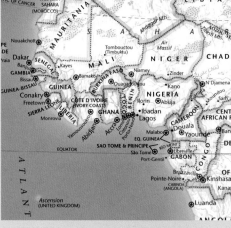

POLITICAL MAPS. These maps represent characteristics of the landscape created by humans, such as boundaries, cities, and place-names. Natural features are added only for reference. On the map above, capital cities are represented with a star inside a circle, while other cities are shown with black dots.

THEMATIC MAPS. Patterns related to a particular topic or theme, such as population distribution, appear on these maps. The map above displays the region's climate zones, which range from tropical wet (bright green) to tropical wet and dry (light green) to semiarid (dark yellow) to arid or desert (light yellow).

GEOGRAPHIC FEATURES

From roaring rivers to parched deserts, from underwater canyons to jagged mountains, Earth is covered with beautiful and diverse environments. Here are examples of the most common types of geographic features found around the world.

DESERT
Deserts are land features created by climate, specifically by a lack of water. Here, a camel caravan crosses the Sahara in North Africa.

VALLEY
Valleys, cut by running water or moving ice, may be broad and flat or narrow and steep, such as the Indus River Valley in Ladakh, India (above).

RIVER
As a river moves through flatlands, it twists and turns. Above, the Rio Los Amigos winds through a rain forest in Peru.

MOUNTAIN
Mountains are Earth's tallest landforms, and Mount Everest (above) rises highest of all, at 29,035 feet (8,850 m) above sea level.

GLACIER
Glaciers—"rivers" of ice— such as Alaska's Hubbard Glacier (above) move slowly from mountains to the sea. Global warming is shrinking them.

CANYON
Steep-sided valleys called canyons are created mainly by running water. Buckskin Gulch in Utah (above) is the deepest "slot" canyon in the American Southwest.

WATERFALL
Waterfalls form when a river reaches an abrupt change in elevation. Above, Kaieteur Falls, in Guyana, has a sheer drop of 741 feet (226 m).

SPOTLIGHT ON
AFRICA

Verreaux's sifaka

With powerful hind legs, a sifaka can jump over 30 feet (9 m).

About 70 percent of the world's cocoa is grown in Africa.

The massive continent of Africa, where humankind began millions of years ago, is second to only Asia in size. Stretching nearly as far from west to east as it does from north to south, Africa is home to both the longest river in the world (the Nile) and the largest hot desert on Earth (Sahara).

Zulu woman in native costume

Pyramids Plus

Egypt isn't the only place where you can find pyramids in Africa. Sudan is home to more than 200 pyramids dating back 2,000 years—twice as many as in Egypt.

Fast Growth

Thanks to better quality health care and more access to medicine, Africa's population is expected to more than double to at least 2.4 billion people by 2050.

Beautiful Baskets

Young girls and women weave brightly colored baskets from grass and straw that have become a trademark of African cultures. The baskets are used for decoration and to store food.

Great Lakes

Three of the world's ten biggest lakes are in Africa. Lake Victoria, Lake Tanganyika, and Lake Malawi are found in the Great Rift Valley, which stretches from Ethiopia to Mozambique.

Protecting the Environment

Namibia	43.2%*
Seychelles	42.0%
Zambia	37.8%
Botswana	37.2%
Tanzania	32.2%
Congo	30.4%

Figures represent percent of total land area set aside as protected area

The Great Sphinx at Giza in Egypt

263

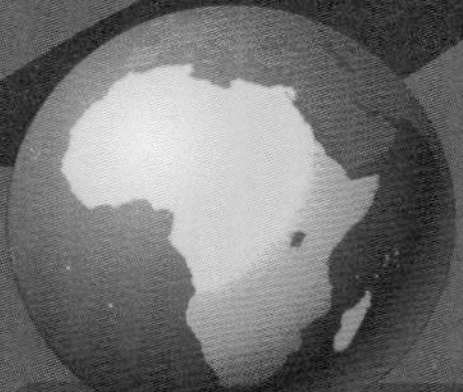

PHYSICAL

LAND AREA
11,608,000 sq mi (30,065,000 sq km)

LOWEST POINT
Lake Assal, Djibouti
-509 ft (-155 m)

LARGEST LAKE
Victoria
26,800 sq mi (69,500 sq km)

HIGHEST POINT
Kilimanjaro, Tanzania
19,340 ft (5,895 m)

LONGEST RIVER
Nile
4,400 mi (7,081 km)

POLITICAL

POPULATION
1,136,000,000

LARGEST METROPOLITAN AREA
Cairo, Egypt
Pop. 18,772,000

LARGEST COUNTRY
Algeria
919,595 sq mi (2,381,741 sq km)

MOST DENSELY POPULATED COUNTRY
Mauritius 1,650 people per sq mi (618 per sq km)

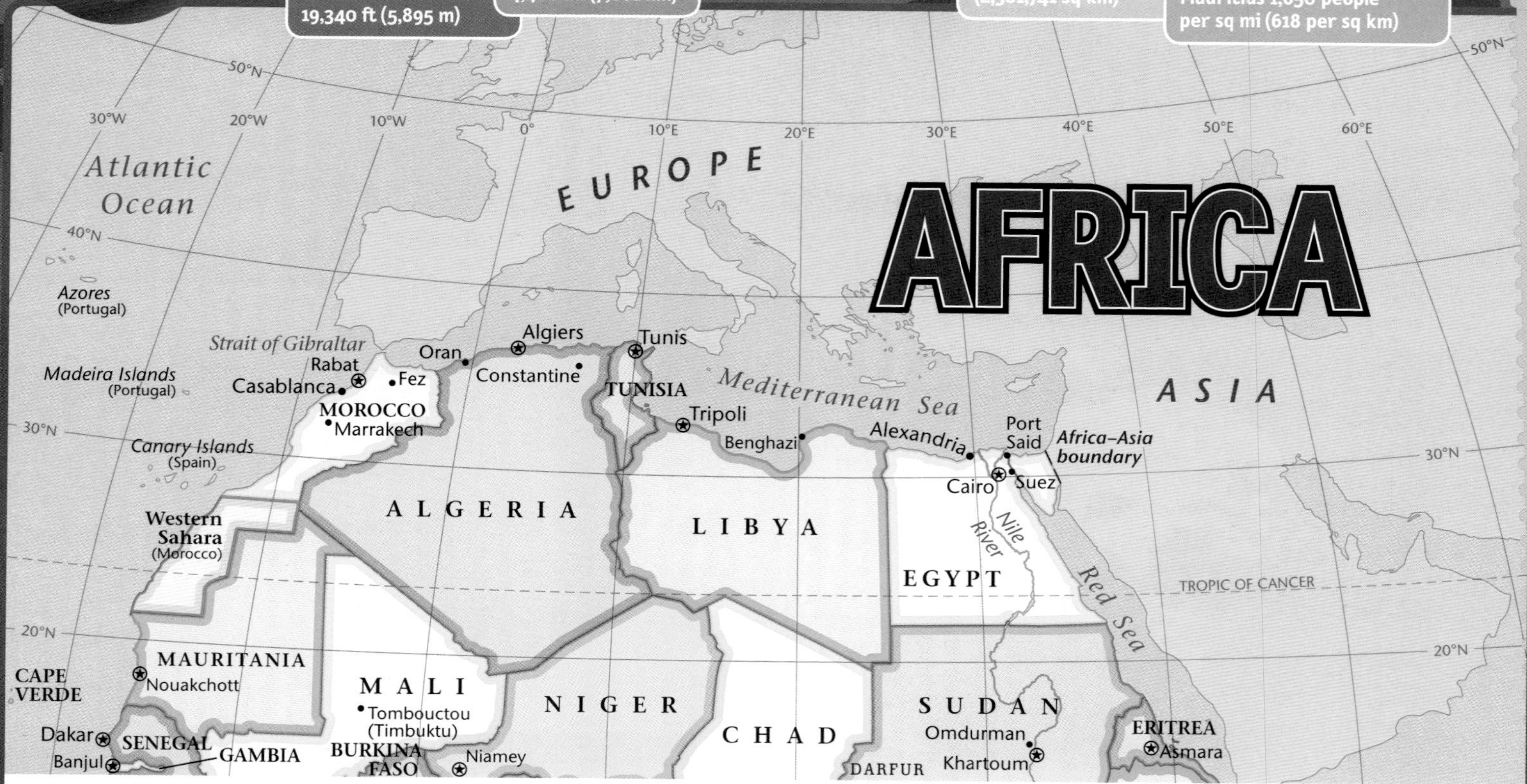

AFRICA
EUROPE
ASIA
Atlantic Ocean
Mediterranean Sea
Red Sea
50°N
40°N
30°N
20°N
30°W
20°W
10°W
0°
10°E
20°E
30°E
40°E
50°E
60°E
TROPIC OF CANCER
Azores (Portugal)
Madeira Islands (Portugal)
Canary Islands (Spain)
Strait of Gibraltar
Rabat
Casablanca
Fez
MOROCCO
Marrakech
Oran
Algiers
Constantine
Tunis
TUNISIA
Tripoli
Benghazi
Alexandria
Port Said
Cairo
Suez
Africa–Asia boundary
Nile River
ALGERIA
LIBYA
EGYPT
Western Sahara (Morocco)
MAURITANIA
Nouakchott
CAPE VERDE
Dakar
SENEGAL
Banjul
GAMBIA
MALI
Tombouctou (Timbuktu)
BURKINA FASO
Niamey
NIGER
CHAD
SUDAN
Omdurman
Khartoum
DARFUR
ERITREA
Asmara

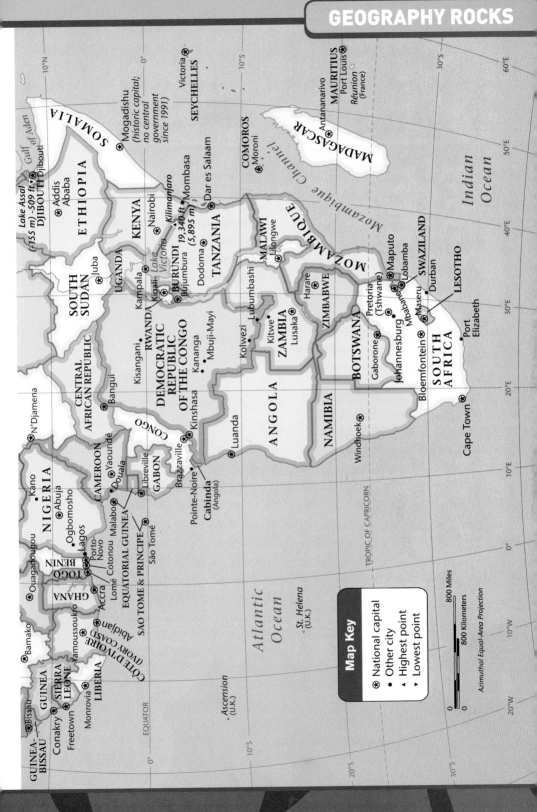

Gulf of Aden

Gulf of Djibouti

SOMALIA

Mogadishu
(historic capital;
no central
government
since 1991)

Lake Assal
(-155 m) -509 ft.▼
DJIBOUTI Djibouti

Addis
Ababa

ETHIOPIA

Victoria ⊛

SEYCHELLES

COMOROS
Moroni

MAURITIUS ⊛
Port Louis
Réunion
(France)

Antananarivo

MADAGASCAR

Indian
Ocean

SOUTH
SUDAN

Juba

UGANDA

Kampala

KENYA

Nairobi

Mombasa

Dar es Salaam

Mozambique Channel

Kigali Lake
Victoria Kilimanjaro
19,340 ft.
(5,895 m) ▲

RWANDA

BURUNDI

Bujumbura

TANZANIA

Dodoma

MALAWI

Lilongwe

MOZAMBIQUE

SWAZILAND

Maputo
Lobamba
Mbabane

LESOTHO

Maseru
Durban

CENTRAL
AFRICAN REPUBLIC

Bangui

N'Djamena

DEMOCRATIC
REPUBLIC
OF THE CONGO

Kisangani

Kananga

Mbuji-Mayi

Lubumbashi

Kolwezi

Kitwe

ZAMBIA

Lusaka

Harare

ZIMBABWE

Pretoria
(Tshwane)

Gaborone

BOTSWANA

Johannesburg

Bloemfontein

SOUTH
AFRICA

Port
Elizabeth

CONGO

Libreville

GABON

Brazzaville

Kinshasa

Luanda

ANGOLA

Cabinda
(Angola)

Pointe-Noire

NAMIBIA

Windhoek ⊛

Cape Town

CAMEROON

Yaoundé

Douala

EQUATORIAL GUINEA

Malabo

Cotonou

SAO TOME & PRINCIPE

São Tomé

NIGERIA

Kano

Abuja

Ogbomosho

Lagos

Porto-
Novo

BENIN

TOGO

GHANA

Lomé

Accra

Ouagadougou

Bamako

GUINEA

Conakry

SIERRA
LEONE

Freetown

LIBERIA

Monrovia

CÔTE D'IVOIRE
(IVORY COAST)

Yamoussoukro

Abidjan

GUINEA-
BISSAU

Bissau

Atlantic
Ocean

St. Helena
(U.K.)

Ascension
(U.K.)

EQUATOR

TROPIC OF CAPRICORN

Map Key

⊛ National capital
• Other city
▲ Highest point
▼ Lowest point

800 Miles

800 Kilometers

Azimuthal Equal-Area Projection

SPOTLIGHT ON
ANTARCTICA

There is an ice sheet in Antarctica that is 1.5 million years old.

About 37,000 tourists travel to Antarctica each year.

Iceberg

This frozen continent may be a cool place to visit, but unless you're a penguin, you probably wouldn't want to hang out in Antarctica for long. The fact that it's the coldest, windiest, and driest continent helps explain why humans never colonized this ice-covered land surrounding the South Pole.

A seasonal Argentine scientific research station, Almirante Brown is also a popular stop for tourists.

Whale World

At least 12 species of whales and dolphins can be found in Antarctic waters, including the minke whale, which spends much of its time near the ice-edge. Most species are seen only seasonally.

Warm Waters

Deception Island's geothermal pools are a popular spot for the tourists who visit Antarctica each year. Activity from an underwater active volcano keeps the waters warm.

A Long Waddle

After building their stone-lined nests along Antarctica's coasts, Adélie penguins may have to waddle up to 30 miles (50 km) across seasonal ice sheets to reach the shore.

Not All Ice

The Antarctic Peninsula is known as the "Banana Belt" since it has a mild climate and gets just 14 to 20 inches (35 to 50 cm) of annual precipitation, about the same as Denver, Colorado, U.S.A.

Earth's Largest Deserts

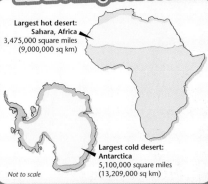

Largest hot desert:
Sahara, Africa
3,475,000 square miles
(9,000,000 sq km)

Largest cold desert:
Antarctica
5,100,000 square miles
(13,209,000 sq km)

Not to scale

Weddell seal

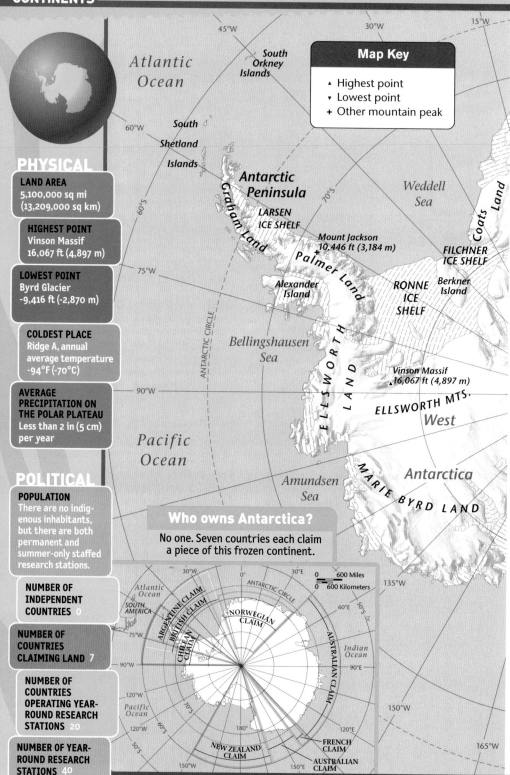

Atlantic
Ocean

South
Orkney
Islands

60°W

South
Shetland
Islands

45°W

30°W

15°W

Map Key

▲ Highest point
▼ Lowest point
+ Other mountain peak

Antarctic
Peninsula

Graham Land

70°S

Weddell
Sea

Coats Land

LARSEN
ICE SHELF

Mount Jackson
10,446 ft (3,184 m)

FILCHNER
ICE SHELF

75°W

Alexander
Island

Palmer Land

RONNE
ICE
SHELF

Berkner
Island

ANTARCTIC CIRCLE

Bellingshausen
Sea

E L L S W O R T H   L A N D

Vinson Massif
16,067 ft (4,897 m)

90°W

ELLSWORTH MTS.
West

Pacific
Ocean

Amundsen
Sea

M A R I E   B Y R D   L A N D

Antarctica

135°W

PHYSICAL

LAND AREA
5,100,000 sq mi
(13,209,000 sq km)

HIGHEST POINT
Vinson Massif
16,067 ft (4,897 m)

LOWEST POINT
Byrd Glacier
-9,416 ft (-2,870 m)

COLDEST PLACE
Ridge A, annual
average temperature
-94°F (-70°C)

**AVERAGE
PRECIPITATION ON
THE POLAR PLATEAU**
Less than 2 in (5 cm)
per year

POLITICAL

POPULATION
There are no indig-
enous inhabitants,
but there are both
permanent and
summer-only staffed
research stations.

**NUMBER OF
INDEPENDENT
COUNTRIES** 0

**NUMBER OF
COUNTRIES
CLAIMING LAND** 7

**NUMBER OF
COUNTRIES
OPERATING YEAR-
ROUND RESEARCH
STATIONS** 20

**NUMBER OF YEAR-
ROUND RESEARCH
STATIONS** 40

Who owns Antarctica?

No one. Seven countries each claim
a piece of this frozen continent.

30°W

0°

ANTARCTIC CIRCLE

30°E

0   600 Miles
0   600 Kilometers

Atlantic
Ocean

SOUTH
AMERICA

ARGENTINE CLAIM

BRITISH CLAIM

75°W

CHILEAN
CLAIM

NORWEGIAN
CLAIM

60°E

AUSTRALIAN CLAIM

Indian
Ocean

90°W

90°E

120°W

Pacific
Ocean

120°W

60°S

180°

120°E

150°W

NEW ZEALAND
CLAIM

FRENCH
CLAIM

165°W

150°W

AUSTRALIAN
CLAIM

ANTARCTICA

FIMBUL
ICE SHELF

0°

15°E

30°E

45°E

RIISER-LARSEN
ICE SHELF

60°E

QUEEN MAUD LAND

ENDERBY
LAND

Indian
Ocean

Valkyrie
Dome

MacKenzie Bay

75°E

AMERY ICE SHELF

Lambert
Glacier

AMERICAN

Ridge A +

HIGHLAND

WEST
ICE SHELF

TRANSANTARCTIC MOUNTAINS

POLAR PLATEAU

East

90°E

★ South Pole

Antarctica

SHACKLETON
ICE SHELF

80°S

ROSS
ICE
SHELF

105°E

Byrd Glacier
-9,416 ft (-2,870 m)

Roosevelt
Island

Taylor
Glacier

WILKES LAND

Ross Island

VICTORIA LAND

70°S

Mount Erebus
12,448 ft
(3,794 m)

120°E

Ross
Sea

60°S

Talos
Dome

180°

0   600 Miles

0   600 Kilometers

* South
Magnetic
Pole (2015)

Indian
Ocean

Azimuthal Equidistant Projection

150°E

135°E

SPOTLIGHT ON
ASIA

The mango is the national fruit of India, and the capital of Thailand, Bangkok, is known as the Big Mango.

The endangered Philippine eagle, which has a seven-foot (2.1-m) wingspan, eats monkeys.

Women sell fruit and flowers at Damnoen Saduak floating market in Bangkok, Thailand.

Made up of 46 countries, Asia is the world's largest continent. And just how big is it? From western Turkey to the eastern tip of Russia, Asia spans nearly half the globe! Home to four billion citizens—that's three out of five people on the planet—Asia's population is bigger than that of all the other continents combined.

Hong Kong

Rare Breed

Native to Indonesia, Southeast Asia, and Malaysia, the rare binturong—or bear cat—has a cat's face, a bear's body, and a tail that's as long as its body.

What Lies Beneath

At the bottom of China's Fuxian Lake lie the ruins of a city. Researchers think that over 1,700 years ago, an entire section of the city broke off and slid into the lake during an earthquake.

Young Mountains

Stretching across South Asia, the Himalaya include Mount Everest, the world's tallest peak. Formed about 50 million years ago, it's one of the youngest mountain ranges on Earth.

Egg-citing Find

In 2007, explorers in India discovered a site that held more than 100 sauropod dinosaur eggs. Some of the eggs were so big that you'd need two hands to hold them.

Asia's 6 Most Visited Cities*

1. **Bangkok, Thailand**
   16.42 million visitors

2. **Singapore**
   12.47 million visitors

3. **Dubai, U.A.E.**
   11.95 million visitors

4. **Kuala Lumpur, Malaysia**
   10.81 million visitors

5. **Hong Kong**
   8.84 million visitors

6. **Seoul, South Korea**
   8.63 million visitors

*2014

Giant panda

ASIA

PHYSICAL

LAND AREA
17,208,000 sq mi
(44,570,000 sq km)

HIGHEST POINT
Mount Everest,
China–Nepal
29,035 ft (8,850 m)

LOWEST POINT
Dead Sea,
Israel–Jordan
-1,388 ft (-423 m)

LONGEST RIVER
Yangtze, China
3,880 mi (6,244 km)

**LARGEST LAKE
ENTIRELY IN ASIA**
Lake Baikal, Russia
12,200 sq mi
(31,500 sq km)

POLITICAL

POPULATION
4,351,000,000

**LARGEST
METROPOLITAN AREA**
Tokyo, Japan
Pop. 38,001,000

**LARGEST COUNTRY
ENTIRELY IN ASIA**
China
3,705,405 sq mi
(9,596,960 sq km)

**MOST DENSELY
POPULATED COUNTRY**
Singapore
21,520 people
per sq mi
(8,314 per sq km)

EUROPE

Europe
Asia

Nizhniy Tagil
Yekaterinburg
Tyumen'
Magnitogorsk
Chelyabinsk
Omsk

İzmir
Ankara
ARMENIA
GEORGIA
Tbilisi
TURKMENISTAN
Astana
Qaraghandy
Yerevan
Baku
KAZAKHSTAN

Dardanelles
Bosporus
TURKEY
Mediterranean Sea

LEBANON
Beirut
SYRIA
Damascus
Jerusalem
Amman
ISRAEL
Dead Sea
-1,388 ft
(-423 m)
JORDAN
IRAQ
Baghdad
Basra

AZERBAIJAN
UZBEKISTAN
Bishkek
Ashgabat
Tashkent
Almaty
Tehran
Samarqand
Mashhad
Dushanbe
KYRGYZSTAN
TAJIKISTAN

Medina
KUWAIT
Kuwait
City
IRAN
AFGHANISTAN
Hotan
Jeddah
SAUDI ARABIA
Kabul
Islamabad
Mecca
Manama
Rawalpindi
Riyadh
BAHRAIN
Doha
Lahore
Faisalabad
QATAR
Dubai
PAKISTAN
Delhi
Abu Dhabi
New Delhi
NEPAL
Muscat
Jaipur
Kanpur
Sanaa
Karachi
Indore
Bhopal
YEMEN
OMAN
Surat
Aden
UNITED ARAB
EMIRATES
Mumbai
(Bombay)
INDIA
Pune

AFRICA
Arabian
Sea
Hyderabad

Bangalore
(Bengaluru)
Chennai
(Madras)

EQUATOR
Colombo
SRI
LANKA
Sri Jayewardenepura Kotte
Male

0   800 Miles
0   800 Kilometers
Two-point Equidistant Projection
MALDIVES

Indian Ocean

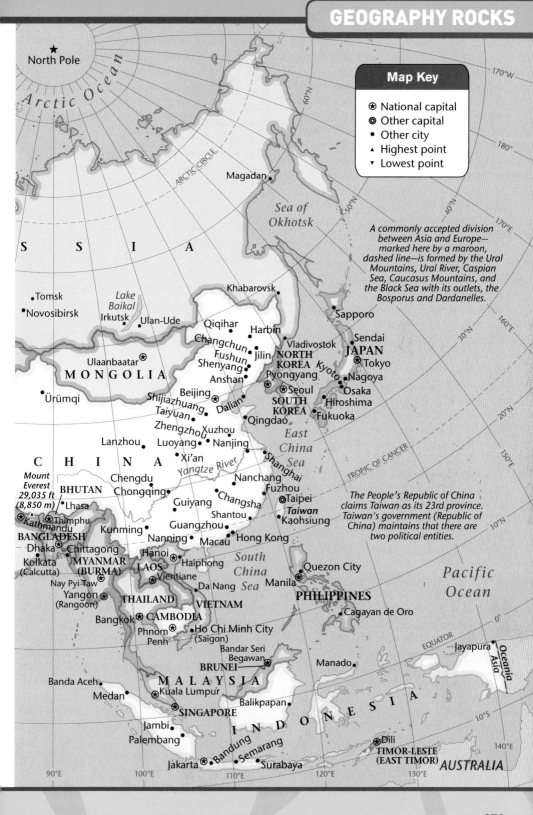

★ North Pole

Arctic Ocean

170°W

180°

170°E

160°E

150°E

40°N

30°N

20°N

10°N

0°

10°S

Map Key

⊛ National capital
◎ Other capital
• Other city
▲ Highest point
▼ Lowest point

ARCTIC CIRCLE

R U S S I A

Magadan

Sea of
Okhotsk

60°N

50°N

A commonly accepted division
between Asia and Europe—
marked here by a maroon,
dashed line—is formed by the Ural
Mountains, Ural River, Caspian
Sea, Caucasus Mountains, and
the Black Sea with its outlets, the
Bosporus and Dardanelles.

•Tomsk
•Novosibirsk

Lake
Baikal

Irkutsk •Ulan-Ude

Khabarovsk

Sapporo

Qiqihar   Harbin

Vladivostok

Sendai

JAPAN

Changchun
Fushun
Jilin
NORTH
KOREA
Kyoto
⊛Tokyo

Ulaanbaatar ⊛

M O N G O L I A

Shenyang
Anshan
Pyongyang
Nagoya

•Ürümqi

Beijing
Shijiazhuang
Dalian
⊛Seoul
SOUTH
KOREA
Osaka
Hiroshima
Fukuoka

Taiyuan
Qingdao

Zhengzhou
Xuzhou

Lanzhou   Luoyang • Nanjing

Xi'an

East
China
Sea

TROPIC OF CANCER

C H I N A

Mount
Everest
29,035 ft
(8,850 m)

BHUTAN

Chengdu
Chongqing

Yangtze River

Shanghai

Nanchang
Fuzhou

The People's Republic of China
claims Taiwan as its 23rd province.
Taiwan's government (Republic of
China) maintains that there are
two political entities.

•Lhasa

Guiyang   Changsha

◎Taipei

Shantou

Taiwan

Kaohsiung

⊛Thimphu
⊛Kathmandu

Kunming

Guangzhou

BANGLADESH
Dhaka ⊛
Chittagong

Nanning • Macau Hong Kong

Hanoi

Kolkata
(Calcutta)

MYANMAR
(BURMA)

⊛Haiphong

South
China
Sea

Quezon City

*Pacific
Ocean*

LAOS

Nay Pyi Taw
Yangon ⊛
(Rangoon)

⊛Vientiane

Da Nang

Manila

PHILIPPINES

THAILAND

VIETNAM

Bangkok ⊛ CAMBODIA

Phnom ⊛
Penh

Ho Chi Minh City
(Saigon)

Cagayan de Oro

EQUATOR

Jayapura

Oceania
Asia

Bandar Seri
Begawan

Manado

Banda Aceh •

BRUNEI

M A L A Y S I A

•Medan

⊛Kuala Lumpur

Balikpapan

⊛SINGAPORE

I N D O N E S I A

AUSTRALIA

Jambi
Palembang

Bandung
Semarang

Jakarta ⊛

Surabaya

◎Dili

TIMOR-LESTE
(EAST TIMOR)

90°E   100°E   110°E   120°E   130°E   140°E

SPOTLIGHT ON
AUSTRALIA,
NEW ZEALAND, AND OCEANIA

New Zealand has two national anthems.

In the hot Australian desert, kangaroos lick their arms to stay cool.

Kangaroo and joey

274

G'day, mate! This vast region, covering almost 3.3 million square miles (8.5 million sq km), includes Australia—the world's smallest and flattest continent—and New Zealand, as well as a fleet of mostly tiny islands scattered across the Pacific Ocean. Also known as "down under," all of the countries in this region are in the Southern Hemisphere, and below the Equator.

Aboriginal children in ceremonial markings

Fenced In

A 1,550-mile (2,500-km) fence protects farmland in southeast Australia by keeping sheep and cattle in—and wild dogs out. That's longer than the distance between Miami and Montreal.

Big, Bad Bird

Australia and New Guinea are home to the wild cassowary, a giant flightless bird. Taller than an adult human with daggerlike claws, it's considered the world's most dangerous bird.

Girl Power

In 1893, Kiwi women were the first women to vote in a national election. New Zealand is also the first country to have its three top government positions held simultaneously by women.

Helen Clark, Prime Minister, 1999–2008

Giant Reef

The Great Barrier Reef, found off the east coast of Australia, is big enough to be seen from space. It's teeming with sea life, like whales, dolphins, sea turtles, snakes, coral, and fish.

Australia: Continent or Island?

Greenland: 836,330 sq mi (2,166,086 sq km)

Australia: 2,988,901 sq mi (7,741,220 sq km)

How does Australia compare to Greenland, the world's largest island?

Uluru (Ayers Rock) in Northern Territory, Australia

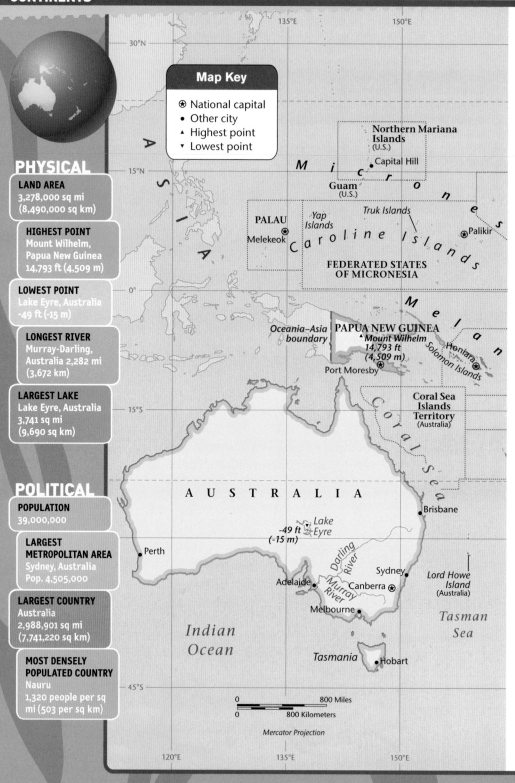

Map Key

- ⊛ National capital
- • Other city
- ▲ Highest point
- ▼ Lowest point

PHYSICAL

LAND AREA
3,278,000 sq mi
(8,490,000 sq km)

HIGHEST POINT
Mount Wilhelm,
Papua New Guinea
14,793 ft (4,509 m)

LOWEST POINT
Lake Eyre, Australia
-49 ft (-15 m)

LONGEST RIVER
Murray-Darling,
Australia 2,282 mi
(3,672 km)

LARGEST LAKE
Lake Eyre, Australia
3,741 sq mi
(9,690 sq km)

POLITICAL

POPULATION
39,000,000

**LARGEST
METROPOLITAN AREA**
Sydney, Australia
Pop. 4,505,000

LARGEST COUNTRY
Australia
2,988,901 sq mi
(7,741,220 sq km)

**MOST DENSELY
POPULATED COUNTRY**
Nauru
1,320 people per sq
mi (503 per sq km)

Northern Mariana
Islands
(U.S.)
• Capital Hill

Guam
(U.S.)

ASIA

Micronesia

PALAU
Melekeok ⊛

Yap
Islands

Truk Islands

Caroline Islands

⊛ Palikir

FEDERATED STATES
OF MICRONESIA

Melanesia

Oceania–Asia
boundary

PAPUA NEW GUINEA
▲ Mount Wilhelm
14,793 ft
(4,509 m)

Port Moresby

Honiara
Solomon Islands

Coral Sea
Islands
Territory
(Australia)

Coral Sea

AUSTRALIA

Brisbane •

-49 ft ▼ Lake
(-15 m)   Eyre

Darling River

Sydney •

Lord Howe
Island
(Australia)

Perth •

Adelaide •

Murray River

Canberra ⊛

Melbourne •

Indian
Ocean

Tasman
Sea

Tasmania

Hobart •

0   800 Miles
0   800 Kilometers

Mercator Projection

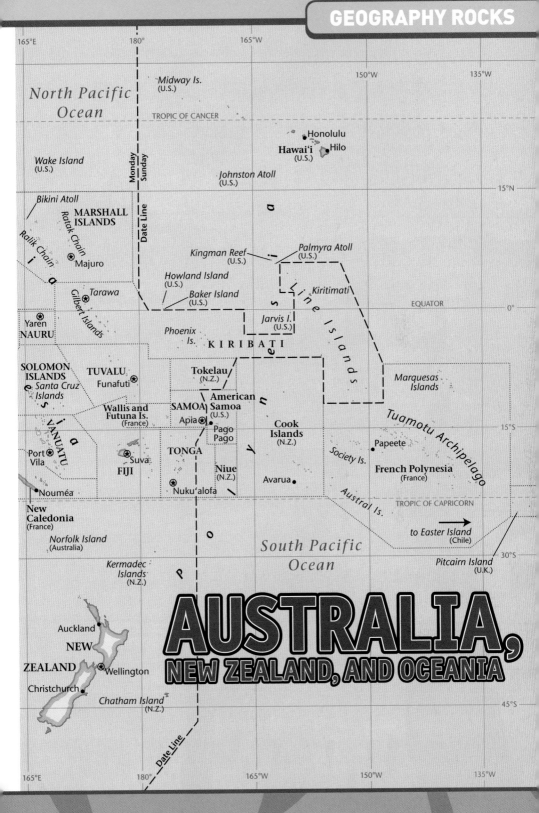

North Pacific Ocean

Midway Is. (U.S.)

TROPIC OF CANCER

Honolulu
Hawai'i • Hilo
(U.S.)

Wake Island (U.S.)

Monday | Sunday

Date Line

Johnston Atoll (U.S.)

15°N

Bikini Atoll

MARSHALL ISLANDS

Ratak Chain

Ralik Chain

⊛ Majuro

M i c r o n e s i a

Kingman Reef (U.S.)

Palmyra Atoll (U.S.)

Howland Island (U.S.)

Baker Island (U.S.)

Kiritimati

EQUATOR 0°

⊛ Yaren
NAURU

Tarawa

Gilbert Islands

Jarvis I. (U.S.)

Phoenix Is.

K I R I B A T I

L i n e   I s l a n d s

Marquesas Islands

SOLOMON ISLANDS
Santa Cruz Islands

TUVALU
Funafuti ⊛

Tokelau (N.Z.)

SAMOA
Apia ⊛

American Samoa
(U.S.)
Pago Pago

P o l y n e s i a

Cook Islands (N.Z.)

Society Is.

Papeete •

Tuamotu Archipelago

15°S

M e l a n e s i a

VANUATU

Port ⊛ Vila

⊛ Suva
FIJI

TONGA

Niue (N.Z.)

Avarua •

French Polynesia
(France)

Nouméa •

Wallis and Futuna Is. (France)

Nuku'alofa

Austral Is.

TROPIC OF CAPRICORN

New Caledonia (France)

Norfolk Island (Australia)

to Easter Island (Chile)

Pitcairn Island (U.K.)

30°S

Kermadec Islands (N.Z.)

South Pacific Ocean

Auckland •

NEW ZEALAND
⊛ Wellington

Christchurch •

Chatham Island (N.Z.)

Date Line

45°S

AUSTRALIA, NEW ZEALAND, AND OCEANIA

165°E   180°   165°W   150°W   135°W

SPOTLIGHT ON
EUROPE

Legend says Holy Roman Emperor Charles IV ordered builders to use egg yolks to make the mortar for the Charles Bridge harder.

In Austria, bouquets with an even number of flowers are considered bad luck.

The Charles Bridge in Prague, Czech Republic, was built from 1357 to 1402.

A cluster of islands and peninsulas jutting west from Asia, Europe is bordered by the Atlantic and Arctic Oceans and more than a dozen seas. Here you'll find a variety of scenery, from mountains to countryside to coastlines. Europe is also known for its rich culture and fascinating history, which make it one of the most visited continents on the planet.

Bagpiper in Scotland, U.K.

Happy People

According to one survey, seven of the ten World's Happiest Countries are in Europe—Norway, Switzerland, Sweden, Denmark, Finland, Netherlands, and Luxembourg.

Fiery Mountain

Italy's Mount Etna, one of the most active volcanoes on Earth, erupts almost every year. Towering 10,900 feet (3,322 m) above Sicily, it can be seen from much of the island.

Rock Monkeys

Macaques are the only nonhuman primates found in Europe. They have been living on Gibraltar, a narrow peninsula at the southern edge of Spain, for centuries.

Ship (Un)Wrecked

Visitors to Sweden's Vasa Museum can check out an intact royal warship that sank in Stockholm harbor on its maiden voyage in 1628. It's the only preserved 17th-century ship in the world.

Europe's 6 Most Visited Cities*

1. **London, England**
   15.96 million visitors

2. **Paris, France**
   13.92 million visitors

3. **Istanbul, Turkey**
   10.37 million visitors

4. **Barcelona, Spain**
   8.41 million visitors

5. **Milan, Italy**
   6.83 million visitors

6. **Rome, Italy**
   6.71 million visitors

*2013

Saint Bernards in the Swiss Alps

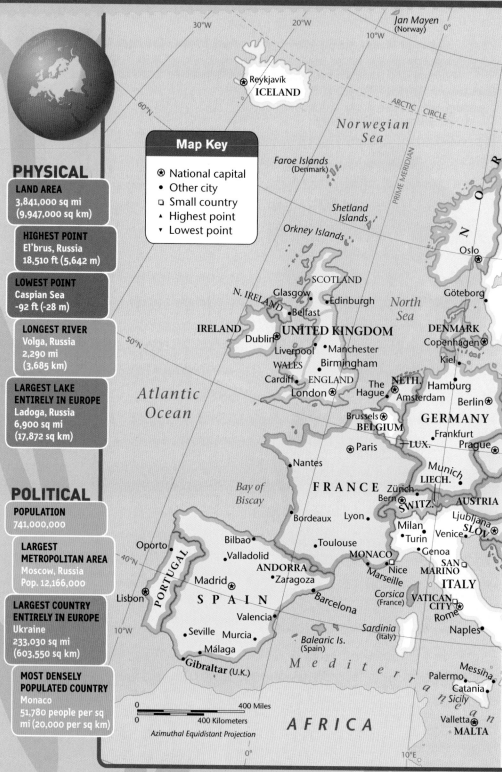

PHYSICAL

LAND AREA
3,841,000 sq mi
(9,947,000 sq km)

HIGHEST POINT
El'brus, Russia
18,510 ft (5,642 m)

LOWEST POINT
Caspian Sea
-92 ft (-28 m)

LONGEST RIVER
Volga, Russia
2,290 mi
(3,685 km)

**LARGEST LAKE
ENTIRELY IN EUROPE**
Ladoga, Russia
6,900 sq mi
(17,872 sq km)

POLITICAL

POPULATION
741,000,000

**LARGEST
METROPOLITAN AREA**
Moscow, Russia
Pop. 12,166,000

**LARGEST COUNTRY
ENTIRELY IN EUROPE**
Ukraine
233,030 sq mi
(603,550 sq km)

**MOST DENSELY
POPULATED COUNTRY**
Monaco
51,780 people per sq
mi (20,000 per sq km)

Map Key

⊛ National capital
• Other city
▫ Small country
▲ Highest point
▾ Lowest point

30°W   20°W   10°W   0°

Jan Mayen
(Norway)

Reykjavík
ICELAND

ARCTIC CIRCLE

*Norwegian
Sea*

PRIME MERIDIAN

Faroe Islands
(Denmark)

Shetland
Islands

Orkney Islands

60°N

N
O
R

Oslo

SCOTLAND
Glasgow   •Edinburgh
N. IRELAND
•Belfast

Göteborg

*North
Sea*

IRELAND
Dublin⊛

UNITED KINGDOM
Liverpool•   •Manchester
WALES   Birmingham
Cardiff• ENGLAND
London⊛

DENMARK
Copenhagen⊛

Kiel•

50°N

*Atlantic
Ocean*

The
Hague•
NETH. Hamburg
•Amsterdam
Berlin⊛

Brussels⊛
BELGIUM

GERMANY
•Frankfurt
Prague⊛

⊛ Paris

LUX.

•Nantes

Munich

LIECH.

*Bay of
Biscay*

F R A N C E   Zürich
Bern⊛ **SWITZ.**

AUSTRIA
Ljubljana⊛
SLOV.

Lyon•

Milan•

Venice•

•Bordeaux

Turin•

40°N

Oporto•

Bilbao•
•Valladolid

•Toulouse

MONACO
Nice

Genoa•

**SAN
MARINO** ▫

10°W

PORTUGAL

Madrid⊛

ANDORRA
•Zaragoza

Marseille

ITALY

Lisbon•

S P A I N

Barcelona•

Corsica
(France)

**VATICAN
CITY** ⊛

Valencia•

Rome•

•Seville Murcia•

•Málaga

Sardinia
(Italy)

Naples•

Balearic Is.
(Spain)

⊛Gibraltar (U.K.)

M e d i t e r r

Palermo•

Messina

•Catania

a   n Sicily
e

0   400 Miles

0   400 Kilometers
Azimuthal Equidistant Projection

A F R I C A

Valletta⊛
MALTA

0°   10°E

280

EUROPE

10°E 20°E 30°E 40°E 50°E 60°E 70°E

Barents Sea

ASIA

RUSSIA

Murmansk

Archangel

N O R W A Y

S W E D E N

FINLAND

Lake Ladoga

Helsinki

Stockholm

Tallinn

ESTONIA

Baltic Sea

Rīga

LATVIA

LITHUANIA

Kaliningrad
(Russia)

Kaunas

Vilnius

Minsk

BELARUS

Homyel'

Vitsyebsk

Gdańsk

POLAND

Warsaw

Bydgoszcz

Łódź

Wrocław

Kraków

CZECH REP.
(CZECHIA)

Vienna

SLOVAKIA

Bratislava

Budapest

HUNGARY

Zagreb

CROATIA

BOSNIA &
HERZEGOVINA

Sarajevo

MONTENEGRO

Podgorica

Tirana

ALBANIA

GREECE

Athens

Crete

Sea

St. Petersburg

Tver'

Moscow

Ryazan'

Smolensk

Bryansk

Kursk

Kiev

Poltava

L'viv

UKRAINE

Donets'k

Vinnytsya

Dnipropetrovs'k

MOLDOVA

Chişinău

ROMANIA

Odesa

Simferopol'

Bucharest

Sevastopol'

Belgrade

SERBIA

Varna

KOSOVO

Prishtina

BULGARIA

Sofia

Skopje

MACED.

Thessaloniki

Dardanelles

Istanbul

Bosporus

Black Sea

T U R K E Y

Nicosia

CYPRUS

Yaroslavl'

Volga River

Kazan'

Ufa

Nizhniy
Novgorod

Samara

Orenburg

Penza

Saratov

KAZAKHSTAN

Volgograd

Rostov

Astrakhan'

-92 ft
(-28 m)

Caspian Sea

Groznyy

El'brus
(5,642 m) 18,510 ft

Sochi

GEORGIA

Baku

AZERBAIJAN

40°N

50°N

60°N

Asia
Europe

A commonly accepted division
between Asia and Europe—
marked here by a maroon,
dashed line—is formed by the
Ural Mountains, Ural River, Caspian
Sea, Caucasus Mountains, and
the Black Sea with its outlets, the
Bosporus and Dardanelles.

20°E 30°E 40°E

SPOTLIGHT ON

NORTH AMERICA

One World Trade Center in
New York City, New York, U.S.A.

At 1,776 feet
(541.3 m), One World
Trade Center is the
tallest building in
the Western
Hemisphere.

Alaska, U.S.A.,
has more
earthquakes than
anywhere else
in North
America.

From the Great Plains of the United States and Canada to the rain forests of Panama, North America stretches 5,500 miles (8,850 km) from north to south. The third largest continent, North America can be divided into five regions: the mountainous west (including parts of Mexico and Central America's western coast), the Great Plains, the Canadian Shield, the varied eastern region (including Central America's lowlands and coastal plains), and the Caribbean.

Mexican children perform mariachi music.

Puppy Love

The United States has one of the highest pet populations in the world. About 56 percent of American households report sharing their home with at least one dog or cat.

Going Deep

Popular with divers and snorkelers, Belize's Giant Blue Hole is known as the largest sea hole on the planet. At 1,000 feet (304 m) across, it is about as deep as a 37-story building is tall!

Colossal Crystals

Mexico's Cave of Crystals contains some of the world's largest known natural crystals. They measure as long as 37.4 feet (11.4 m). That's almost as long as a school bus!

Tale of the Shrew

Found throughout most of Canada and the U.S., the northern short-tailed shrew is North America's only native venomous mammal. The mouse-size animal uses its venom to paralyze prey.

5 Most Visited National Parks*

1. Great Smoky Mountains, U.S.A. 9.35 million
2. Grand Canyon, U.S.A. 4.56 million
3. Yosemite, U.S.A. 3.69 million
4. Banff, Canada 3.27 million**
5. Yellowstone, U.S.A. 3.19 million

Snowy owl

*2013 (National Park Service); **2013-2014 (Parks Canada)

PHYSICAL

LAND AREA
9,449,000 sq mi
(24,474,000 sq km)

HIGHEST POINT
Mount McKinley, Alaska
20,320 ft (6,194 m)

LOWEST POINT
Death Valley, California
-282 ft (-86 m)

LONGEST RIVER
Mississippi–Missouri,
United States
3,780 mi (6,083 km)

LARGEST LAKE
Lake Superior,
U.S.–Canada
31,700 sq mi
(82,100 sq km)

POLITICAL

POPULATION
561,000,000

LARGEST COUNTRY
Canada
3,855,103 sq mi
(9,984,670 sq km)

LARGEST METROPOLITAN AREA
Mexico City, Mexico
Pop. 20,999,000

MOST DENSELY POPULATED COUNTRY
Barbados / 1,709 people
per sq mi (660 per sq km)

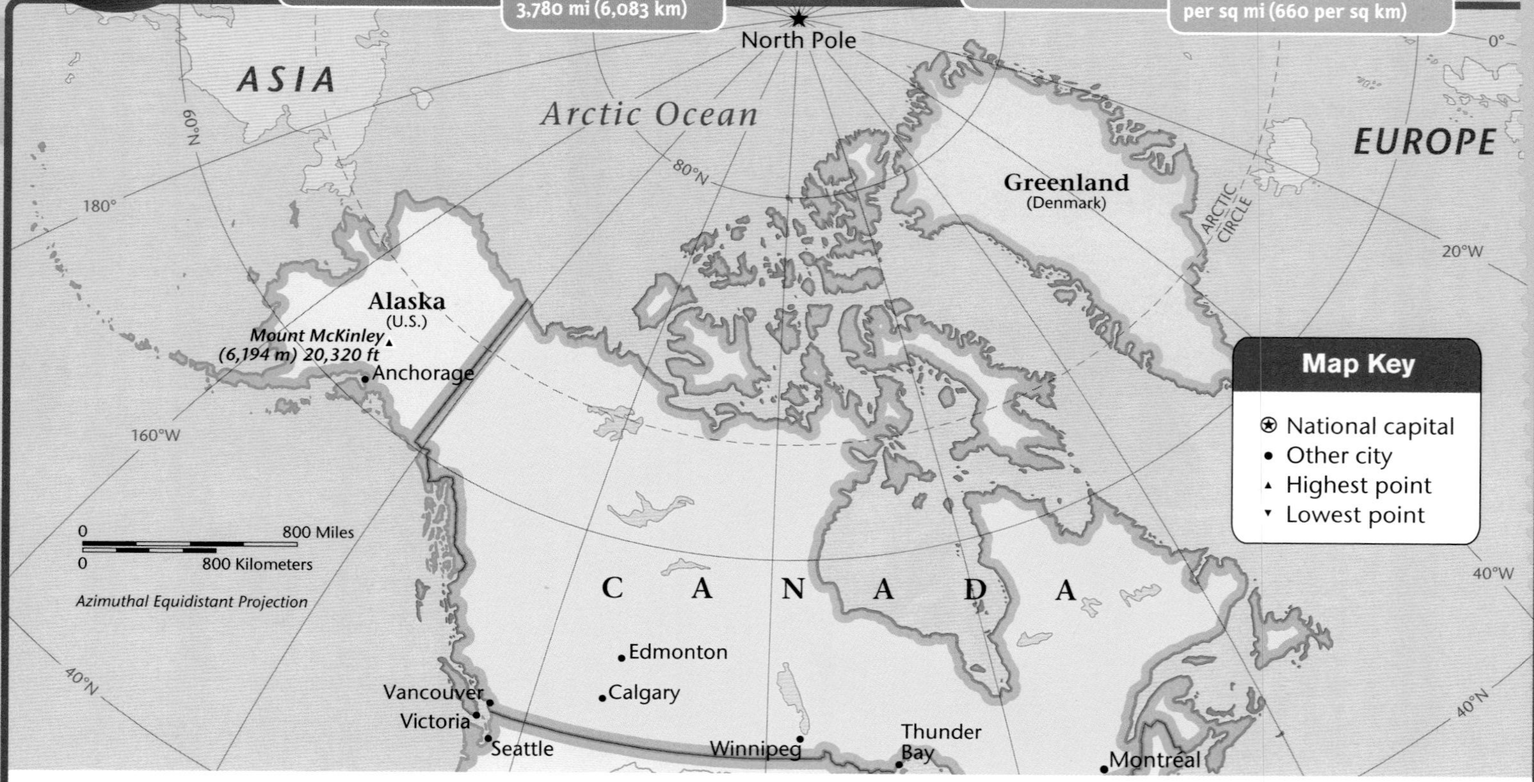

Map Key

⊛ National capital
• Other city
▲ Highest point
▼ Lowest point

EUROPE

ASIA

0°
20°W
40°W
40°W

ARCTIC CIRCLE

Greenland
(Denmark)

North Pole

Arctic Ocean

80°N

C A N A D A

Montréal

Thunder Bay

Winnipeg

Edmonton

Calgary

Seattle

Vancouver

Victoria

Alaska
(U.S.)

Mount McKinley
(6,194 m) 20,320 ft ▲

Anchorage

160°W

180°

60°N

40°N

800 Miles
800 Kilometers
0
0
Azimuthal Equidistant Projection

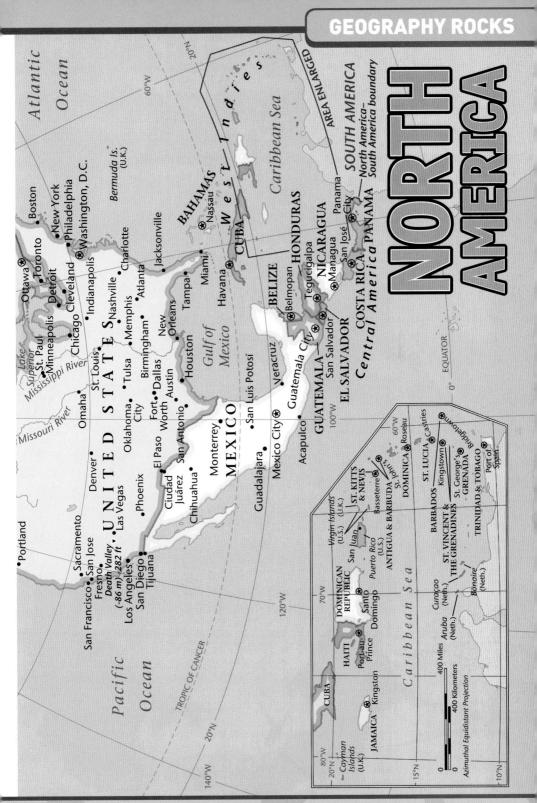

NORTH AMERICA

Atlantic Ocean

20°N

60°W

Bermuda Is. (U.K.)

West Indies

Caribbean Sea

AREA ENLARGED

SOUTH AMERICA

North America–
South America boundary

Boston
New York
Philadelphia
Washington, D.C.

Toronto
Ottawa
Detroit
Cleveland
Charlotte
Indianapolis
Atlanta
Jacksonville

BAHAMAS
Nassau

CUBA

Panama
City
San José

PANAMA
Central America
COSTA RICA
NICARAGUA
Managua
HONDURAS
Tegucigalpa
BELIZE
Belmopan

Miami
Havana
Tampa
New
Orleans

Gulf of
Mexico

Lake Superior
St. Paul
Minneapolis
Chicago
St. Louis
UNITED STATES
Nashville
Memphis
Birmingham

Mississippi River
Missouri River
Omaha

Houston

Veracruz
San Luis Potosí

EL SALVADOR
San Salvador
GUATEMALA
Guatemala City

EQUATOR
0°

Portland

San Francisco
San Jose
Sacramento
Fresno
Death Valley
(-86 m) -282 ft
Los Angeles
San Diego
Tijuana

Denver
Las Vegas
Phoenix
El Paso
Ciudad
Juárez
Chihuahua

Oklahoma
City
Fort
Worth
Dallas
Austin
San Antonio

Monterrey
MEXICO

Guadalajara
Mexico City
Acapulco

TROPIC OF CANCER

120°W

100°W

Pacific Ocean

140°W

20°N

80°W

20°N
15°N

CUBA
JAMAICA
Kingston
Cayman
Islands
(U.K.)

HAITI
Port-au-
Prince

DOMINICAN
REPUBLIC
Santo
Domingo

Aruba
(Neth.)

Caribbean Sea

70°W

Virgin Islands
(U.S.)
San Juan
Puerto Rico
(U.S.)

ST. KITTS
& NEVIS
Basseterre
ANTIGUA & BARBUDA
St. John's
DOMINICA
Roseau
ST. LUCIA
Castries
BARBADOS
Bridgetown
ST. VINCENT &
THE GRENADINES
Kingstown
St. George's
GRENADA
TRINIDAD & TOBAGO
Port of
Spain

Curaçao
(Neth.)
Bonaire
(Neth.)

60°W

10°N

400 Miles
0
0
400 Kilometers
Azimuthal Equidistant Projection

SPOTLIGHT ON
SOUTH AMERICA

Blue-footed booby

The blue-footed booby gets its unusual foot color from pigments found in the fish it eats.

A rhino once won an election for city council in São Paulo, Brazil.

286

South America is bordered by three major bodies of water—the Caribbean Sea, Atlantic Ocean, and Pacific Ocean. The world's fourth largest continent extends over a range of climates from tropical in the north to subarctic in the south. South America produces a rich diversity of natural resources, including nuts, fruits, sugar, grains, coffee, and chocolate.

A boy celebrates Carnival in Rio de Janeiro, Brazil.

Mirror, Mirror

Once a prehistoric salt lake, Salar de Uyuni in Bolivia is now a vast salt desert stretching over 4,633 square miles (12,000 sq km). During rainy season, it reflects all around it like a mirror.

Surf's Up

With 1,500 miles (2,414 km) of coastline, Peru is a hot spot for surfers. The waves off the country's northwest coast are among the world's longest, often stretching over a mile (1.6 km).

Big Bird

The Andean condor, which lives exclusively in the mountains and valleys of the Andes, is the largest raptor in the world and the largest flying bird in South America.

Friend's Day

In July, people throughout South America celebrate Día del Amigo (Friend's Day). The holiday is so popular that the amount of well-wishing pals calling each other has disrupted phone service.

World's Tallest Waterfalls

Angel Falls 3,212 feet (979 m) Venezuela

Tugela Falls 3,110 feet (948 m) South Africa

Three Sisters Falls (Tres Hermanas, Cataratas Las) 3,000 feet (914 m) Peru

Olo'upena Falls 2,953 feet (900 m) Hawaii, U.S.A.

Yumbilla, Catarata 2,938 feet (896 m) Peru

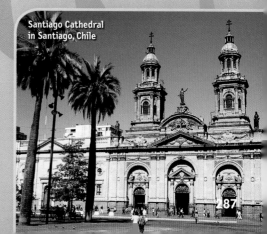

Santiago Cathedral in Santiago, Chile

PHYSICAL

LAND AREA
6,880,000 sq mi
(17,819,000 sq km)

HIGHEST POINT
Cerro Aconcagua,
Argentina
22,831 ft (6,959 m)

LOWEST POINT
Laguna del Carbón,
Argentina
-344 ft (-105 m)

LONGEST RIVER
Amazon
4,150 m (6,679 km)

LARGEST LAKE
Lake Maracaibo,
Venezuela
5,127 sq mi
(13,280 sq km)

POLITICAL

POPULATION
410,000,000

LARGEST COUNTRY
Brazil
3,287,612 sq mi
(8,514,877 sq km)

LARGEST METROPOLITAN AREA
São Paulo, Brazil
Pop. 21,066,000

MOST DENSELY POPULATED COUNTRY
Ecuador / 148 people per
sq mi (57 per sq km)

Map Key
⊛ National capital
• Other city
▲ Highest point
▼ Lowest point

Central America

Caribbean Sea

South America–North America boundary

80°W
70°W
60°W
50°W
40°W
10°N
0°
10°S

EQUATOR

Barranquilla
Maracaibo
Lake Maracaibo
Medellín
⊛ Bogotá
Cali
COLOMBIA
Quito
⊛
ECUADOR
Guayaquil

Caracás
Valencia
Barquisimeto
VENEZUELA

Georgetown
⊛
GUYANA

Paramaribo
⊛
SURINAME

Cayenne
French Guiana
(France)

Belém

Manaus

Amazon River

P E R U
Trujillo
Lima
⊛
Cusco

B O L I V I A

B R A Z I L
⊛ Brasília
Fortaleza
Natal
Recife
Salvador
(Bahia)

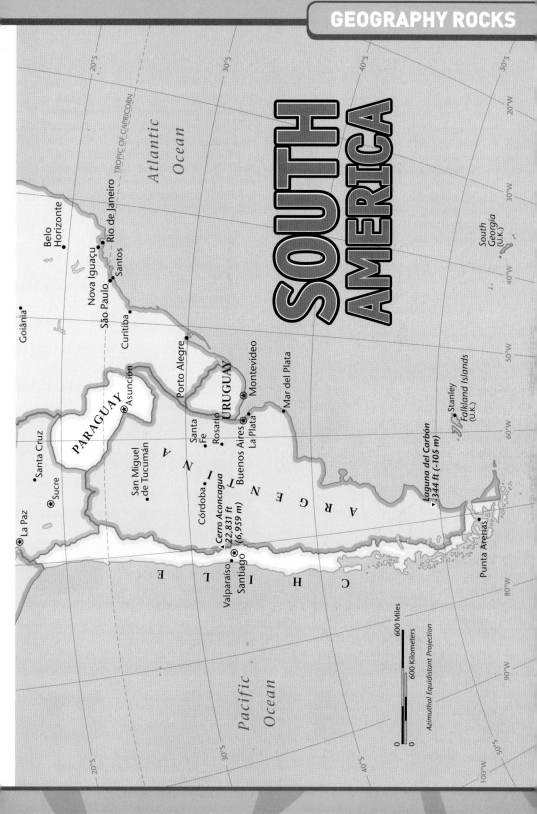

SOUTH AMERICA

Atlantic Ocean

Pacific Ocean

TROPIC OF CAPRICORN

Goiânia

Belo Horizonte

Rio de Janeiro

Nova Iguaçu
São Paulo
Santos

Curitiba

Porto Alegre

La Paz

Sucre

Santa Cruz

PARAGUAY

Asunción

San Miguel
de Tucumán

Córdoba

Cerro Aconcagua
22,831 ft
(6,959 m)

Valparaíso
Santiago

E

L

I

H

C

A R G E N T I N A

Santa
Fe

Rosario

URUGUAY

Montevideo

Buenos Aires
La Plata

Mar del Plata

Laguna del Carbón
-344 ft (-105 m)

Punta Arenas

Stanley
Falkland Islands
(U.K.)

South
Georgia
(U.K.)

600 Miles

600 Kilometers

Azimuthal Equidistant Projection

COUNTRIES OF THE WORLD

The following pages present a general overview of all 195 independent countries recognized by the National Geographic Society, including the newest nation, South Sudan, which gained independence in 2011.

The flags of each independent country symbolize diverse cultures and histories. The statistical data cover highlights of geography and demography and provide a brief overview of each country. They present general characteristics and are not intended to be comprehensive. For example, not every language spoken in a specific country can be listed. Thus, languages shown are the most representative of that area. This is also true of the religions mentioned.

A country is defined as a political body with its own independent government, geographical space, and, in most cases, laws, military, and taxes.

Disputed areas such as Northern Cyprus and Taiwan, and dependencies of independent nations, such as Bermuda and Puerto Rico, are not included in this listing.

Note the color key at the bottom of the pages and the locator map below, which assign a color to each country based on the continent on which it is located. All information is accurate as of press time.

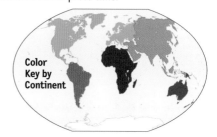

Color Key by Continent

Afghanistan

Area: 251,773 sq mi (652,090 sq km)
Population: 31,300,000
Capital: Kabul, pop. 4,436,000
Currency: afghani
Religions: Sunni Muslim, Shiite Muslim
Languages: Afghan Persian (Dari), Pashto, Turkic languages (primarily Uzbek and Turkmen), Baluchi, 30 minor languages (including Pashai)

Albania

Area: 11,100 sq mi (28,748 sq km)
Population: 3,000,000
Capital: Tirana, pop. 445,000
Currency: lek
Religions: Muslim, Albanian Orthodox, Roman Catholic
Languages: Albanian, Greek, Vlach, Romani, Slavic dialects

Algeria

Area: 919,595 sq mi (2,381,741 sq km)
Population: 39,100,000
Capital: Algiers, pop. 2,559,000
Currency: Algerian dinar
Religion: Sunni Muslim
Languages: Arabic, French, Berber dialects

Andorra

Area: 181 sq mi (469 sq km)
Population: 100,000
Capital: Andorra la Vella, pop. 23,000
Currency: euro
Religion: Roman Catholic
Languages: Catalan, French, Castilian, Portuguese

Angola

Area: 481,354 sq mi (1,246,700 sq km)
Population: 22,400,000
Capital: Luanda, pop. 5,288,000
Currency: kwanza
Religions: indigenous beliefs, Roman Catholic, Protestant
Languages: Portuguese, Bantu, and other African languages

Antigua and Barbuda

Area: 171 sq mi (442 sq km)
Population: 100,000
Capital: St. John's, pop. 22,000
Currency: East Caribbean dollar
Religions: Anglican, Seventh-day Adventist, Pentecostal, Moravian, Roman Catholic, Methodist, Baptist, Church of God, other Christian
Languages: English, local dialects

Argentina

Area: 1,073,518 sq mi
(2,780,400 sq km)
Population: 42,700,000
Capital: Buenos Aires,
pop. 15,024,000
Currency: Argentine peso
Religion: Roman Catholic
Languages: Spanish, English, Italian, German, French

Armenia

Area: 11,484 sq mi
(29,743 sq km)
Population: 3,000,000
Capital: Yerevan,
pop. 1,049,000
Currency: dram
Religions: Armenian Apostolic, other Christian
Language: Armenian

Australia

Area: 2,988,901 sq mi
(7,741,220 sq km)
Population: 23,500,000
Capital: Canberra,
pop. 415,000
Currency: Australian dollar
Religions: Roman Catholic, Anglican
Language: English

Austria

Area: 32,378 sq mi (83,858 sq km)
Population: 8,500,000
Capital: Vienna, pop. 1,743,000
Currency: euro
Religions: Roman Catholic, Protestant, Muslim
Language: German

Azerbaijan

Area: 33,436 sq mi
(86,600 sq km)
Population: 9,500,000
Capital: Baku, pop. 2,317,000
Currency: Azerbaijani manat
Religion: Muslim
Language: Azerbaijani (Azeri)

Bahamas

Area: 5,382 sq mi
(13,939 sq km)
Population: 400,000
Capital: Nassau, pop. 267,000
Currency: Bahamian dollar
Religions: Baptist, Anglican, Roman Catholic,
Pentecostal, Church of God
Languages: English, Creole

Bahrain

Area: 277 sq mi (717 sq km)
Population: 1,300,000
Capital: Manama, pop. 398,000
Currency: Bahraini dinar
Religions: Shiite Muslim, Sunni Muslim, Christian
Languages: Arabic, English, Farsi, Urdu

Bangladesh

Area: 55,598 sq mi
(143,998 sq km)
Population: 158,500,000
Capital: Dhaka, pop. 16,982,000
Currency: taka
Religions: Muslim, Hindu
Languages: Bangla (Bengali), English

Barbados

Area: 166 sq mi (430 sq km)
Population: 300,000
Capital: Bridgetown, pop. 90,000
Currency: Barbadian dollar
Religions: Anglican, Pentecostal, Methodist, other
Protestant, Roman Catholic
Language: English

Belarus

Area: 80,153 sq mi
(207,595 sq km)
Population: 9,500,000
Capital: Minsk, pop. 1,905,000
Currency: Belarusian ruble
Religions: Eastern Orthodox, other (includes Roman
Catholic, Protestant, Jewish, Muslim)
Languages: Belarusian, Russian

Belgium

Area: 11,787 sq mi (30,528 sq km)
Population: 11,200,000
Capital: Brussels, pop. 2,029,000
Currency: euro
Religions: Roman Catholic, other (includes Protestant)
Languages: Dutch, French

Belize

Area: 8,867 sq mi (22,965 sq km)
Population: 400,000
Capital: Belmopan, pop. 17,000
Currency: Belizean dollar
Religions: Roman Catholic, Protestant (includes Pentecostal, Seventh-day Adventist, Mennonite, Methodist)
Languages: Spanish, Creole, Mayan dialects, English, Garifuna (Carib), German

Benin

Area: 43,484 sq mi (112,622 sq km)
Population: 10,300,000
Capitals: Porto-Novo, pop. 268,000; Cotonou, pop. 680,000
Currency: Communauté Financière Africaine franc
Religions: Christian, Muslim, Vodoun
Languages: French, Fon, Yoruba, tribal languages

Bhutan

Area: 17,954 sq mi (46,500 sq km)
Population: 700,000
Capital: Thimphu, pop. 152,000
Currencies: ngultrum; Indian rupee
Religions: Lamaistic Buddhist, Indian- and Nepalese-influenced Hindu
Languages: Dzongkha, Tibetan dialects, Nepalese dialects

Bolivia

Area: 424,164 sq mi (1,098,581 sq km)
Population: 10,300,000
Capitals: La Paz, pop. 1,800,000; Sucre, pop. 358,000
Currency: boliviano
Religions: Roman Catholic, Protestant (includes Evangelical Methodist)
Languages: Spanish, Quechua, Aymara

Bosnia and Herzegovina

Area: 19,741 sq mi (51,129 sq km)
Population: 3,800,000
Capital: Sarajevo, pop. 322,000
Currency: konvertibilna marka (convertible mark)
Religions: Muslim, Orthodox, Roman Catholic
Languages: Bosnian, Croatian, Serbian

Botswana

Area: 224,607 sq mi (581,730 sq km)
Population: 2,000,000
Capital: Gaborone, pop. 247,000
Currency: pula
Religions: Christian, Badimo
Languages: Setswana, Kalanga

Brazil

Area: 3,287,612 sq mi (8,514,877 sq km)
Population: 202,800,000
Capital: Brasília, pop. 4,074,000
Currency: real
Religions: Roman Catholic, Protestant
Language: Portuguese

Brunei

Area: 2,226 sq mi (5,765 sq km)
Population: 400,000
Capital: Bandar Seri Begawan, pop. 14,000
Currency: Bruneian dollar
Religions: Muslim, Buddhist, Christian, other (includes indigenous beliefs)
Languages: Malay, English, Chinese

Bulgaria

Area: 42,855 sq mi (110,994 sq km)
Population: 7,200,000
Capital: Sofia, pop. 1,222,000
Currency: lev
Religions: Bulgarian Orthodox, Muslim
Languages: Bulgarian, Turkish, Roma

Burkina Faso

Area: 105,869 sq mi
(274,200 sq km)
Population: 17,900,000
Capital: Ouagadougou,
pop. 2,565,000
Currency: Communauté Financière Africaine franc
Religions: Muslim, indigenous beliefs, Christian
Languages: French, native African languages

Cambodia

Area: 69,898 sq mi (181,035 sq km)
Population: 14,800,000
Capital: Phnom Penh,
pop. 1,684,000
Currency: riel
Religion: Theravada Buddhist
Language: Khmer

Burundi

Area: 10,747 sq mi (27,834 sq km)
Population: 10,500,000
Capital: Bujumbura, pop. 707,000
Currency: Burundi franc
Religions: Roman Catholic, indigenous beliefs,
Muslim, Protestant
Languages: Kirundi, French, Swahili

Cameroon

Area: 183,569 sq mi
(475,442 sq km)
Population: 22,800,000
Capital: Yaoundé, pop. 2,930,000
Currency: Communauté Financière Africaine franc
Religions: indigenous beliefs, Christian, Muslim
Languages: 24 major African language groups,
English, French

You Are There!

The Amazon, Brazil

pink river dolphins

Cruising along the Amazon River on a boat, you look down to spot a large, shadowy figure lurking just beneath the water's surface. Is it a massive fish? A dolphin? A manatee? In the Amazon, it just may be any of those things. This iconic river is home to thousands of species, including threatened animals like the giant arapaima fish, the Amazonian manatee, and the pink river dolphin. A trip along any stretch of this 4,150-mile (6,679-km) water-way is an ideal way to spot such rare species in their natural habitat. Just make sure you stay safe inside the boat: There are plenty of alligators and piranhas in that water, too, so you're better off admiring everything from afar—and above.

Canada

Area: 3,855,101 sq mi
(9,984,670 sq km)
Population: 35,500,000
Capital: Ottawa, pop. 1,306,000
Currency: Canadian dollar
Religions: Roman Catholic, Protestant (includes United Church, Anglican), other Christian
Languages: English, French

Cape Verde

Area: 1,558 sq mi (4,036 sq km)
Population: 500,000
Capital: Praia, pop. 145,000
Currency: Cape Verdean escudo
Religions: Roman Catholic (infused with indigenous beliefs), Protestant (mostly Church of the Nazarene)
Languages: Portuguese, Crioulo

Central African Republic

Area: 240,535 sq mi
(622,984 sq km)
Population: 4,800,000
Capital: Bangui, pop. 781,000
Currency: Communauté Financière Africaine franc
Religions: indigenous beliefs, Protestant, Roman Catholic, Muslim
Languages: French, Sangho, tribal languages

Chad

Area: 495,755 sq mi
(1,284,000 sq km)
Population: 13,300,000
Capital: N'Djamena, pop. 1,212,000
Currency: Communauté Financière Africaine franc
Religions: Muslim, Catholic, Protestant, animist
Languages: French, Arabic, Sara, more than 120 languages and dialects

Chile

Area: 291,930 sq mi
(756,096 sq km)
Population: 17,700,000
Capital: Santiago, pop. 6,472,000
Currency: Chilean peso
Religions: Roman Catholic, Evangelical
Language: Spanish

China

Area: 3,705,406 sq mi
(9,596,961 sq km)
Population: 1,364,100,000
Capital: Beijing, pop. 19,520,000
Currency: renminbi (yuan)
Religions: Taoist, Buddhist, Christian
Languages: Standard Chinese or Mandarin, Yue, Wu, Minbei, Minnan, Xiang, Gan, Hakka dialects

Colombia

Area: 440,831 sq mi
(1,141,748 sq km)
Population: 47,700,000
Capital: Bogotá, pop. 9,558,000
Currency: Colombian peso
Religion: Roman Catholic
Language: Spanish

Comoros

Area: 863 sq mi (2,235 sq km)
Population: 700,000
Capital: Moroni, pop. 56,000
Currency: Comoran franc
Religion: Sunni Muslim
Languages: Arabic, French, Shikomoro

5 cool things about COMOROS

1. Comoros is named after the Arabic word *qamar*, meaning "moon."

2. The country is nicknamed the "Perfume Islands" as it exports much of the world's vanilla and perfume oil.

3. Green turtles lay eggs year-round on Comoros's Mohéli Island, one of the key nesting spots for the reptiles.

4. Comoros's Karthala volcano is one of the most active in the world.

5. Comoros is the only place in the world where you'll see the endangered Livingstone's fruit bats.

COLOR KEY ● Africa ● Australia, New Zealand, and Oceania

Congo

Area: 132,047 sq mi (342,000 sq km)
Population: 4,600,000
Capital: Brazzaville, pop. 1,827,000
Currency: Communauté Financière Africaine franc
Religions: Christian, animist
Languages: French, Lingala, Monokutuba, local languages

Costa Rica

Area: 19,730 sq mi (51,100 sq km)
Population: 4,800,000
Capital: San José, pop. 1,160,000
Currency: Costa Rican colón
Religions: Roman Catholic, Evangelical
Languages: Spanish, English

Côte d'Ivoire (Ivory Coast)

Area: 124,503 sq mi (322,462 sq km)
Population: 20,800,000
Capitals: Abidjan, pop. 4,708,000; Yamoussoukro, pop. 259,000
Currency: Communauté Financière Africaine franc
Religions: Muslim, indigenous beliefs, Christian
Languages: French, Dioula, other native dialects

Croatia

Area: 21,831 sq mi (56,542 sq km)
Population: 4,200,000
Capital: Zagreb, pop. 687,000
Currency: kuna
Religions: Roman Catholic, Orthodox
Language: Croatian

Cuba

Area: 42,803 sq mi (110,860 sq km)
Population: 11,200,000
Capital: Havana, pop. 2,146,000
Currency: Cuban peso
Religions: Roman Catholic, Protestant, Jehovah's Witnesses, Jewish, Santería
Language: Spanish

Cyprus

Area: 3,572 sq mi (9,251 sq km)
Population: 1,200,000
Capital: Nicosia, pop. 251,000
Currencies: euro; new Turkish lira in Northern Cyprus
Religions: Greek Orthodox, Muslim, Maronite, Armenian Apostolic
Languages: Greek, Turkish, English

Czech Republic (Czechia)

Area: 30,450 sq mi (78,866 sq km)
Population: 10,500,000
Capital: Prague, pop. 1,303,000
Currency: koruny
Religion: Roman Catholic
Language: Czech

Democratic Republic of the Congo

Area: 905,365 sq mi (2,344,885 sq km)
Population: 71,200,000
Capital: Kinshasa, pop. 11,116,000
Currency: Congolese franc
Religions: Roman Catholic, Protestant, Kimbanguist, Muslim, syncretic sects, indigenous beliefs
Languages: French, Lingala, Kingwana, Kikongo, Tshiluba

Denmark

Area: 16,640 sq mi (43,098 sq km)
Population: 5,600,000
Capital: Copenhagen, pop. 1,255,000
Currency: Danish krone
Religions: Evangelical Lutheran, other Protestant, Roman Catholic
Languages: Danish, Faroese, Greenlandic, German, English as second language

A man in **HAVANA, CUBA,** built a bicycle that's as **TALL AS AN ELEPHANT!**

Djibouti

Area: 8,958 sq mi
(23,200 sq km)
Population: 900,000
Capital: Djibouti, pop. 522,000
Currency: Djiboutian franc
Religions: Muslim, Christian
Languages: French, Arabic, Somali, Afar

Dominican Republic

Area: 18,704 sq mi
(48,442 sq km)
Population: 10,400,000
Capital: Santo Domingo,
pop. 2,873,000
Currency: Dominican peso
Religion: Roman Catholic
Language: Spanish

Dominica

Area: 290 sq mi (751 sq km)
Population: 100,000
Capital: Roseau, pop. 15,000
Currency: East Caribbean
dollar
Religions: Roman Catholic, Seventh-day Adventist,
Pentecostal, Baptist, Methodist, other Christian
Languages: English, French patois

Ecuador

Area: 109,483 sq mi
(283,560 sq km)
Population: 16,000,000
Capital: Quito, pop. 1,699,000
Currency: U.S. dollar
Religion: Roman Catholic
Languages: Spanish, Quechua, other
Amerindian languages

You Are There!

Fiji Barrier Reef

After slipping on some fins and a snorkel mask, you plunge into the turquoise Pacific Ocean. The water is so clear, you can see straight to the bottom as the sunlight filters down in glittering rays around you. This is what it's like to snorkel in Fiji: a network of some 320 islands all surrounded by about 4,000 square miles (10,360 sq km) of coral reef. Hundreds of species, like turtles, seabirds, and fish, call the "Soft Coral Capital of the World" home, and a dip into the waters will welcome you with breathtaking sights, like schools of tropical fish in a rainbow of colors and giant clams that grow as long as a baseball bat. It's like swimming in your very own aquarium!

Egypt

Area: 386,874 sq mi
(1,002,000 sq km)
Population: 87,900,000
Capital: Cairo, pop. 18,419,000
Currency: Egyptian pound
Religions: Muslim (mostly Sunni), Coptic Christian
Languages: Arabic, English, French

El Salvador

Area: 8,124 sq mi
(21,041 sq km)
Population: 6,400,000
Capital: San Salvador,
pop. 1,097,000
Currency: U.S. dollar
Religions: Roman Catholic, Protestant
Languages: Spanish, Nahua

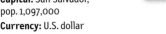

Equatorial Guinea

Area: 10,831 sq mi (28,051 sq km)
Population: 800,000
Capital: Malabo, pop. 145,000
Currency: Communauté
Financière Africaine franc
Religions: Christian (predominantly Roman Catholic),
pagan practices
Languages: Spanish, French, Fang, Bubi

Eritrea

Area: 45,406 sq mi
(117,600 sq km)
Population: 6,500,000
Capital: Asmara, pop. 775,000
Currency: nakfa
Religions: Muslim, Coptic Christian, Roman Catholic
Languages: Afar, Arabic, Tigre, Kunama, Tigrinya, other
Cushitic languages

Estonia

Area: 17,462 sq mi (45,227 sq km)
Population: 1,300,000
Capital: Tallinn, pop. 392,000
Currency: euro
Religions: Evangelical Lutheran, Orthodox
Languages: Estonian, Russian

Ethiopia

Area: 426,373 sq mi
(1,104,300 sq km)
Population: 95,900,000
Capital: Addis Ababa,
pop. 3,168,000
Currency: birr
Religions: Christian, Muslim, traditional
Languages: Amharic, Oromigna, Tigrinya, Guaragigna

Fiji

Area: 7,095 sq mi
(18,376 sq km)
Population: 900,000
Capital: Suva, pop. 176,000
Currency: Fijian dollar
Religions: Christian (Methodist, Roman Catholic,
Assembly of God), Hindu (Sanatan), Muslim (Sunni)
Languages: English, Fijian, Hindustani

Finland

Area: 130,558 sq mi
(338,145 sq km)
Population: 5,500,000
Capital: Helsinki, pop. 1,170,000
Currency: euro
Religion: Lutheran Church of Finland
Languages: Finnish, Swedish

France

Area: 210,026 sq mi
(543,965 sq km)
Population: 64,100,000
Capital: Paris, pop. 10,764,000
Currency: euro
Religions: Roman Catholic, Muslim
Language: French

Gabon

Area: 103,347 sq mi (267,667 sq km)
Population: 1,700,000
Capital: Libreville, pop. 695,000
Currency: Communauté Financière
Africaine franc
Religions: Christian, animist
Languages: French, Fang, Myene, Nzebi, Bapounou/
Eschira, Bandjabi

Gambia

Area: 4,361 sq mi (11,295 sq km)
Population: 1,900,000
Capital: Banjul, pop. 489,000
Currency: dalasi
Religions: Muslim, Christian
Languages: English, Mandinka, Wolof, Fula, other indigenous vernaculars

Greece

Area: 50,949 sq mi (131,957 sq km)
Population: 11,000,000
Capital: Athens, pop. 3,060,000
Currency: euro
Religion: Greek Orthodox
Languages: Greek, English, French

Georgia

Area: 26,911 sq mi (69,700 sq km)
Population: 4,800,000
Capital: Tbilisi, pop. 1,150,000
Currency: lari
Religions: Orthodox Christian, Muslim, Armenian-Gregorian
Languages: Georgian, Russian, Armenian, Azeri, Abkhaz

Grenada

Area: 133 sq mi (344 sq km)
Population: 100,000
Capital: St. George's, pop. 38,000
Currency: East Caribbean dollar
Religions: Roman Catholic, Anglican, other Protestant
Languages: English, French patois

Germany

Area: 137,847 sq mi (357,022 sq km)
Population: 80,900,000
Capital: Berlin, pop. 3,547,000
Currency: euro
Religions: Protestant, Roman Catholic, Muslim
Language: German

Guatemala

Area: 42,042 sq mi (108,889 sq km)
Population: 15,900,000
Capital: Guatemala City, pop. 2,874,000
Currency: quetzal
Religions: Roman Catholic, Protestant, indigenous Maya beliefs
Languages: Spanish, 23 official Amerindian languages

Ghana

Area: 92,100 sq mi (238,537 sq km)
Population: 27,000,000
Capital: Accra, pop. 2,242,000
Currency: Ghana cedi
Religions: Christian (Pentecostal/Charismatic, Protestant, Roman Catholic, other), Muslim, traditional beliefs
Languages: Asante, Ewe, Fante, Boron (Brong), Dagomba, Dangme, Dagarte (Dagaba), Akyem, Ga, English

Guinea

Area: 94,926 sq mi (245,857 sq km)
Population: 11,600,000
Capital: Conakry, pop. 1,886,000
Currency: Guinean franc
Religions: Muslim, Christian, indigenous beliefs
Languages: French, ethnic languages

In 2010, a downhill skier from **GHANA** became the country's first-ever **WINTER OLYMPIAN.**

Guinea-Bissau

Area: 13,948 sq mi (36,125 sq km)
Population: 1,700,000
Capital: Bissau, pop. 473,000
Currency: Communauté Financière Africaine franc
Religions: indigenous beliefs, Muslim, Christian
Languages: Portuguese, Crioulo, African languages

COLOR KEY ● Africa ● Australia, New Zealand, and Oceania

Guyana

Area: 83,000 sq mi
(214,969 sq km)
Population: 700,000
Capital: Georgetown, pop. 124,000
Currency: Guyanese dollar
Religions: Christian, Hindu, Muslim
Languages: English, Amerindian dialects, Creole, Hindustani, Urdu

Honduras

Area: 43,433 sq mi
(112,492 sq km)
Population: 8,200,000
Capital: Tegucigalpa,
pop. 1,101,000
Currency: lempira
Religions: Roman Catholic, Protestant
Languages: Spanish, Amerindian dialects

Haiti

Area: 10,714 sq mi (27,750 sq km)
Population: 10,800,000
Capital: Port-au-Prince,
pop. 2,376,000
Currency: gourde
Religions: Roman Catholic, Protestant
(Baptist, Pentecostal, other)
Languages: French, Creole

Hungary

Area: 35,919 sq mi (93,030 sq km)
Population: 9,900,000
Capital: Budapest, pop. 1,717,000
Currency: forint
Religions: Roman Catholic, Calvinist, Lutheran
Language: Hungarian

You Are There!

Copán, Honduras

Face of Jaguar Sun God of Underworld on western stairway of East Court of Mayan ruin of Copan

Take a trip back in time with a visit to the ruins of Copán, the site of some of Central America's greatest Maya temples and tombs. Examine Maya artifacts and check out intricately carved sculptures and architectural highlights, such as the hieroglyphic stairway, which features 1,800 individual glyphs. Then imagine what life was like in this bustling and influential city over a thousand years ago.

Iceland

Area: 39,769 sq mi
(103,000 sq km)
Population: 300,000
Capital: Reykjavík, pop. 184,000
Currency: Icelandic krona
Religion: Lutheran Church of Iceland
Languages: Icelandic, English, Nordic
languages, German

Indonesia

Area: 742,308 sq mi
(1,922,570 sq km)
Population: 251,500,000
Capital: Jakarta, pop. 10,176,000
Currency: Indonesian rupiah
Religions: Muslim, Protestant, Roman Catholic
Languages: Bahasa Indonesia (modified form of Malay),
English, Dutch, Javanese, local dialects

India

Area: 1,269,221 sq mi (3,287,270 sq km)
Population: 1,296,200,000
Capital: New Delhi, pop. 24,953,000
(part of Delhi metropolitan area)
Currency: Indian rupee
Religions: Hindu, Muslim
Languages: Hindi, 21 other official languages,
Hindustani (popular Hindi/Urdu variant in the north)

Iran

Area: 636,296 sq mi
(1,648,000 sq km)
Population: 77,400,000
Capital: Tehran, pop. 8,353,000
Currency: Iranian rial
Religions: Shiite Muslim, Sunni Muslim
Languages: Persian, Turkic, Kurdish, Luri,
Baluchi, Arabic

You Are There!
Tanjung Puting, Indonesia

There are only two places on the planet where you can spot a wild orangutan— the islands of Borneo and Sumatra. To get a glance of these big orange apes in person, head to Indonesia's Tanjung Puting National Park on the island of Borneo. Here, you can travel with a tour group deep within the forest to ogle orangutans. Tour guides dole out bananas and vitamin-rich milk to lure the animals as visitors stand at a safe distance to watch the apes in action. Don't forget to bring your camera: Orangutans—which share much of the same genetic code as humans—just may strike some funny poses as you snap away!

COLOR KEY ● Africa ● Australia, New Zealand, and Oceania

Iraq

Area: 168,754 sq mi
(437,072 sq km)
Population: 35,100,000
Capital: Baghdad, pop. 6,483,000
Currency: Iraqi dinar
Religions: Shiite Muslim, Sunni Muslim
Languages: Arabic, Kurdish, Assyrian, Armenian

Ireland

Area: 27,133 sq mi
(70,273 sq km)
Population: 4,600,000
Capital: Dublin, pop. 1,155,000
Currency: euro
Religions: Roman Catholic, Church of Ireland
Languages: Irish (Gaelic), English

Israel

Area: 8,550 sq mi (22,145 sq km)
Population: 8,200,000
Capital: Jerusalem, pop. 829,000
Currency: new Israeli sheqel
Religions: Jewish, Muslim
Languages: Hebrew, Arabic, English

Italy

Area: 116,345 sq mi
(301,333 sq km)
Population: 61,300,000
Capital: Rome, pop. 3,697,000
Currency: euro
Religions: Roman Catholic, Protestant, Jewish, Muslim
Languages: Italian, German, French, Slovene

Jamaica

Area: 4,244 sq mi
(10,991 sq km)
Population: 2,700,000
Capital: Kingston, pop. 587,000
Currency: Jamaican dollar
Religions: Protestant (Church of God, Seventh-day Adventist, Pentecostal, Baptist, Anglican, other)
Languages: English, English patois

Japan

Area: 145,902 sq mi (377,887 sq km)
Population: 127,100,000
Capital: Tokyo, pop. 37,833,000
Currency: yen
Religions: Shinto, Buddhist
Language: Japanese

Jordan

Area: 34,495 sq mi
(89,342 sq km)
Population: 7,600,000
Capital: Amman, pop. 1,148,000
Currency: Jordanian dinar
Religions: Sunni Muslim, Christian
Languages: Arabic, English

Kazakhstan

Area: 1,049,155 sq mi
(2,717,300 sq km)
Population: 17,300,000
Capital: Astana, pop. 741,000
Currency: tenge
Religions: Muslim, Russian Orthodox
Languages: Kazakh (Qazaq), Russian

Kenya

Area: 224,081 sq mi (580,367 sq km)
Population: 43,200,000
Capital: Nairobi, pop. 3,768,000
Currency: Kenyan shilling
Religions: Protestant, Roman Catholic, Muslim, indigenous beliefs
Languages: English, Kiswahili, many indigenous languages

Kiribati

Area: 313 sq mi (811 sq km)
Population: 100,000
Capital: Tarawa, pop. 46,000
Currency: Australian dollar
Religions: Roman Catholic, Protestant (Congregational)
Languages: I-Kiribati, English

● Asia ● Europe ● North America ● South America

Kosovo

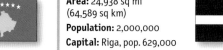

Area: 4,203 sq mi (10,887 sq km)
Population: 1,800,000
Capital: Prishtina, pop. 207,500
Currency: euro
Religions: Muslim, Serbian Orthodox, Roman Catholic
Languages: Albanian, Serbian, Bosnian, Turkish, Roma

Latvia

Area: 24,938 sq mi (64,589 sq km)
Population: 2,000,000
Capital: Riga, pop. 629,000
Currency: Latvian lat
Religions: Lutheran, Roman Catholic, Russian Orthodox
Languages: Latvian, Russian, Lithuanian

Kuwait

Area: 6,880 sq mi (17,818 sq km)
Population: 3,700,000
Capital: Kuwait City, pop. 2,680,000
Currency: Kuwaiti dinar
Religions: Sunni Muslim, Shiite Muslim
Languages: Arabic, English

Lebanon

Area: 4,036 sq mi (10,452 sq km)
Population: 5,000,000
Capital: Beirut, pop. 2,179,000
Currency: Lebanese pound
Religions: Muslim, Christian
Languages: Arabic, French, English, Armenian

Kyrgyzstan

Area: 77,182 sq mi (199,900 sq km)
Population: 5,800,000
Capital: Bishkek, pop. 858,000
Currency: som
Religions: Muslim, Russian Orthodox
Languages: Kyrgyz, Uzbek, Russian

Lesotho

Area: 11,720 sq mi (30,355 sq km)
Population: 1,900,000
Capital: Maseru, pop. 267,000
Currencies: loti; South African rand
Religions: Christian, indigenous beliefs
Languages: Sesotho, English, Zulu, Xhosa

Laos

Area: 91,429 sq mi (236,800 sq km)
Population: 6,800,000
Capital: Vientiane, pop. 946,000
Currency: kip
Religions: Buddhist, animist
Languages: Lao, French, English, various ethnic languages

Liberia

Area: 43,000 sq mi (111,370 sq km)
Population: 4,400,000
Capital: Monrovia, pop. 1,224,000
Currency: Liberian dollar
Religions: Christian, indigenous beliefs, Muslim
Languages: English, some 20 ethnic languages

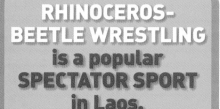

RHINOCEROS-BEETLE WRESTLING is a popular SPECTATOR SPORT in Laos.

Libya

Area: 679,362 sq mi (1,759,540 sq km)
Population: 6,300,000
Capital: Tripoli, pop. 1,126,000
Currency: Libyan dinar
Religion: Sunni Muslim
Languages: Arabic, Italian, English

COLOR KEY ● Africa ● Australia, New Zealand, and Oceania

Liechtenstein

Area: 62 sq mi (160 sq km)
Population: 40,000
Capital: Vaduz, pop. 5,000
Currency: Swiss franc
Religions: Roman Catholic, Protestant
Languages: German, Alemannic dialect

Lithuania

Area: 25,212 sq mi (65,300 sq km)
Population: 2,900,000
Capital: Vilnius, pop. 519,000
Currency: litas
Religions: Roman Catholic, Russian Orthodox
Languages: Lithuanian, Russian, Polish

Luxembourg

Area: 998 sq mi (2,586 sq km)
Population: 600,000
Capital: Luxembourg, pop. 107,000
Currency: euro
Religions: Roman Catholic, Protestant, Jewish, Muslim
Languages: Luxembourgish, German, French

Macedonia

Area: 9,928 sq mi (25,713 sq km)
Population: 2,100,000
Capital: Skopje, pop. 501,000
Currency: Macedonian denar
Religions: Macedonian Orthodox, Muslim
Languages: Macedonian, Albanian, Turkish

Madagascar

Area: 226,658 sq mi (587,041 sq km)
Population: 22,400,000
Capital: Antananarivo, pop. 2,487,000
Currency: Madagascar ariary
Religions: indigenous beliefs, Christian, Muslim
Languages: English, French, Malagasy

Malawi

Area: 45,747 sq mi (118,484 sq km)
Population: 16,800,000
Capital: Lilongwe, pop. 867,000
Currency: Malawian kwacha
Religions: Christian, Muslim
Languages: Chichewa, Chinyanja, Chiyao, Chitumbuka

5 cool things about MALAWI

1. Lake Malawi, Africa's third largest lake, is home to more than 600 species of fish.

2. The Mulanje cedar, the national tree of Malawi, can grow taller than a 12-story building.

3. A 14-year-old boy in Malawi used recycled junk to build windmills that brought electricity to his village.

4. In 1923, researchers discovered the *Malawisaurus,* an elephant-size dinosaur that roamed the earth over 100 million years ago.

5. The Chongoni Rock Art Area in central Malawi is home to hundreds of rock paintings dating back to the Stone Age.

Malaysia

Area: 127,355 sq mi (329,847 sq km)
Population: 30,100,000
Capital: Kuala Lumpur, pop. 6,629,000
Currency: ringgit
Religions: Muslim, Buddhist, Christian, Hindu
Languages: Bahasa Malaysia, English, Chinese, Tamil, Telugu, Malayalam, Panjabi, Thai, indigenous languages

Maldives

Area: 115 sq mi (298 sq km)
Population: 400,000
Capital: Male, pop. 156,000
Currency: rufiyaa
Religion: Sunni Muslim
Languages: Maldivian Dhivehi, English

Mali

Area: 478,841 sq mi (1,240,192 sq km)
Population: 15,900,000
Capital: Bamako, pop. 2,386,000
Currency: Communauté Financière Africaine franc
Religions: Muslim, indigenous beliefs
Languages: Bambara, French, numerous African languages

Marshall Islands

Area: 70 sq mi (181 sq km)
Population: 100,000
Capital: Majuro, pop. 31,000
Currency: U.S. dollar
Religions: Protestant, Assembly of God, Roman Catholic
Language: Marshallese

Malta

Area: 122 sq mi (316 sq km)
Population: 400,000
Capital: Valletta, pop. 197,000
Currency: euro
Religion: Roman Catholic
Languages: Maltese, English

Mauritania

Area: 397,955 sq mi (1,030,700 sq km)
Population: 4,000,000
Capital: Nouakchott, pop. 945,000
Currency: ouguiya
Religion: Muslim
Languages: Arabic, Pulaar, Soninke, French, Hassaniya, Wolof

You Are There!

Monte Carlo, Monaco

Monaco may be one of the smallest countries in the world, but that doesn't mean it lacks pizazz. Luxury cars, yachts, and hotels are commonplace in this three-mile (4.8-km)-long by half-mile (0.8-km)-wide principality. Adding to the glamour? The Monaco Grand Prix, which welcomes dozens of Formula One cars and their drivers from around the world each year.

COLOR KEY ● Africa ● Australia, New Zealand, and Oceania

Mauritius

Area: 788 sq mi (2,040 sq km)
Population: 1,300,000
Capital: Port Louis, pop. 135,000
Currency: Mauritian rupee
Religions: Hindu, Roman Catholic, Muslim, other Christian
Languages: Creole, Bhojpuri, French

Mexico

Area: 758,449 sq mi (1,964,375 sq km)
Population: 119,700,000
Capital: Mexico City, pop. 20,843,000
Currency: Mexican peso
Religions: Roman Catholic, Protestant
Languages: Spanish, Mayan, other indigenous languages

Micronesia

Area: 271 sq mi (702 sq km)
Population: 100,000
Capital: Palikir, pop. 7,000
Currency: U.S. dollar
Religions: Roman Catholic, Protestant
Languages: English, Trukese, Pohnpeian, Yapese, other indigenous languages

Moldova

Area: 13,050 sq mi (33,800 sq km)
Population: 4,100,000
Capital: Chisinau, pop. 721,000
Currency: Moldovan leu
Religion: Eastern Orthodox
Languages: Moldovan, Russian, Gagauz

Monaco

Area: 0.8 sq mi (2.0 sq km)
Population: 40,000
Capital: Monaco, pop. 38,000
Currency: euro
Religion: Roman Catholic
Languages: French, English, Italian, Monegasque

Mongolia

Area: 603,909 sq mi (1,564,116 sq km)
Population: 2,900,000
Capital: Ulaanbaatar, pop. 1,334,000
Currency: togrog/tugrik
Religions: Buddhist Lamaist, Shamanist, Christian
Languages: Khalkha Mongol, Turkic, Russian

Montenegro

Area: 5,333 sq mi (13,812 sq km)
Population: 600,000
Capital: Podgorica, pop. 165,000
Currency: euro
Religions: Orthodox, Muslim, Roman Catholic
Languages: Serbian (Ijekavian dialect), Bosnian, Albanian, Croatian

Morocco

Area: 172,414 sq mi (446,550 sq km)
Population: 33,300,000
Capital: Rabat, pop. 1,932,000
Currency: Moroccan dirham
Religion: Muslim
Languages: Arabic, Berber dialects, French

Mozambique

Area: 308,642 sq mi (799,380 sq km)
Population: 25,100,000
Capital: Maputo, pop. 1,174,000
Currency: metical
Religions: Roman Catholic, Muslim, Zionist Christian
Languages: Emakhuwa, Xichangana, Portuguese, Elomwe, Cisena, Echuwabo, other local languages

Myanmar (Burma)

Area: 261,218 sq mi (676,552 sq km)
Population: 53,700,000
Capitals: Nay Pyi Taw, pop. 1,016,000; Yangon (Rangoon), pop. 4,802,000
Currency: kyat
Religions: Buddhist, Christian, Muslim
Languages: Burmese, minority ethnic languages

Namibia

Area: 318,261 sq mi
(824,292 sq km)
Population: 2,300,000
Capital: Windhoek, pop. 356,000
Currencies: Namibian dollar;
South African rand
Religions: Lutheran, other Christian, indigenous beliefs
Languages: Afrikaans, German, English

Nauru

Area: 8 sq mi (21 sq km)
Population: 10,000
Capital: Yaren, pop. 10,000
Currency: Australian dollar
Religions: Protestant, Roman Catholic
Languages: Nauruan, English

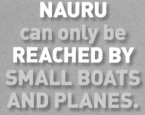

NAURU can only be REACHED BY SMALL BOATS AND PLANES.

Nepal

Area: 56,827 sq mi
(147,181 sq km)
Population: 27,100,000
Capital: Kathmandu, pop. 1,142,000
Currency: Nepalese rupee
Religions: Hindu, Buddhist, Muslim, Kirant
Languages: Nepali, Maithali, Bhojpuri, Tharu, Tamang, Newar, Magar

Netherlands

Area: 16,034 sq mi
(41,528 sq km)
Population: 16,900,000
Capital: Amsterdam, pop. 1,084,000
Currency: euro
Religions: Roman Catholic, Dutch Reformed, Calvinist, Muslim
Languages: Dutch, Frisian

New Zealand

Area: 104,454 sq mi
(270,534 sq km)
Population: 4,300,000
Capital: Wellington, pop. 380,000
Currency: New Zealand dollar
Religions: Anglican, Roman Catholic, Presbyterian, other Christian
Languages: English, Maori

Nicaragua

Area: 50,193 sq mi
(130,000 sq km)
Population: 6,200,000
Capital: Managua, pop. 951,000
Currency: gold cordoba
Religions: Roman Catholic, Evangelical
Language: Spanish

Niger

Area: 489,191 sq mi (1,267,000 sq km)
Population: 18,200,000
Capital: Niamey, pop. 1,058,000
Currency: Communauté
Financière Africaine franc
Religions: Muslim, other (includes indigenous beliefs and Christian)
Languages: French, Hausa, Djerma

Nigeria

Area: 356,669 sq mi
(923,768 sq km)
Population: 177,500,000
Capital: Abuja, pop. 2,301,000
Currency: naira
Religions: Muslim, Christian, indigenous beliefs
Languages: English, Hausa, Yoruba, Igbo (Ibo), Fulani

North Korea

Area: 46,540 sq mi
(120,538 sq km)
Population: 24,900,000
Capital: Pyongyang,
pop. 2,856,000
Currency: North Korean won
Religions: Buddhist, Confucianist, some Christian and syncretic Chondogyo
Language: Korean

Norway

Area: 125,004 sq mi
(323,758 sq km)
Population: 5,100,000
Capital: Oslo, pop. 970,000
Currency: Norwegian krone
Religion: Church of Norway (Lutheran)
Languages: Bokmal Norwegian, Nynorsk
Norwegian, Sami

Pakistan

Area: 307,374 sq mi
(796,095 sq km)
Population: 194,000,000
Capital: Islamabad, pop. 1,297,000
Currency: Pakistani rupee
Religions: Sunni Muslim, Shiite Muslim
Languages: Punjabi, Sindhi, Siraiki, Pashto, Urdu,
Baluchi, Hindko, English

Oman

Area: 119,500 sq mi
(309,500 sq km)
Population: 4,100,000
Capital: Muscat, pop. 812,000
Currency: Omani rial
Religions: Ibadhi Muslim, Sunni Muslim,
Shiite Muslim, Hindu
Languages: Arabic, English, Baluchi, Urdu, Indian dialects

Palau

Area: 189 sq mi (489 sq km)
Population: 20,000
Capital: Melekeok, pop. 1,000
Currency: U.S. dollar
Religions: Roman Catholic, Protestant, Modekngei,
Seventh-day Adventist
Languages: Palauan, Filipino, English, Chinese

You Are There!
Namib-Naukluft Park, Namibia

Sand dunes as tall as a skyscraper? Only in this national park, where high winds form these star-shaped dunes in the Sossusvlei area, rising from the ground like reddish orange mountains. One of the world's largest national parks, Namib-Naukluft covers an area about the size of Costa Rica and is home to an array of animals such as Hartmann's mountain zebras, leopards, baboons, and flamingos. The park's main attraction, of course, is its amazing dunes.

Panama

Area: 29,157 sq mi (75,517 sq km)
Population: 3,900,000
Capital: Panama City, pop. 1,638,000
Currencies: balboa; U.S. dollar
Religions: Roman Catholic, Protestant
Languages: Spanish, English

Papua New Guinea

Area: 178,703 sq mi (462,840 sq km)
Population: 7,600,000
Capital: Port Moresby, pop. 338,000
Currency: kina
Religions: indigenous beliefs, Roman Catholic, Lutheran, other Protestant
Languages: Melanesian Pidgin, 820 indigenous languages

Paraguay

Area: 157,048 sq mi (406,752 sq km)
Population: 6,900,000
Capital: Asunción, pop. 2,307,000
Currency: guarani
Religions: Roman Catholic, Protestant
Languages: Spanish, Guarani

Peru

Area: 496,224 sq mi (1,285,216 sq km)
Population: 30,800,000
Capital: Lima, pop. 9,722,000
Currency: nuevo sol
Religion: Roman Catholic
Languages: Spanish, Quechua, Aymara, minor Amazonian languages

Philippines

Area: 115,831 sq mi (300,000 sq km)
Population: 100,100,000
Capital: Manila, pop. 12,764,000
Currency: Philippine peso
Religions: Roman Catholic, Muslim, other Christian
Languages: Filipino (based on Tagalog), English

Poland

Area: 120,728 sq mi (312,685 sq km)
Population: 38,500,000
Capital: Warsaw, pop. 1,718,000
Currency: zloty
Religion: Roman Catholic
Language: Polish

Portugal

Area: 35,655 sq mi (92,345 sq km)
Population: 10,400,000
Capital: Lisbon, pop. 2,869,000
Currency: euro
Religion: Roman Catholic
Languages: Portuguese, Mirandese

5 cool things about PORTUGAL

1. A chapel in Évora, Portugal, is decorated with thousands of human bones.

2. There are more cork trees in Portugal than anywhere else on the planet.

3. Portugal is home to the world's first commercial wave farm, which uses the power of ocean waves to create energy.

4. The 10.5-mile (17-km)-long Vasco da Gama Bridge in Lisbon is Europe's longest bridge.

5. Established in 1732, a bookstore in Lisbon is the world's oldest bookshop.

Qatar

Area: 4,448 sq mi (11,521 sq km)
Population: 2,300,000
Capital: Doha, pop. 699,000
Currency: Qatari rial
Religions: Muslim, Christian
Languages: Arabic; English commonly a second language

COLOR KEY ● Africa ● Australia, New Zealand, and Oceania

Romania

Area: 92,043 sq mi
(238,391 sq km)
Population: 20,000,000
Capital: Bucharest, pop. 1,872,000
Currency: new leu
Religions: Eastern Orthodox, Protestant, Roman Catholic
Languages: Romanian, Hungarian

Russia

Area: 6,592,850 sq mi
(17,075,400 sq km)
Population: 143,700,000
Capital: Moscow, pop. 12,063,000
Currency: ruble
Religions: Russian Orthodox, Muslim
Languages: Russian, many minority languages
Note: Russia is in both Europe and Asia, but its capital is in Europe, so it is classified here as a European country.

Rwanda

Area: 10,169 sq mi
(26,338 sq km)
Population: 11,100,000
Capital: Kigali, pop. 1,223,000
Currency: Rwandan franc
Religions: Roman Catholic, Protestant, Adventist, Muslim
Languages: Kinyarwanda, French, English, Kiswahili

Samoa

Area: 1,093 sq mi (2,831 sq km)
Population: 200,000
Capital: Apia, pop. 37,000
Currency: tala
Religions: Congregationalist, Roman Catholic, Methodist, Church of Jesus Christ of Latter-day Saints, Assembly of God, Seventh-day Adventist
Languages: Samoan (Polynesian), English

San Marino

Area: 24 sq mi (61 sq km)
Population: 30,000
Capital: San Marino, pop. 4,000
Currency: euro
Religion: Roman Catholic
Language: Italian

Sao Tome and Principe

Area: 386 sq mi (1,001 sq km)
Population: 200,000
Capital: São Tomé, pop. 71,000
Currency: dobra
Religions: Roman Catholic, Evangelical
Language: Portuguese

Saudi Arabia

Area: 756,985 sq mi
(1,960,582 sq km)
Population: 30,800,000
Capital: Riyadh, pop. 6,195,000
Currency: Saudi riyal
Religion: Muslim
Language: Arabic

Senegal

Area: 75,955 sq mi
(196,722 sq km)
Population: 13,900,000
Capital: Dakar, pop. 3,393,000
Currency: Communauté Financière Africaine franc
Religions: Muslim, Christian (mostly Roman Catholic)
Languages: French, Wolof, Pulaar, Jola, Mandinka

Serbia

Area: 29,913 sq mi (77,474 sq km)
Population: 7,100,000
Capital: Belgrade, pop. 1,181,000
Currency: Serbian dinar
Religions: Serbian Orthodox, Roman Catholic, Muslim
Languages: Serbian, Hungarian

Seychelles

Area: 176 sq mi (455 sq km)
Population: 100,000
Capital: Victoria, pop. 26,000
Currency: Seychelles rupee
Religions: Roman Catholic, Anglican, other Christian
Languages: Creole, English

Sierra Leone

Area: 27,699 sq mi (71,740 sq km)
Population: 6,300,000
Capital: Freetown, pop. 986,000
Currency: leone
Religions: Muslim, indigenous beliefs, Christian
Languages: English, Mende, Temne, Krio

Slovakia

Area: 18,932 sq mi
(49,035 sq km)
Population: 5,400,000
Capital: Bratislava, pop. 403,000
Currency: euro
Religions: Roman Catholic, Protestant, Greek Catholic
Languages: Slovak, Hungarian

Singapore

Area: 255 sq mi (660 sq km)
Population: 5,500,000
Capital: Singapore, pop. 5,500,000
Currency: Singapore dollar
Religions: Buddhist, Muslim, Taoist, Roman Catholic,
Hindu, other Christian
Languages: Mandarin, English, Malay, Hokkien,
Cantonese, Teochew, Tamil

Slovenia

Area: 7,827 sq mi
(20,273 sq km)
Population: 2,100,000
Capital: Ljubljana,
pop. 279,000
Currency: euro
Religions: Roman Catholic, Muslim, Orthodox
Languages: Slovene, Croatian, Serbian

You Are There!

Singapore Flyer, Singapore

Imagine strapping yourself into a Ferris wheel and being lifted so high in the sky, you can see nearly 30 miles (45 km) away. Well, in Singapore, you don't have to imagine: You can do just that in real life! Just take a spin on the Singapore Flyer—one of the world's highest observation wheels, which, at 541 feet (165 m), stands about 50 stories high. A standout on Singapore's iconic skyline along the Singapore River, the Flyer offers an unrivaled 360° view of famous sites and even neighboring countries.

Solomon Islands

Area: 10,954 sq mi
(28,370 sq km)
Population: 600,000
Capital: Honiara, pop. 73,000
Currency: Solomon Islands dollar
Religions: Church of Melanesia, Roman Catholic,
South Seas Evangelical, other Christian
Languages: Melanesian pidgin, 120 indigenous languages

Somalia

Area: 246,201 sq mi
(637,657 sq km)
Population: 10,800,000
Capital: Mogadishu, pop. 2,014,000
Currency: Somali shilling
Religion: Sunni Muslim
Languages: Somali, Arabic, Italian, English

South Africa

Area: 470,693 sq mi (1,219,090 sq km)
Population: 53,700,000
Capitals: Pretoria (Tshwane),
pop. 1,991,000; Bloemfontein,
pop. 496,000; Cape Town, pop. 3,624,000
Currency: rand
Religions: Zion Christian, Pentecostal, Catholic,
Methodist, Dutch Reformed, Anglican, other Christian
Languages: IsiZulu, IsiXhosa, Afrikaans, Sepedi, English

South Korea

Area: 38,321 sq mi
(99,250 sq km)
Population: 50,400,000
Capital: Seoul, pop. 9,775,000
Currency: South Korean won
Religions: Christian, Buddhist
Languages: Korean, English

South Sudan

Area: 248,777 sq mi
(644,329 sq km)
Population: 11,700,000
Capital: Juba, pop. 307,000
Currency: South Sudan pound
Religions: animist, Christian
Languages: English, Arabic, regional languages (Dinke,
Nuer, Bari, Zande, Shilluk)

Spain

Area: 195,363 sq mi (505,988 sq km)
Population: 46,500,000
Capital: Madrid, pop. 6,133,000
Currency: euro
Religion: Roman Catholic
Languages: Castilian Spanish, Catalan,
Galician, Basque

Sri Lanka

Area: 25,299 sq mi
(65,525 sq km)
Population: 20,700,000
Capitals: Colombo, pop. 704,000;
Sri Jayewardenepura Kotte, pop. 128,000
Currency: Sri Lankan rupee
Religions: Buddhist, Muslim, Hindu, Christian
Languages: Sinhala, Tamil

St. Kitts and Nevis

Area: 104 sq mi (269 sq km)
Population: 55,000
Capital: Basseterre, pop. 14,000
Currency: East Caribbean dollar
Religions: Anglican, other Protestant,
Roman Catholic
Language: English

St. Lucia

Area: 238 sq mi (616 sq km)
Population: 200,000
Capital: Castries, pop. 22,000
Currency: East Caribbean
dollar
Religions: Roman Catholic, Seventh-day Adventist,
Pentecostal
Languages: English, French patois

St. Vincent and the Grenadines

Area: 150 sq mi (389 sq km)
Population: 100,000
Capital: Kingstown, pop. 27,000
Currency: East Caribbean dollar
Religions: Anglican, Methodist, Roman Catholic
Languages: English, French patois

Sudan

Area: 718,722 sq mi (1,861,484 sq km)
Population: 38,800,000
Capital: Khartoum, pop. 5,000,000
Currency: Sudanese pound
Religions: Sunni Muslim, indigenous beliefs, Christian
Languages: Arabic, Nubian, Ta Bedawie, many diverse dialects of Nilotic, Nilo-Hamitic, Sudanic languages

Syria

Area: 71,498 sq mi (185,180 sq km)
Population: 22,000,000
Capital: Damascus, pop. 2,574,000
Currency: Syrian pound
Religions: Sunni, other Muslim (includes Alawite, Druze), Christian
Languages: Arabic, Kurdish, Armenian, Aramaic, Circassian

Suriname

Area: 63,037 sq mi (163,265 sq km)
Population: 600,000
Capital: Paramaribo, pop. 234,000
Currency: Suriname dollar
Religions: Hindu, Protestant (predominantly Moravian), Roman Catholic, Muslim, indigenous beliefs
Languages: Dutch, English, Sranang Tongo, Hindustani, Javanese

Tajikistan

Area: 55,251 sq mi (143,100 sq km)
Population: 8,300,000
Capital: Dushanbe, pop. 801,000
Currency: somoni
Religions: Sunni Muslim, Shiite Muslim
Languages: Tajik, Russian

Swaziland

Area: 6,704 sq mi (17,363 sq km)
Population: 1,300,000
Capitals: Mbabane, pop. 66,000; Lobamba, pop. 4,600
Currency: lilangeni
Religions: Zionist, Roman Catholic, Muslim
Languages: English, siSwati

Tanzania

Area: 364,900 sq mi (945,087 sq km)
Population: 50,800,000
Capitals: Dar es Salaam, pop. 5,116,000; Dodoma, pop. 228,000
Currency: Tanzanian shilling
Religions: Muslim, indigenous beliefs, Christian
Languages: Kiswahili, Kiunguja, English, Arabic, local languages

Sweden

Area: 173,732 sq mi (449,964 sq km)
Population: 9,700,000
Capital: Stockholm, pop. 1,464,000
Currency: Swedish krona
Religion: Lutheran
Languages: Swedish, Sami, Finnish

Thailand

Area: 198,115 sq mi (513,115 sq km)
Population: 66,400,000
Capital: Bangkok, pop. 9,098,000
Currency: baht
Religions: Buddhist, Muslim
Languages: Thai, English, ethnic dialects

Switzerland

Area: 15,940 sq mi (41,284 sq km)
Population: 8,200,000
Capital: Bern, pop. 358,000
Currency: Swiss franc
Religions: Roman Catholic, Protestant, Muslim
Languages: German, French, Italian, Romansh

Timor-Leste (East Timor)

Area: 5,640 sq mi (14,609 sq km)
Population: 1,200,000
Capital: Dili, pop. 228,000
Currency: U.S. dollar
Religion: Roman Catholic
Languages: Tetum, Portuguese, Indonesian, English, indigenous languages

Togo

Area: 21,925 sq mi (56,785 sq km)
Population: 7,000,000
Capital: Lomé, pop. 930,000
Currency: Communauté Financière Africaine franc
Religions: indigenous beliefs, Christian, Muslim
Languages: French, Ewe, Mina, Kabye, Dagomba

Trinidad and Tobago

Area: 1,980 sq mi (5,128 sq km)
Population: 1,300,000
Capital: Port of Spain, pop. 34,000
Currency: Trinidad and Tobago dollar
Religions: Roman Catholic, Hindu, Anglican, Baptist
Languages: English, Caribbean Hindustani, French, Spanish, Chinese

Tonga

Area: 289 sq mi (748 sq km)
Population: 100,000
Capital: Nuku'alofa, pop. 25,000
Currency: pa'anga
Religion: Christian
Languages: Tongan, English

Tunisia

Area: 63,170 sq mi (163,610 sq km)
Population: 11,000,000
Capital: Tunis, pop. 1,978,000
Currency: Tunisian dinar
Religion: Muslim
Languages: Arabic, French

You Are There!

The Matterhorn, Switzerland

One of the most iconic peaks on the planet, this pyramid-shaped mountain stands apart among the stunning Swiss Alps. While only the most expert mountaineers should even attempt to climb to the top of the Matterhorn, you can enjoy a swift ride that gets you pretty close. The Klein-Matterhorn cable car lifts you more than two miles (3,820 m) above sea level to the highest scenic overlook in Europe.

● Asia ● Europe ● North America ● South America

Turkey

Area: 300,948 sq mi
(779,452 sq km)
Population: 77,200,000
Capital: Ankara, pop. 4,644,000
Currency: new Turkish lira
Religion: Muslim (mostly Sunni)
Languages: Turkish, Kurdish, Dimli (Zaza), Azeri, Kabardian, Gagauz

Turkmenistan

Area: 188,456 sq mi
(488,100 sq km)
Population: 5,300,000
Capital: Ashgabat, pop. 735,000
Currency: Turkmen manat
Religions: Muslim, Eastern Orthodox
Languages: Turkmen, Russian, Uzbek

Tuvalu

Area: 10 sq mi (26 sq km)
Population: 10,000
Capital: Funafuti, pop. 6,000
Currencies: Australian dollar; Tuvaluan dollar
Religion: Church of Tuvalu (Congregationalist)
Languages: Tuvaluan, English, Samoan, Kiribati

Uganda

Area: 93,104 sq mi
(241,139 sq km)
Population: 38,800,000
Capital: Kampala, pop. 1,863,000
Currency: Ugandan shilling
Religions: Protestant, Roman Catholic, Muslim
Languages: English, Ganda, other local languages, Kiswahili, Arabic

Ukraine

Area: 233,090 sq mi
(603,700 sq km)
Population: 42,900,000
Capital: Kiev, pop. 2,917,000
Currency: hryvnia
Religions: Ukrainian Orthodox, Orthodox, Ukrainian Greek Catholic
Languages: Ukrainian, Russian

United Arab Emirates

Area: 30,000 sq mi
(77,700 sq km)
Population: 9,400,000
Capital: Abu Dhabi, pop. 1,114,000
Currency: Emirati dirham
Religion: Muslim
Languages: Arabic, Persian, English, Hindi, Urdu

United Kingdom

Area: 93,788 sq mi
(242,910 sq km)
Population: 64,500,000
Capital: London, pop. 10,189,000
Currency: British pound
Religions: Anglican, Roman Catholic, Presbyterian, Methodist
Languages: English, Welsh, Scottish form of Gaelic

United States

Area: 3,794,083 sq mi
(9,826,630 sq km)
Population: 317,700,000
Capital: Washington, D.C., pop. 646,449
Currency: U.S. dollar
Religions: Protestant, Roman Catholic
Languages: English, Spanish

5 cool things about the UNITED STATES

1. The U.S.A. grows nearly all the corn used for popcorn around the world.

2. About 1,200 tornadoes touch down in the U.S.A. each year—more than in any other country.

3. The U.S.A. is one of the few countries without an official language.

4. The American flag's official colors are "Old Glory Red," "White," and "Old Glory Blue."

5. The U.S.A. has 35,000 museums.

Uruguay

Area: 68,037 sq mi
(176,215 sq km)
Population: 3,400,000
Capital: Montevideo, pop. 1,698,000
Currency: Uruguayan peso
Religion: Roman Catholic
Language: Spanish

Uzbekistan

Area: 172,742 sq mi
(447,400 sq km)
Population: 30,700,000
Capital: Tashkent,
pop. 2,241,000
Currency: Uzbekistani sum
Religions: Muslim (mostly Sunni), Eastern Orthodox
Languages: Uzbek, Russian, Tajik

Vanuatu

Area: 4,707 sq mi (12,190 sq km)
Population: 300,000
Capital: Port Vila, pop. 53,000
Currency: vatu
Religions: Presbyterian, Anglican, Roman Catholic, other Christian, indigenous beliefs
Languages: more than 100 local languages, pidgin (known as Bislama or Bichelama)

Vatican City

Area: 0.2 sq mi (0.4 sq km)
Population: 1,000
Capital: Vatican City, pop. 1,000
Currency: euro
Religion: Roman Catholic
Languages: Italian, Latin, French

Venezuela

Area: 352,144 sq mi
(912,050 sq km)
Population: 30,200,000
Capital: Caracas, pop. 2,912,000
Currency: bolivar
Religion: Roman Catholic
Languages: Spanish, numerous indigenous dialects

Vietnam

Area: 127,844 sq mi
(331,114 sq km)
Population: 90,700,000
Capital: Hanoi, pop. 3,470,000
Currency: dong
Religions: Buddhist, Roman Catholic
Languages: Vietnamese, English, French, Chinese, Khmer

Vietnam is home to Son Doong Cave— the BIGGEST CAVE in the WORLD.

Yemen

Area: 207,286 sq mi
(536,869 sq km)
Population: 26,000,000
Capital: Sanaa, pop. 2,833,000
Currency: Yemeni rial
Religions: Muslim, including Shaf'i (Sunni) and Zaydi (Shiite)
Language: Arabic

Zambia

Area: 290,586 sq mi
(752,614 sq km)
Population: 15,100,000
Capital: Lusaka, pop. 2,078,000
Currency: Zambian kwacha
Religions: Christian, Muslim, Hindu
Languages: English, Bemba, Kaonda, Lozi, Lunda, Luvale, Nyanja, Tonga, about 70 other indigenous languages

Zimbabwe

Area: 150,872 sq mi
(390,757 sq km)
Population: 14,700,000
Capital: Harare, pop. 1,495,000
Currency: Zimbabwean dollar
Religions: Syncretic (part Christian, part indigenous beliefs), Christian, indigenous beliefs
Languages: English, Shona, Sindebele, tribal dialects

THE POLITICAL
UNITED STATES

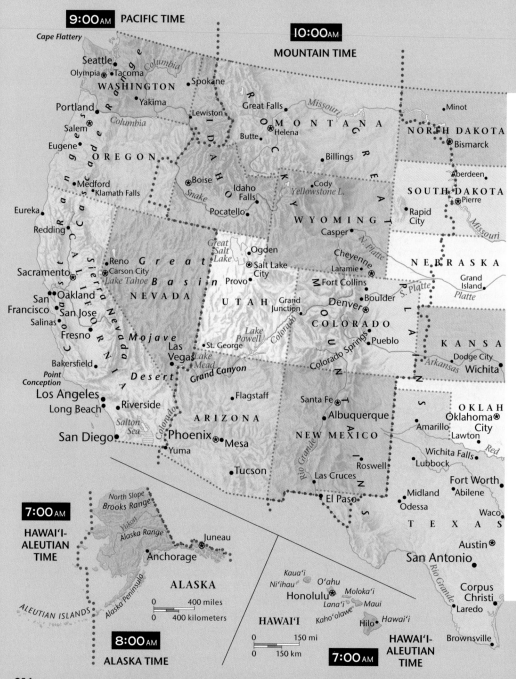

9:00AM PACIFIC TIME

10:00AM
MOUNTAIN TIME

Cape Flattery

Seattle
Olympia⊛ •Tacoma
WASHINGTON •Spokane
Portland• •Yakima
Columbia
Salem⊛ •Lewiston
Eugene•
OREGON
•Medford •Boise⊛
•Klamath Falls Snake
Eureka•
Redding•

Great Falls
MONTANA
Butte• •Helena
•Billings

•Minot
NORTH DAKOTA
⊛Bismarck

•Aberdeen
SOUTH DAKOTA
•Cody ⊛Pierre
Yellowstone L.
Idaho
Falls
Pocatello•
WYOMING
•Casper
N. Platte
•Rapid
City
Missouri

Great
Salt
Lake •Ogden
Reno Great •Carson City ⊛ Salt Lake
Lake Tahoe City
Sacramento• Basin Provo•
San• •Oakland NEVADA
Francisco• San Jose UTAH Grand
Salinas• Junction
•Fresno Mojave •St. George
Lake
Bakersfield• Las Powell
Point Vegas Lake
Conception Desert Mead Grand Canyon
Los Angeles•
Long Beach• •Riverside Salton
Sea
San Diego• Phoenix⊛•Mesa
•Yuma
ARIZONA

Cheyenne
•Laramie
•Fort Collins
•Boulder
Denver⊛
COLORADO
•Colorado Springs •Pueblo

NEBRASKA
Grand
Island
Platte

KANSA
Dodge City
Arkansas Wichita

Santa Fe⊛
•Albuquerque
NEW MEXICO
•Flagstaff

Oklahoma⊛
Amarillo• City
•Lawton
OKLAH

•Tucson
Las Cruces•
•El Paso
Rio Grande

•Wichita Falls
•Lubbock Red

Fort Worth
•Midland •Abilene
Odessa• Waco
TEXAS

7:00AM
HAWAI'I-
ALEUTIAN
TIME

North Slope
Brooks Range
Yukon
Alaska Range •Juneau
•Anchorage
ALASKA
ALEUTIAN ISLANDS Alaska Peninsula

Kaua'i
Ni'ihau O'ahu
Honolulu⊛ Moloka'i
Lana'i Maui
HAWAI'I Kaho'olawe
Hilo• Hawai'i

Austin⊛
San Antonio•

Corpus
Christi•
•Laredo

0   400 miles
0   400 kilometers

0   150 mi
0   150 km

8:00AM
ALASKA TIME

7:00AM
HAWAI'I-
ALEUTIAN
TIME

•Brownsville

Like a giant quilt, the United States is made up of 50 states. Each is unique, but together they make a national fabric held together by a constitution and a federal government. State boundaries, outlined in dotted lines on the map, set apart internal political units within the country. The national capital—Washington, D.C.—is marked by a star in a double circle. The capital of each state is marked by a star in a single circle.

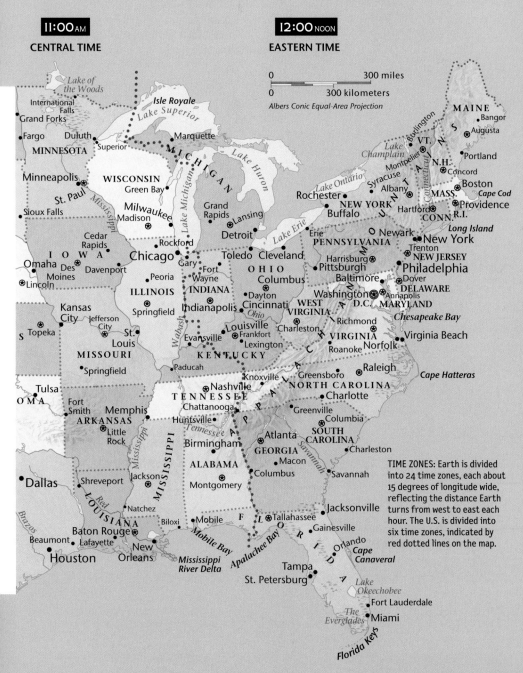

11:00 AM
CENTRAL TIME

12:00 NOON
EASTERN TIME

0   300 miles
0   300 kilometers
Albers Conic Equal-Area Projection

TIME ZONES: Earth is divided into 24 time zones, each about 15 degrees of longitude wide, reflecting the distance Earth turns from west to east each hour. The U.S. is divided into six time zones, indicated by red dotted lines on the map.

THE PHYSICAL
UNITED STATES

Mt. Rainier
14,411 ft
4,392 m

Mt. St. Helens
8,366 ft, 2,550 m

Columbia

Mt. Hood
11,239 ft
3,425 m

Snake

C A S C A D E   R A N G E

Blue Mountains

Great Sandy
Desert

Columbia Plateau

Salmon River
Mountains

Snake

Snake River Plain

Bitterroot Range

R O C K Y

Flathead
Lake

Absaroka Range

Yellowstone
Lake

Grand
Teton
13,770 ft
4,197 m

Milk

Fort Peck
Lake

Missouri

Yellowstone

Bighorn Mts.

Harney
Peak
7,242 ft
2,207 m

Black
Hills

Little Missouri

G R E A T

Lake
Sakakawea

Heart

Missouri

White
Butte
3,506 ft
1,069 m

Lake
Oahe

Geographical Center
of the 50 United States

White

James

Sierra

Sacramento Valley

San Joaquin

Lake
Tahoe

G r e a t

Great
Salt
Lake

Wasatch Range

Uinta Mts.

Great Divide
Basin

Front Range

Laramie Mts.

N. Platte

Niobrara

Sand Hills

S. Platte

Geographical Center
of the 48
Contiguous United States

Platte

Smoky Hills

San Joaquin Valley

Nevada

B a s i n

Mt. Whitney
14,494 ft
4,418 m

Death
Valley

Mojave

Lake
Powell

Colorado

Mt. Elbert
14,433 ft
4,399 m

San Juan Mts.

M O U N T A I N S

Pikes Peak
14,110 ft
4,301 m

Arkansas

Red Hills

R A N G E S

Lowest Point in
North America
-282 ft, -86 m

D e s e r t

Lake
Mead

Grand
Canyon

C o l o r a d o

P l a t e a u

Painted Desert

Black Mesa
4,973 ft
1,516 m

Sangre de Cristo Mts.

Rio Grande

Arkansas

Cimarron

Canadian

Channel

Islands

Salton
Sea

Imperial
Valley

Humphreys Peak
12,637 ft
3,852 m

Colorado

Gila

Sonoran

Desert

Salt

Rio Grande

Sacramento Mts.

Llano
Estacado

Brazos

Colorado

Guadalupe Peak
8,749 ft
2,667 m

Pecos

Edwards
Plateau

0   400 miles

0   400 kilometers

North Slope

Brooks Range

Yukon

Mt. McKinley (Denali)
20,320 ft, 6,194 m

Highest Point in
North America

Alaska Range

Alexander
Archipelago

Aleutian Islands

Alaska Peninsula

Rio Grande

0   150 miles

0   150 kilometers

Kaua'i

Ni'ihau

O'ahu

Moloka'i

Lana'i   Maui

Kaho'olawe

Mauna Kea
13,679 ft
4,169 m

Hawai'i

ALASKA AND HAWAII:
In addition to the states
located on the main landmass,
the U.S. has two states—Alaska
and Hawaii—that are not directly
connected to the other 48 states.
If Alaska and Hawaii were shown in
their correct relative sizes and locations, the map would not fit on these pages.

Stretching from the Atlantic Ocean in the east to the Pacific Ocean in the west, the United States is the third largest country (by area) in the world. Its physical diversity ranges from mountains to fertile plains and dry deserts. Shading on the map indicates changes in elevation, while colors show different vegetation patterns.

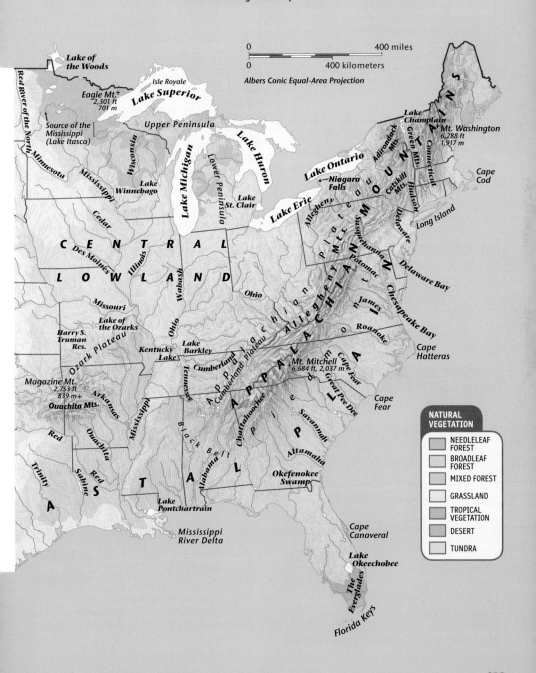

0   400 miles

0   400 kilometers

Albers Conic Equal-Area Projection

Lake of the Woods

Red River of the North

Isle Royale

Lake Superior

Eagle Mt. 2,301 ft 701 m

Source of the Mississippi (Lake Itasca)

Minnesota

Upper Peninsula

Wisconsin

Lake Michigan

Lower Peninsula

Lake Huron

Mississippi

Cedar

Lake Winnebago

Lake St. Clair

Lake Erie

Lake Ontario

Niagara Falls

Allegheny Plateau

Adirondack Mts.

Green Mts.

Lake Champlain

Mt. Washington 6,288 ft 1,917 m

Connecticut

Catskill Mts.

Hudson

Delaware

Cape Cod

Long Island

C E N T R A L

L O W L A N D

Des Moines

Illinois

Wabash

Ohio

Missouri

Lake of the Ozarks

Harry S. Truman Res.

Ozark Plateau

Kentucky Lake

Lake Barkley

Ohio

Tennessee

Cumberland

Appalachian Cumberland Plateau

Allegheny Mts.

Susquehanna

Potomac

James

Roanoke

Chesapeake Bay

Delaware Bay

Cape Hatteras

A P P A L A C H I A N   M O U N T A I N S

Mt. Mitchell 6,684 ft, 2,037 m

Magazine Mt. 2,753 ft 839 m+

Ouachita Mts.

Arkansas

Ouachita

Red

Trinity

Sabine

Red

Mississippi

Black Belt

Chattahoochee

Alabama

Cape Fear

Great Pee Dee

Savannah

Altamaha

Cape Fear

C O A S T A L   P L A I N

Okefenokee Swamp

Lake Pontchartrain

Mississippi River Delta

Cape Canaveral

Lake Okeechobee

The Everglades

Florida Keys

NATURAL VEGETATION

NEEDLELEAF FOREST

BROADLEAF FOREST

MIXED FOREST

GRASSLAND

TROPICAL VEGETATION

DESERT

TUNDRA

THE STATES

From sea to shining sea, the United States of America is a nation of diversity. In the 240 years since its creation, the nation has grown to become home to a wide range of peoples, industries, and cultures. The following pages present a general overview of all 50 states in the U.S.

The country is generally divided into five large regions: the Northeast, the Southeast, the Midwest, the Southwest, and the West. Though loosely defined, these zones tend to share important similarities, including climate, history, and geography. The color key below provides a guide to which states are in each region.

Flags of each state and highlights of demography and industry are also included. These details offer a brief overview of each state.

In addition, each state's official flower and bird are identified.

Color Key by Region

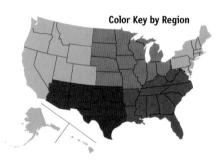

Alabama

Area: 52,419 sq mi (135,765 sq km)
Population: 4,833,722
Capital: Montgomery, pop. 201,332
Largest city: Birmingham, pop. 212,113
Industry: Retail and wholesale trade, services, government, finance, insurance, real estate, transportation, construction, communication
State flower/bird: Camellia/northern flicker

Alaska

Area: 663,267 sq mi (1,717,862 sq km)
Population: 735,132
Capital: Juneau, pop. 32,660
Largest city: Anchorage, pop. 300,950
Industry: Petroleum products, government, services, trade
State flower/bird: Forget-me-not/willow ptarmigan

Arizona

Area: 113,998 sq mi (295,256 sq km)
Population: 6,626,624
Capital: Phoenix, pop. 1,513,367
Largest city: Phoenix, pop. 1,513,367
Industry: Real estate, manufactured goods, retail, state and local government, transportation and public utilities, wholesale trade, health services
State flower/bird: Saguaro/cactus wren

PETRIFIED WOOD is Arizona's official state fossil.

Arkansas

Area: 53,179 sq mi (137,732 sq km)
Population: 2,959,373
Capital: Little Rock, pop. 197,357
Largest city: Little Rock, pop. 197,357
Industry: Services, food processing, paper products, transportation, metal products, machinery, electronics
State flower/bird: Apple blossom/mockingbird

California

Area: 163,696 sq mi (423,972 sq km)
Population: 38,332,521
Capital: Sacramento, pop. 479,686
Largest city: Los Angeles, pop. 3,884,307
Industry: Electronic components and equipment, computers and computer software, tourism, food processing, entertainment, clothing
State flower/bird: Golden poppy/California quail

Colorado

Area: 104,094 sq mi (269,602 sq km)
Population: 5,268,367
Capital: Denver, pop. 649,495
Largest city: Denver, pop. 649,495
Industry: Real estate, government, durable goods, communications, health and other services, nondurable goods, transportation
State flower/bird: Columbine/lark bunting

Connecticut

Area: 5,543 sq mi (14,357 sq km)
Population: 3,596,080
Capital: Hartford, pop. 125,017
Largest city: Bridgeport, pop. 147,216
Industry: Transportation equipment, metal products, machinery, electrical equipment, printing and publishing, scientific instruments, insurance
State flower/bird: Mountain laurel/robin

Delaware

Area: 2,489 sq mi (6,447 sq km)
Population: 925,749
Capital: Dover, pop. 37,366
Largest city: Wilmington, pop. 71,525
Industry: Food processing, chemicals, rubber and plastic products, scientific instruments, printing and publishing, financial services
State flower/bird: Peach blossom/blue hen chicken

Florida

Area: 65,755 sq mi (170,304 sq km)
Population: 19,552,860
Capital: Tallahassee, pop. 186,411
Largest city: Jacksonville, pop. 842,583
Industry: Tourism, health services, business services, communications, banking, electronic equipment, insurance
State flower/bird: Orange blossom/mockingbird

Georgia

Area: 59,425 sq mi (153,910 sq km)
Population: 9,992,167
Capital: Atlanta, pop. 447,841
Largest city: Atlanta, pop. 447,841
Industry: Textiles and clothing, transportation equipment, food processing, paper products, chemicals, electrical equipment, tourism
State flower/bird: Cherokee rose/brown thrasher

Hawaii

Area: 10,931 sq mi (28,311 sq km)
Population: 1,404,054
Capital: Honolulu, pop. 347,884
Largest city: Honolulu, pop. 347,884
Industry: Tourism, trade, finance, food processing, petroleum refining, stone, clay, glass products
State flower/bird: Hibiscus/Hawaiian goose (nene)

Idaho

Area: 83,570 sq mi (216,447 sq km)
Population: 1,612,136
Capital: Boise, pop. 214,237
Largest city: Boise, pop. 214,237
Industry: Electronics and computer equipment, tourism, food processing, forest products, mining
State flower/bird: Syringa (Lewis's mock orange)/mountain bluebird

Illinois

Area: 57,914 sq mi (149,998 sq km)
Population: 12,882,135
Capital: Springfield, pop. 117,006
Largest city: Chicago, pop. 2,718,782
Industry: Industrial machinery, electronic equipment, food processing, chemicals, metals, printing and publishing, rubber and plastics, motor vehicles
State flower/bird: Violet/cardinal

> The state **SNACK FOOD** of Illinois is **POPCORN.**

Indiana

Area: 36,418 sq mi (94,322 sq km)
Population: 6,570,902
Capital: Indianapolis, pop. 843,393
Largest city: Indianapolis, pop. 843,393
Industry: Transportation equipment, steel, pharmaceutical and chemical products, machinery, petroleum, coal
State flower/bird: Peony/cardinal

Iowa

Area: 56,272 sq mi (145,743 sq km)
Population: 3,090,416
Capital: Des Moines, pop. 207,510
Largest city: Des Moines, pop. 207,510
Industry: Real estate, health services, industrial machinery, food processing, construction
State flower/bird: Wild rose/American goldfinch

Kansas

Area: 82,277 sq mi (213,097 sq km)
Population: 2,893,957
Capital: Topeka, pop. 127,679
Largest city: Wichita, pop. 386,552
Industry: Aircraft manufacturing, transportation equipment, construction, food processing, printing and publishing, health care
State flower/bird: Sunflower/western meadowlark

Kentucky

Area: 40,409 sq mi (104,659 sq km)
Population: 4,395,295
Capital: Frankfort, pop. 27,453
Largest city: Louisville, pop. 609,893
Industry: Manufacturing, services, government, finance, insurance, real estate, retail trade, transportation, wholesale trade, construction, mining
State flower/bird: Goldenrod/cardinal

> The song "Happy Birthday to You" was written by two sisters living in Louisville, Kentucky.

Louisiana

Area: 51,840 sq mi (134,265 sq km)
Population: 4,625,470
Capital: Baton Rouge, pop. 229,426
Largest city: New Orleans, pop. 378,715
Industry: Chemicals, petroleum products, food processing, health services, tourism, oil and natural gas extraction, paper products
State flower/bird: Magnolia/brown pelican

Maine

Area: 35,385 sq mi (91,646 sq km)
Population: 1,328,302
Capital: Augusta, pop. 18,793
Largest city: Portland, pop. 66,318
Industry: Health services, tourism, forest products, leather products, electrical equipment
State flower/bird: White pine cone and tassel/chickadee

Maryland

Area: 12,407 sq mi (32,133 sq km)
Population: 5,928,814
Capital: Annapolis, pop. 38,772
Largest city: Baltimore, pop. 622,104
Industry: Real estate, federal government, health services, business services, engineering services
State flower/bird: Black-eyed Susan/northern (Baltimore) oriole

Massachusetts

Area: 10,555 sq mi (27,336 sq km)
Population: 6,692,824
Capital: Boston, pop. 645,966
Largest city: Boston, pop. 645,966
Industry: Electrical equipment, machinery, metal products, scientific instruments, printing and publishing, tourism
State flower/bird: Mayflower/chickadee

Michigan

Area: 96,716 sq mi (250,495 sq km)
Population: 9,895,622
Capital: Lansing, pop. 113,972
Largest city: Detroit, pop. 688,701
Industry: Motor vehicles and parts, machinery, metal products, office furniture, tourism, chemicals
State flower/bird: Apple blossom/robin

Minnesota

Area: 86,939 sq mi (225,172 sq km)
Population: 5,420,380
Capital: St. Paul, pop. 294,873
Largest city: Minneapolis, pop. 400,070
Industry: Real estate, banking and insurance, industrial machinery, printing and publishing, food processing, scientific equipment
State flower/bird: Showy lady's slipper/common loon

Mississippi

Area: 48,430 sq mi (125,434 sq km)
Population: 2,991,207
Capital: Jackson, pop. 172,638
Largest city: Jackson, pop. 172,638
Industry: Petroleum products, health services, electronic equipment, transportation, banking, forest products, communications
State flower/bird: Magnolia/mockingbird

Missouri

Area: 69,704 sq mi (180,534 sq km)
Population: 6,044,171
Capital: Jefferson City, pop. 43,330
Largest city: Kansas City, pop. 467,007
Industry: Transportation equipment, food processing, chemicals, electrical equipment, metal products
State flower/bird: Hawthorn/eastern bluebird

Montana

Area: 147,042 sq mi (380,840 sq km)
Population: 1,015,165
Capital: Helena, pop. 29,596
Largest city: Billings, pop. 109,059
Industry: Forest products, food processing, mining, construction, tourism
State flower/bird: Bitterroot/western meadowlark

Nebraska

Area: 77,354 sq mi (200,346 sq km)
Population: 1,868,516
Capital: Lincoln, pop. 268,738
Largest city: Omaha, pop. 434,353
Industry: Food processing, machinery, electrical equipment, printing and publishing
State flower/bird: Goldenrod/western meadowlark

NEBRASKA has counties named ANTELOPE and BUFFALO.

Nevada

Area: 110,561 sq mi (286,352 sq km)
Population: 2,790,136
Capital: Carson City, pop. 54,080
Largest city: Las Vegas, pop. 603,488
Industry: Tourism and gaming, mining, printing and publishing, food processing, electrical equipment
State flower/bird: Sagebrush/mountain bluebird

New Hampshire

Area: 9,350 sq mi (24,216 sq km)
Population: 1,323,459
Capital: Concord, pop. 42,419
Largest city: Manchester, pop. 110,378
Industry: Machinery, electronics, metal products
State flower/bird: Purple lilac/purple finch

New Jersey

Area: 8,721 sq mi (22,588 sq km)
Population: 8,899,339
Capital: Trenton, pop. 84,349
Largest city: Newark, pop. 278,427
Industry: Machinery, electronics, metal products, chemicals
State flower/bird: Violet/American goldfinch

New Mexico

Area: 121,590 sq mi (314,917 sq km)
Population: 2,085,287
Capital: Santa Fe, pop. 69,976
Largest city: Albuquerque, pop. 556,495
Industry: Electronic equipment, state and local government, real estate, business services, federal government, oil and gas extraction, health services
State flower/bird: Yucca/roadrunner

New York

Area: 54,556 sq mi (141,300 sq km)
Population: 19,651,127
Capital: Albany, pop. 98,424
Largest city: New York City, pop. 8,405,837
Industry: Printing and publishing, machinery, computer products, finance, tourism
State flower/bird: Rose/eastern bluebird

North Carolina

Area: 53,819 sq mi (139,390 sq km)
Population: 9,848,060
Capital: Raleigh, pop. 431,746
Largest city: Charlotte, pop. 792,862
Industry: Real estate, health services, chemicals, tobacco products, finance, textiles
State flower/bird: Flowering dogwood/cardinal

North Dakota

Area: 70,700 sq mi (183,113 sq km)
Population: 723,393
Capital: Bismarck, pop. 67,034
Largest city: Fargo, pop. 113,658
Industry: Services, government, finance, construction, transportation, oil and gas
State flower/bird: Wild prairie rose/western meadowlark

Ohio

Area: 44,825 sq mi (116,097 sq km)
Population: 11,570,808
Capital: Columbus, pop. 822,553
Largest city: Columbus, pop. 822,553
Industry: Transportation equipment, metal products, machinery, food processing, electrical equipment
State flower/bird: Scarlet carnation/cardinal

Oklahoma

Area: 69,898 sq mi (181,036 sq km)
Population: 3,850,568
Capital: Oklahoma City, pop. 610,613
Largest city: Oklahoma City, pop. 610,613
Industry: Manufacturing, services, government, finance, insurance, real estate
State flower/bird: Mistletoe/scissor-tailed flycatcher

Oregon

Area: 98,381 sq mi (254,806 sq km)
Population: 3,930,065
Capital: Salem, pop. 160,614
Largest city: Portland, pop. 609,456
Industry: Real estate, retail and wholesale trade, electronic equipment, health services, construction, forest products, business services
State flower/bird: Oregon grape/western meadowlark

Pennsylvania

Area: 46,055 sq mi (119,283 sq km)
Population: 12,773,801
Capital: Harrisburg, pop. 49,188
Largest city: Philadelphia, pop. 1,553,165
Industry: Machinery, printing and publishing, forest products, metal products
State flower/bird: Mountain laurel/ruffed grouse

Rhode Island

Area: 1,545 sq mi (4,002 sq km)
Population: 1,051,511
Capital: Providence, pop. 177,994
Largest city: Providence, pop. 177,994
Industry: Health services, business services, silver and jewelry products, metal products
State flower/bird: Violet/Rhode Island red

South Carolina

Area: 32,020 sq mi (82,932 sq km)
Population: 4,774,839
Capital: Columbia, pop. 133,358
Largest city: Columbia, pop. 133,358
Industry: Service industries, tourism, chemicals, textiles, machinery, forest products
State flower/bird: Yellow jessamine/Carolina wren

South Dakota

Area: 77,117 sq mi (199,732 sq km)
Population: 844,877
Capital: Pierre, pop. 13,984
Largest city: Sioux Falls, pop. 164,676
Industry: Finance, services, manufacturing, government, retail trade, transportation and utilities, wholesale trade, construction, mining
State flower/bird: Pasqueflower/ring-necked pheasant

5 cool things about PENNSYLVANIA

1. Philadelphia served as the nation's capital from 1790 until 1800.

2. Milk is the state drink of Pennsylvania.

3. Pennsylvania is the home of Crayola crayons, Hershey's chocolate, and Silly Putty.

4. The Philadelphia Zoo, which opened its gates in 1874, is America's first zoo.

5. Pennsylvania has more covered bridges than any other state.

COLOR KEY ● Northeast ● Southeast

Tennessee

Area: 42,143 sq mi (109,151 sq km)
Population: 6,495,978
Capital: Nashville, pop. 634,464
Largest city: Memphis, pop. 653,450
Industry: Service industries, chemicals, transportation equipment, processed foods, machinery
State flower/bird: Iris/mockingbird

Texas

Area: 268,581 sq mi (695,624 sq km)
Population: 26,448,193
Capital: Austin, pop. 885,400
Largest city: Houston, pop. 2,195,914
Industry: Chemicals, machinery, electronics and computers, food products, petroleum and natural gas, transportation equipment
State flower/bird: Bluebonnet/mockingbird

Utah

Area: 84,899 sq mi (219,888 sq km)
Population: 2,900,872
Capital: Salt Lake City, pop. 191,180
Largest city: Salt Lake City, pop. 191,180
Industry: Government, manufacturing, real estate, construction, health services, business services, banking
State flower/bird: Sego lily/California gull

> There are 190-MILLION-year-old DINOSAUR FOOTPRINTS near Moab, Utah.

Vermont

Area: 9,614 sq mi (24,901 sq km)
Population: 626,630
Capital: Montpelier, pop. 7,755
Largest city: Burlington, pop. 42,284
Industry: Health services, tourism, finance, real estate, computer components, electrical parts, printing and publishing, machine tools
State flower/bird: Red clover/hermit thrush

Virginia

Area: 42,774 sq mi (110,785 sq km)
Population: 8,260,405
Capital: Richmond, pop. 214,114
Largest city: Virginia Beach, pop. 448,479
Industry: Food processing, communication and electronic equipment, transportation equipment, printing, shipbuilding, textiles
State flower/bird: Flowering dogwood/cardinal

Washington

Area: 71,300 sq mi (184,666 sq km)
Population: 6,971,406
Capital: Olympia, pop. 48,388
Largest city: Seattle, pop. 652,405
Industry: Aerospace, tourism, food processing, forest products, paper products, industrial machinery, printing and publishing, metals, computer software
State flower/bird: Coast rhododendron/Amer. goldfinch

West Virginia

Area: 24,230 sq mi (62,755 sq km)
Population: 1,854,304
Capital: Charleston, pop. 50,821
Largest city: Charleston, pop. 50,821
Industry: Tourism, coal mining, chemicals, metal manufacturing, forest products, stone, clay, oil, glass products
State flower/bird: Rhododendron/cardinal

Wisconsin

Area: 65,498 sq mi (169,639 sq km)
Population: 5,742,713
Capital: Madison, pop. 243,344
Largest city: Milwaukee, pop. 599,164
Industry: Industrial machinery, paper products, food processing, metal products, electronic equipment, transportation
State flower/bird: Wood violet/robin

Wyoming

Area: 97,814 sq mi (253,337 sq km)
Population: 582,658
Capital: Cheyenne, pop. 62,448
Largest city: Cheyenne, pop. 62,448
Industry: Oil and natural gas, mining, generation of electricity, chemicals, tourism
State flower/bird: Indian paintbrush/western meadowlark

THE TERRITORIES

The United States has 14 territories—political divisions that are not states. Three of these are in the Caribbean Sea, and the other eleven are in the Pacific Ocean.

St. John, U.S. Virgin Islands

Convention Center, San Juan, Puerto Rico

Talofofo Falls, Guam

U.S. CARIBBEAN TERRITORIES

Puerto Rico
Area: 3,508 sq mi (9,086 sq km)
Population: 3,615,086
Capital: San Juan, pop. 2,466,000
Languages: Spanish, English

U.S. Virgin Islands
Area: 149 sq mi (386 sq km)
Population: 104,170
Capital: Charlotte Amalie, pop. 52,000
Languages: English, Spanish or Spanish Creole, French or French Creole

U.S. PACIFIC TERRITORIES

American Samoa
Area: 77 sq mi (199 sq km)
Population: 54,517
Capital: Pago Pago, pop. 48,000
Language: Samoan

Guam
Area: 217 sq mi (561 sq km)
Population: 161,001
Capital: Hagåtña (Agana), pop. 143,000
Languages: English, Chamorro, Philippine languages

Northern Mariana Islands
Area: 184 sq mi (477 sq km)
Population: 51,483
Capital: Saipan, pop. 49,000
Languages: Philippine languages, Chinese, Chamorro, English

Other U.S. Territories
Baker Island, Howland Island, Jarvis Island, Johnston Atoll, Kingman Reef, Midway Islands, Palmyra Atoll, Wake Island, Navassa Island (in the Caribbean)

Figures for capital cities vary widely between sources because of differences in the way the area is defined and other projection methods.

THE U.S. CAPITAL

District of Columbia
Area: 68 sq mi (177 sq km)
Population: 646,449

Abraham Lincoln, who was President during the Civil War and a strong opponent of slavery, is remembered in the Lincoln Memorial, located at the opposite end of the National Mall from the U.S. Capitol Building.

COLOR KEY ● Territories ● Northeast

DESTINATION GUIDE
NATIONAL PARKS

HAPPY BIRTHDAY, NATIONAL PARKS! In 2016, the U.S. National Park System will celebrate its 100th anniversary. What started as a way to protect and preserve land and wildlife has evolved into an extensive system showcasing the most beautiful places in the country. Today millions of visitors flock to America's 401 national parks each year. Here are some must-see sites.

ACADIA

YOSEMITE

DENALI

EVERGLADES

ZION

Acadia National Park
Where: Maine
What to See: Glacial lakes, granite cliffs, sandy beaches, dense forests, and 120-plus miles of hiking trails.
Cool Fact: Native Americans first inhabited Acadia's Mount Desert Island more than 5,000 years ago.

Yosemite National Park
Where: California
What to See: Towering trees, mirrored lakes, majestic mountains, and flowing waterfalls.
Cool Fact: At 2,425 feet (739 m) tall, Yosemite Falls is one of the highest waterfalls in North America.

Denali National Park and Preserve
Where: Alaska
What to See: Mount McKinley, North America's highest peak; delicate tundra—home to caribou, moose, and more.
Cool Fact: *Denali* means "the high one" in an indigenous language.

Everglades National Park
Where: Florida
What to See: Over 1,000 kinds of plants, 120 types of trees, and countless animals, including many endangered species.
Cool Fact: Everglades National Park is the only place in the world where alligators and crocodiles coexist.

Zion National Park
Where: Utah
What to See: Soaring cliffs, deep green natural pools, and red sandstone canyons.
Cool Fact: Zion's Kolob Arch is one of the world's largest freestanding natural arches.

Cool Things About BUCKINGHAM PALACE

With its 775 rooms, Buckingham Palace makes regular mansions look tiny. Now home to Queen Elizabeth II, it's been the British monarchy's official London digs since 1837. Let's look behind the guarded gates to find the palace's coolest features.

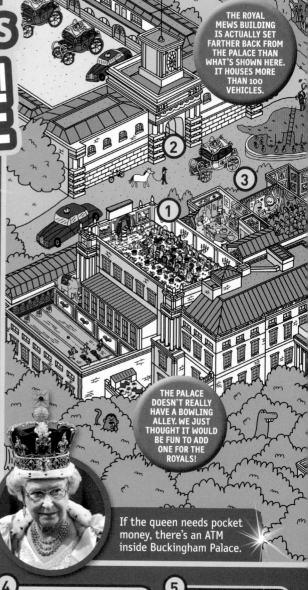

THE ROYAL MEWS BUILDING IS ACTUALLY SET FARTHER BACK FROM THE PALACE THAN WHAT'S SHOWN HERE. IT HOUSES MORE THAN 100 VEHICLES.

THE PALACE DOESN'T REALLY HAVE A BOWLING ALLEY. WE JUST THOUGHT IT WOULD BE FUN TO ADD ONE FOR THE ROYALS!

If the queen needs pocket money, there's an ATM inside Buckingham Palace.

1 FANCY FEAST
For special dinners, a team of 21 chefs whips up dishes that are served on solid-gold platters. Even Her Majesty's pet corgis receive gourmet meals in sterling silver bowls. Good thing the kitchen is well stocked—the queen welcomes about 50,000 dining guests each year.

2 CLASSY COACH
The queen's glitziest ride may be the Gold State Coach, parked in the palace's Royal Mews building and used in every coronation, or crowning of a king or queen, since 1821. Covered with heavy gold, it's pulled by eight horses.

3 MOVIE NIGHT
The royal family hosts private screenings of movies in their very own cinema, sometimes seeing new flicks before they hit theaters.

4 WHAT'S UP, DOC?
Forget a medicine cabinet. Buckingham Palace houses a doctor's office run by the queen's physician. Surgeons have performed operations in other parts of the palace. In 1902, for instance, doctors operated on King Edward VII's appendix in a room facing the garden.

5 BLINGED-OUT BEDROOMS
The palace has 52 bedrooms. Chambers such as those inside the Belgian Suite contain chandeliers, gilded mirrors, fireplaces, canopy beds, and more.

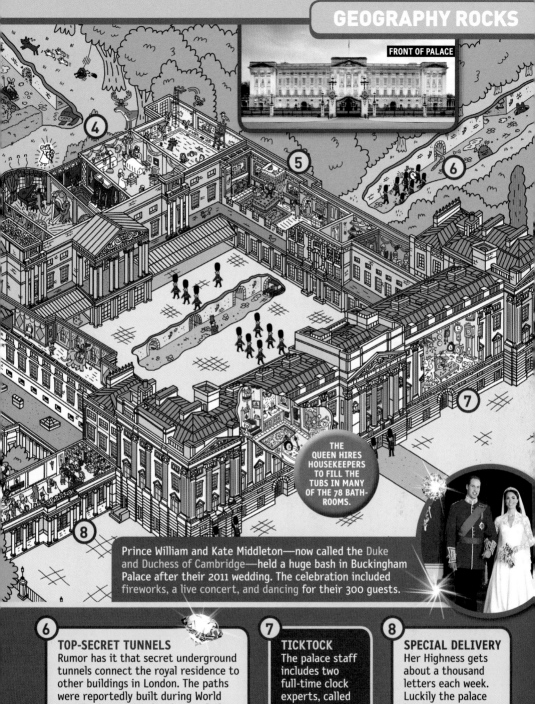

FRONT OF PALACE

THE QUEEN HIRES HOUSEKEEPERS TO FILL THE TUBS IN MANY OF THE 78 BATHROOMS.

Prince William and Kate Middleton—now called the Duke and Duchess of Cambridge—held a huge bash in Buckingham Palace after their 2011 wedding. The celebration included fireworks, a live concert, and dancing for their 300 guests.

6 TOP-SECRET TUNNELS

Rumor has it that secret underground tunnels connect the royal residence to other buildings in London. The paths were reportedly built during World War II, when enemy bombs regularly pounded the city. Weaving deep under London's bustling streets, the tunnels would have provided the royals safe passage during an attack. But even now officials won't reveal much about these under-the-radar routes.

7 TICKTOCK

The palace staff includes two full-time clock experts, called horologists. Their job is to wind the more than 350 clocks and watches and keep them ticking.

8 SPECIAL DELIVERY

Her Highness gets about a thousand letters each week. Luckily the palace has its very own post office. People also send the queen hundreds of boxes of chocolates a year. Being a royal must be sweet!

1

At the **Edinburgh Zoo** in Scotland, **penguins are let out** of their exhibit to walk with guests.

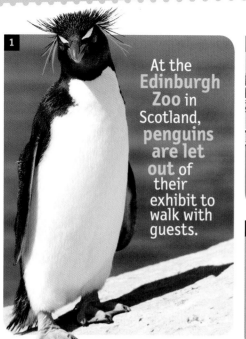

2

THE THUNDER DOLPHIN ROLLER COASTER IN TOKYO, JAPAN, PASSES THROUGH THE CENTER OF A FERRIS WHEEL.

3

A park in Fairbanks, Alaska, U.S.A., has slides, mazes, and animal sculptures— **ALL MADE OF ICE.**

16 COOL THINGS ABOUT

4

GUESTS EAT ABOUT **7,000 HAMBURGERS** A WEEK ON ONE POPULAR CRUISE SHIP.

5

VIRGINIA

IN 1816, President James Madison WENT TO MONTPELIER STATION, VIRGINIA, U.S.A., for a four-month vacation—THE LONGEST EVER OF ANY PRESIDENT.

6

A SKI RESORT IN PARK CITY, UTAH, U.S.A., OFFERS GUESTS AT LEAST EIGHT TYPES of hot chocolate.

7

A HOTEL IN LHASA, TIBET, HAS A SWIMMING POOL LINED WITH **GOLD TILES.**

8

AT SPACE CAMP IN ALABAMA, U.S.A., **A LOW-GRAVITY SIMULATOR** LETS YOU FEEL WHAT IT'S LIKE TO **WALK ON THE MOON.**

9

AT NEW YORK CITY'S BRONX ZOO, KIDS CAN RIDE A CAROUSEL ON **GIANT INSECTS** INSTEAD OF HORSES.

10 ON ONE COASTER WITH A **90-DEGREE DROP** IN QUEENSLAND, AUSTRALIA, YOU FEEL WEIGHTLESS FOR 6.5 SECONDS.

11 VACATIONERS TO CALIFORNIA, U.S.A.'S PFEIFFER BEACH WALK ON **PURPLE SAND.**

12

One round-the-world luxury cruise costs more than **$150,000** a ticket.

13 MORE THAN **40 MILLION** AMERICANS GO CAMPING EACH YEAR.

VACATIONS

14 An ice-cream shop in Mérida, Venezuela, serves visitors more than **850 flavors of ice cream.**

15

16 A HUGE ARCADE in Laconia, New Hampshire, U.S.A., FEATURES MORE THAN **500** VIDEO GAMES.

A waterslide in the Bahamas runs through a clear tunnel in a shark-filled lagoon.

Coolest Coasters

Check out the tallest, fastest, loopiest rides on the planet.

hurl
-o-
meter

hurl
-o-
meter

THE LOOPIEST: COLOSSUS

WHERE Thorpe Park in Surrey, England

RIDE Riders on Colossus blast through ten upside-down loops, including two dizzying corkscrew turns and a loop shaped like a snake's head. One last loop awaits just when you think the ride is over.

COOL SCIENCE As riders enter a loop, the acceleration produces a force that pushes them away from the center of the circle. The force presses riders into their seats—even while upside down.

THE FASTEST: FORMULA ROSSA

WHERE Ferrari World in Abu Dhabi, United Arab Emirates

RIDE This coaster jumps from 0 to 149 miles an hour (0 to 240 kph) in less than five seconds. Because of its launch system, which is similar to those used in jet planes, riders must wear goggles to protect their eyes from sand and bugs.

COOL SCIENCE Formula Rossa's launch system is powered by hydraulics, which uses the pressure of fluids to build power. This power can be stored up and released with so much force that the ride hits incredible speeds.

hurl
-o-
meter

THE TALLEST: KINGDA KA

WHERE Six Flags Great Adventure in Jackson, New Jersey, U.S.A.

RIDE Ka launches riders up a record-breaking 456-foot (139-m)-tall tower—higher than a 40-story building.

COOL SCIENCE When the ride reaches the top of the tower, it has built up potential energy for later. Once it begins to roll back down, potential energy becomes kinetic energy—the energy of motion, which helps the ride move without additional motors.

EXTREME WEIRDNESS

From AROUND the WORLD

NOW THAT'S A SMART PHONE.

PHONE GROWS BRAIN

WHAT Brain-shaped phone booth

WHERE São Paulo, Brazil

DETAILS Need a little extra brain-power? This brain-shaped phone booth was part of a design competition. A hundred designs—including a disco ball, a ladybug, an ear, and a clown—were installed over public telephones in Brazil's largest city. Cell phones have never seemed so boring.

HAT FOR BREAKFAST

WHAT English breakfast hat

WHERE Ascot, England

DETAILS Some people wear their pride on their sleeve—this fashionable woman wears hers on her hat. British patriotism is big at Royal Ascot, an English horse-racing event held every June. Among the hats worn by the crowd was this English breakfast: bacon, sausages, tomatoes, eggs, mushrooms, and beans. Wonder if she's willing to share.

EXCUSE ME, MADAM. YOU'VE GOT SOMETHING IN YOUR HAIR.

SWANS TAKE BOAT RIDE

WHAT Swan roundup

WHERE Hamburg, Germany

DETAILS This is one weird water taxi. Every fall before the water gets too cold, swans living in Alster River are gathered into boats and driven to a nearby ice-free pond. In the spring, they'll return to their warm-weather waters. These birds are swimming on easy street.

HONK, HONK!

333

WILD Vacations

Car Hotel THE V8 HOTEL

WHERE Böblingen, Germany

WHY IT'S COOL The V8 Hotel fuels the fun. Rooms have couches made of car bumpers and tables made from gasoline barrels. The Car Wash Room (shown here) boasts a bed inside a car frame, with car-wash brushes and a roller as a headboard. The Garage Room bed (below) is set up on a hydraulic lift with a mechanic's "legs" underneath. You can even take the hotel's $80,000 Wiesmann Roadster MF3 sports car for a spin. That'll *really* kick things into high gear.

SLEEP HERE!

CARWASH

W 108 - 280 S

MORRIS MINOR

FAKE LEGS!

COOL THINGS ABOUT GERMANY

Gummy bears and gummy worms were both invented in Germany.

It's illegal to run out of gas or unnecessarily stop on the autobahn, Germany's vast network of highways famous for not having a speed limit in many areas.

Germans usually answer the phone by saying their last name.

THINGS TO DO IN GERMANY

Take a horse-drawn carriage to the Neuschwanstein Castle, the inspiration for Disneyland's Sleeping Beauty Castle.

Bike the historic 99-mile (159-km) trail where the Berlin Wall (which divided the city from 1961 to 1989) once stood.

Hike the Eifel region, home to some of Germany's dormant volcanoes and an ancient Roman mine.

Snow Hotel
THE SNOWCASTLE OF KEMI

WHERE Kemi, Finland

WHY IT'S COOL With an indoor temperature of 32°F (0°C), this place is always cool—literally! Built entirely out of snow every winter, this 21-room castle has stunning ice sculptures, an outdoor playground with snow slides, and a SnowRestaurant with tables made of ice. (Cold smoked salmon soup, anyone?) At night you're given a cold-weather sleeping bag and a lambskin cover to keep you extra warm. Just don't forget to actually sleep *on top* of your clothes—if you leave them exposed, they'll freeze. And you sure don't want that happening when bundling up to walk outside to the bathroom.

EAT HERE

FIND YOUR ROOM HERE

SLEEP HERE

COOL THINGS ABOUT FINLAND

Finland is called "the land of a thousand lakes," but the country actually has 187,888 of them.

To stay safe in the brutal winters, Finnish drivers are required to have snow tires on their cars.

A popular sweet in Finland is salmiakki—licorice covered in salt.

Taking a sauna—steaming in a superheated room—and then jumping into an icy lake is a tradition in Finland.

THINGS TO DO IN FINLAND

Ride the icebreaker *Sampo*, a giant ship built to sail through thick ice.

Snowmobile under the glowing northern lights (also known as the aurora borealis).

Canoe in Lake Saimaa to look for the endangered Saimaa ringed seal.

QUIZ WHIZ

Are you a geography genius? Map out your skills with this quiz

ANSWERS BELOW

1 **Which is not found at Buckingham Palace?**
a. cinema
b. doctor's office
c. bowling alley
d. post office

2 **What's at the bottom of Fuxian Lake in China?**
a. underwater trees
b. a sunken airplane
c. ruins of an ancient city
d. buried treasure

3 **Where is the world's fastest roller coaster?**
a. Tokyo, Japan
b. Abu Dhabi, United Arab Emirates
c. New Jersey, U.S.A.
d. Surrey, England

4 **Penguins at Scotland's Edinburgh Zoo _____.**
a. can't swim
b. are let out of their exhibit
c. come from Madagascar
d. all of the above

5 **True or false?** One of the world's most active volcanoes is in Italy.

Not **STUMPED** yet? Check out the
NATIONAL GEOGRAPHIC KIDS QUIZ WHIZ collection
for more crazy **GEOGRAPHY** questions!

ANSWERS:
1. c; 2. c; 3. b; 4. b; 5. True. Mount Etna in Sicily is among the world's most active volcanoes.

HOMEWORK HELP

Finding Your Way Around

Every map has a story to tell, but first you have to know how to read one. Maps represent information by using a language of symbols. Knowing how to read these symbols provides access to a wide range of information. Look at the scale and compass rose or arrow to understand distance and direction (see box below).

To find out what each symbol on a map means, you must use the key. It's your secret decoder— identifying information by each symbol on the map.

90°N (North Pole)
75°N
60°N
45°N
30°N
15°N
0° (Equator)
15°S
30°S
45°S

Latitude

Longitude

LATITUDE AND LONGITUDE

Latitude and longitude lines (above) help us determine locations on Earth. Every place on Earth has a special address called absolute location. Imaginary lines called lines of latitude run west to east, parallel to the Equator. These lines measure distance in degrees north or south from the Equator (0° latitude) to the North Pole (90°N) or to the South Pole (90°S). One degree of latitude is approximately 70 miles (113 km).

Lines of longitude run north to south, meeting at the Poles. These lines measure distance in degrees east or west from 0° longitude (prime meridian) to 180° longitude. The prime meridian runs through Greenwich, England.

SCALE AND DIRECTION

The scale on a map can be shown as a fraction, as words, or as a line or bar. It relates distance on the map to distance in the real world. Sometimes the scale identifies the type of map projection. Maps may include an arrow or compass rose to indicate north on the map.

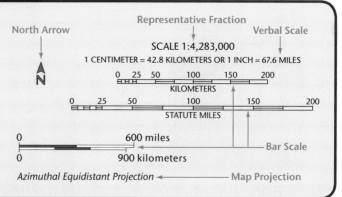

North Arrow

Representative Fraction

Verbal Scale

SCALE 1:4,283,000
1 CENTIMETER = 42.8 KILOMETERS OR 1 INCH = 67.6 MILES

0 25 50   100   150   200
KILOMETERS

0   25   50   100   150   200
STATUTE MILES

Bar Scale

0   600 miles
0   900 kilometers

Azimuthal Equidistant Projection ← Map Projection

337

GAME ANSWERS

Find the Hidden Animals, page 160

1. C, 2. D, 3. B, 4. F, 5. A, 6. E.

What in the World? page 161

Top row: cloud, rope, leaf.
Middle row: flower, islands, potato.
Bottom row: computer mouse, ravioli, door handle.
Bonus: You eat it.

Roman Holiday, page 162

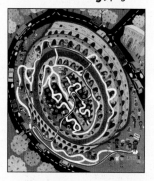

Signs of the Times, page 164

Signs #2 and #5 are fake.

Green Scene, page 165

What in the World? page 166

Top row: daisy, plums, yarn.
Middle row: glitter, sea star, mushroom.
Bottom row: jellyfish, calculator, amethyst.
Bonus: It ran out of juice.

Animal Jam, page 168

Hidden Hike, page 171

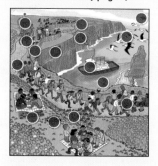

Undersea Stars, page 175

The secret animal and the key to unlock the digital extras is **Komodo dragon.**

Your World 2016 (8–17)

p. 10 "Superlab at Sea" by April Capochino Myers; p. 11 "Gator Gets New Tail" by Kitson Jazynka; p. 15 "Dino Robot" by Crispin Boyer; all other articles in section by Sarah Wassner Flynn

Awesome Adventure (18–35)

pp. 20–23 "Dare to Explore" by C. M. Tomlin; pp. 24–25 "Secrets of the Blue Holes" by Kristin Baird Rattini; p. 27 "Mystery in the Skies" by Sarah Wassner Flynn; pp. 28–29 "Getting the Shot" by April Capochino Myers; p. 32 "Orangutan to the Rescue" by Sarah Wassner Flynn; p. 33 "How to Survive a Killer Bee Attack!" & "How to Survive a Bee Sting!" by Rachel Buchholz

Amazing Animals (36–99)

pp. 38–43 "16 Cutest Animals of 2016" by April Capochino Myers, Kate Olesin, and Sarah Wassner Flynn; pp. 44–45 "How to Speak Dog" by Aline Alexander Newman and Gary Weitzman, D.V.M.; pp. 46–47 "5 Silly Pet Tricks" by Kitson Jazynka; p. 49 "Real Animal Heroes!" by Aline Alexander Newman; pp. 50–51 "Paw Enforcement" by Scott Elder; pp. 52–53 "Blind Pup Has Guide Dog" & "Penguins Play With iPad" by Kitson Jazynka, "Photobombing Fish!" by April Capochino Myers; pp. 54–55 "Animal Rascals" by Aline Alexander Newman; p. 56 "Owl Snuggles With Duck" by Elisabeth Deffner; p. 57 "Capybara Plays With Puppies" by Kitson Jazynka; pp. 58–59 "Do Animals Love Each Other?" by Aline Alexander Newman; pp. 60–61 "What Is Taxonomy?" & "Vertebrates"/"Invertebrates" by Susan K. Donnelly; pp. 62–63 "Name That Dolphin" by Ruth A. Musgrave; pp. 64–67 "Ocean Superstars" & "Parenting, Puffin Style" by Ruth A. Musgrave; p. 68 "5 Cool Things About Koalas" by Crispin Boyer; p. 69 "Foxes on Ice" by Karen De Seve; pp. 70–71 "Freaky Frogs!" by Ruth A. Musgrave; p. 73 "Wolverine!" by Stephanie Warren; pp. 74–75 "Flying Fox" by Kitson Jazynka; "Seal" by Sarah Rowe, "Wolf" by Scott Elder; p. 76 "Secrets of the Spirit Bear" by Karen De Seve; p. 77 "Panda Party" by Kitson Jazynka; pp. 78–79 "Return of the Missing Lynx" by Crispin Boyer; pp. 80–81 "Big Cats" by Elizabeth Carney; pp. 82–83 "Mission Animal Rescue: Lion" by Scott Elder; p. 84 "Cheetahs: Built for Speed" by Fiona Sunquist; p. 85 "Snow Leopard Secrets" by Karen De Seve; pp. 88–89 "Make a Spiderweb" by Nancy Honovich; p. 90 "What Killed the Dinosaurs?" by Sarah Wassner Flynn; pp. 90–92 "Prehistoric Time Line," "Dino Classification" & "Who Ate What?" by Susan K. Donnelly; pp. 94–95 "Dynamite Dino Awards" by Sarah Wassner Flynn; pp. 96–97 "Dino Myths Busted!" by Suzanne McIntire

Super Science (100–135)

pp. 102–103 "Cool Inventions" by Crispin Boyer; p. 104 "Get Ready for Robots" by Douglas E. Richards; p. 105 "Accidents Happen" by Renee Skelton; pp. 106–107 "...Big Bang" by David A. Aguilar; p. 106 "Powerful Particle" by Sarah Wassner Flynn; p. 110 "Dwarf Planets" by Sarah Wassner Flynn; p. 111 "Super Sun!" by Sarah Wassner Flynn; p. 113 "Solar and Lunar Eclipses" by Sarah Wassner Flynn; p. 117 "Rock Stars" by Steve Tomecek; pp. 118–119 "Name That Rock" by Nancy Honovich; pp. 120–121 "Volcano!" by Renee Skelton; pp. 122–123 "Kaboom!" by Sarah Webb; p. 125 "The Three Domains of Life" by Susan K. Donnelly; pp. 127–128 "Your Amazing Eyes" & "Your Amazing Brain" by Douglas E. Richards; p. 129 "How to Decode Your Dreams" by Sarah Wassner Flynn; pp. 132–133 "That's Gross!" by Crispin Boyer

Wonders of Nature (136–157)

p. 138 "Weather and Climate" by Mark Bockenhauer; p. 140 "How Does Your Garden Grow?" by Susan K. Donnelly; p. 141 "Plant a Butterfly Garden" by Nancy Honovich; pp. 142–143 "Carnivorous Plants" by Sarah Wassner Flynn; pp. 144–145 "Biomes" by Susan K. Donnelly; pp. 146–147 "Typhoon!" & "Wildfire!" & "Flood!" by Sarah Wassner Flynn; pp. 148–151 "What Is a Tornado?" & "The Water Cycle" by Kathy Furgang

Culture Connection (178–203)

pp. 182–183 "Handimals" by Kelley Miller; pp. 184–185 "World's Wackiest Houses" by Zachary Petit; p. 189 "New Year's Party" by Barton Seaver; p. 190 "What's Your Chinese Horoscope?" by Geoff Williams; pp. 192–193 "Money Around the World!" by Kristin Baird Rattini; pp. 194–195 "Chew on This" by Kay Boatner; pp. 198–199 "Mythology" by Susan K. Donnelly; pp. 200–201 "World Religions" by Mark Bockenhauer

Going Green (204–221)

pp. 206–207 "Green Extremes" by Sarah Wassner Flynn; pp. 208–209 "Brown Spider Monkey" by Crispin Boyer and "Manatee Rescue!" by Scott Elder; pp. 210–211 "Global Warming" & "Greenland's Giant Canyon" by Sarah Wassner Flynn; pp. 212–213 "Pollution," "Declining Biodiversity" & "Habitats Threatened" by David George Gordon; p.212 "Seeing the Light" by Sarah Wassner Flynn; pp. 216–217 "Food for Thought" & "Salmon Salad Sandwich" by Barton Seaver; p. 217 "Fighting Food Waste" by Sarah Wassner Flynn; pp. 218–219 "8 Fun Ways to Get Outside" by Sarah Wassner Flynn

History Happens (222–253)

pp. 224–225 "Packing for the Afterlife" by Crispin Boyer; pp. 226–227 "Ancient World Adventure" by Sarah Wassner Flynn; pp. 228–229 "Knight Life" by Crispin Boyer; p. 232 "Mystery of the Stone Giants" by Sean McCollum; p. 233 "Mystery of Atlantis" by John Micklos, Jr.; p. 234 "Treasure!" by Jamie Kiffel-Alech; p. 235 "The Amazing Houdini!" by Michael N. Smith and Debora L. Smith; pp. 236–237 "War!" by Susan K. Donnelly and Sarah Wassner Flynn; p. 237 "Spy Trees" by Sarah Wassner Flynn; pp. 238–239 "The Constitution & the Bill of Rights" & "Branches of Government" by Susan K. Donnelly; p. 240 "George Washington's Rules to Live By" adapted by K. M. Kostyal; p. 241 "The Indian Experience" by Martha B. Sharma; pp. 248–249 "Civil Rights" & "Stone of Hope" by Susan K. Donnelly and Sarah Wassner Flynn; pp. 250–251 "8 Daring Women in U.S. History!" by Sarah Wassner Flynn

Geography Rocks (254–337)

pp. 256–261 by Mark Bockenhauer; pp. 262–289 by Sarah Wassner Flynn, Mark Bockenhauer, and Susan K. Donnelly; pp. 290–315 "You Are There!" by Sarah Wassner Flynn; p. 327 "Destination Guide: National Parks" by Sarah Wassner Flynn; pp. 328–329 "Cool Things About Buckingham Palace" by Sarah Wassner Flynn; pp. 330–331 "16 Cool Things About Vacations" by Alicia Klepeis; p. 332 "Coolest Coasters" by Sean McCollum; p. 333 "Extreme Weirdness From Around the World" by Kay Boatner; pp. 334–335 "Wild Vacations" by Zachary Petit and Sarah Wassner Flynn

All "Homework Help" by Vicki Ariyasu

Nature Picture Library; 86 (spittlebug), John Macgregor/Peter Arnold/GI; 86 (LOLE), Jan Hamrsky/Nature Picture Library; 86 (LORT), domin_domin/IS; 86 (mosquito), jps/SS; 87 (grasshopper), Ed Reschke/Oxford Scientific/GI; 87 (weevil), Thomas Marent/MP; 87 (Moth), Danita Delimont/Gallo Images/GI; 87 (LORT), Ian Dagnall/Alamy; 87 (sea skate), Anthony Smith; 87 (honey), Ljupco Smokovski/SS; 87 (dragonfly), Buddy Mays/Alamy; 87 (ant), Robert Sisson/NG Stock; 88 (CTR), Lori Epstein; 89 (UP), Karen Zieff/Zieffphoto.com; 89 (CTR), Mirvav/SS; 89 (LO), James Ac/SS; 90 (UP), Chris Butler/Science Photo Library/PR, Inc.; 90 (CTR), Publiphoto/PR, Inc.; 90 (LO), Pixeldust Studios/NationalGeographicStock.com; 91 (B), Laurie O'Keefe/PR, Inc.; 91 (C), Chris Butler/PR, Inc.; 91 (D), Publiphoto/PR, Inc.; 91 (E), image courtesy of Project Exploration; 92 (UP), Paul B. Moore/SS; 92 (LO), Andrea Meyer/SS; 93 (CTR), Franco Tempesta; 94 (RT), Franco Tempesta; 94 (LO), Jennifer Hall; 94 (UP), Franco Tempesta; 95 (UPLE), Franco Tempesta; 95 (LOLE), Chuang Zhap; 95 (LORT), Davide Bonadonna/NGC; 95 (UPRT), Franco Tempesta; 96 (LE), Dean Macadam; 97 (UP), Dean Macadam; 97 (LORT), Dean Macadam; 98 (UP), Jouan & Rius/Nature Picture Library; 98 (RT CTR), Courtesy of Zoo Atlanta; 98 (LO), Franco Tempesta; 99 (UPRT), CampCrazy Photography/SS

Super Science (100–135)

100–101 (CTR), ChinaFotoPress/GI; 102 (UP), Courtesy of Push Offices; 102 (LO), Oru Kayak, Inc.; 102 (LO), Oru Kayak, Inc.; 103 (UP CTR), Liquid Image; 103 (LOCTR), Steve Debenport/GI; 103 (RT CTR), Cultura Creative/Alamy; 103 (LO), Double Robotics; 103 (UPRT), Jeff Bozanic, 104 (UP), Aldebaran Robotics; 104 (LO), Aldebaran Robotics; 105 (UP), Art By Joe Rocco; 105 (LO), Art By Joe Rocco; 106 (Background), Take 27 Ltd/PR, Inc.; 107 (A), David Aguilar; 107 (B), David Aguilar; 107 (C), David Aguilar; 107 (D), David Aguilar; 107 (E), David Aguilar; 108 (UP), David Aguilar; 110 (UP), David Aguilar; 111 (UP), NASA/Science Faction/SPS; 111 (LO), NASA; 112 (B), Tony & Daphne Hallas/PR, Inc.; 112 (Background), Gabe Palmer/CO; 112 (UPRT), Walter Myers/Stocktrek Images/CO; 112 (LORT), NASA; 114 (RT), NASA/Johnson Space Center; 114–115 (Background), David Aguilar; 114 (LOLE), Xinhua/RIA/Xinhua/Photoshot/Newscom; 114 (LORT), Reuters/Yevgeni Yemeldinov; 115 (UP), Courtesy of NASA; 115 (LO), Courtesy of NASA; 117 (UP), Ralph Lee Hopkins/NG Stock; 117 (UP CTR LE), Visuals Unlimited/GI; 117 (CTR RT), Visuals Unlimited/GI; 117 (LO CTR LE), Doug Martin/PR, Inc.; 117 (LO CTR RT), DEA/C. Dani/GI; 117 (LO LE), Michael Baranski/SS; 118 (a), Jeff Goulden/IS; 118 (B), Hans Neleman/Photodisc/GI; 119 (C), Dirk Wiersma/Science Source; 119 (D), Alexander Bark/SS; 119 (F), Giovanni Rinaldi/IS; 119 (G), Dr. Ajay Kumar Singh/SS; 120 (CTR), James A. Sugar/CO; 121 (UP), Bruce Omori/EPA/Newscom; 121 (CTR), Bruce Omori/EPA/Newscom; 122 (1), Dykon Explosive Demolition Corp.; 122 (2), Dykon Explosive Demolition Corp.; 122 (3), Dykon Explosive Demolition Corp.; 123 (1), Zou Haibin/Xinhua Press/CO; 123 (2), Zou Haibin/Xinhua Press/CO; 123 (3), Zou Haibin/Xinhua Press/CO; 124 (LO), David Aguilar; 125 (E), Marie C. Fields/SS; 125 (D), Fedor A. Sidorov/SS; 125 (F), sgame/SS; 125 (A), Sebastian Kaulitzki/SS; 125 (B), Steve Gschmeissner/PR, Inc.; 125 (C), Volker Steger/Christian Bardele/PR, Inc.; 125 (G), Benjamin Jessop/IS.com; 127 (UP), Dennis Cooper/CO; 128 (CTR), Robert J. Demarest; 129, Art By Joe Rocco; 130 (4A), Gerrit_de_Vries/SS; 130 (6), CLIPAREA l Custom media/SS; 130

(24), Eric Isselée/SS; 131 (8), Pete Donofrio/SS; 131 (13), David Pruter/SS; 131 (15), mashe/SS; 131 (16), PD Loyd/SS; 131 (17), Computer Earth/SS; 131 (22), markrhiggins/SS; 132 (LO), Linda Nye; 132 (1), Science Photo Library/Alamy; 132 (UP), Irochka/Dreamstime.com; 132 (2), Scimat Scimat/GI; 133 (3), Sebastian Kaulitzki/SS; 133 (4), PR/GI; 133 (RT CTR), Liubov Grigoryeva/Dreamstime.com; 133 (LO CTR RT), Shirley Hu/Dreamstime.com; 133 (LORT), Sebastian Kaulitzki/Dreamstime.com; 134 (UP), Gerrit_de_Vries/SS; 134 (CTR), Linda Nye; 134 (LE CTR), David Aguilar; 134 (LORT), James A. Sugar/CO; 135 (UP), AVAVA/SS; 135 (LO), Chris Gorgio/IS.com

Wonders of Nature (136–157)

136 (Background), Steve & Donna O'Meara/NGC; 137 (LORT), Steve Collender/SS; 138 (UP), Dean Conger/NGC; 139 (UP), Sean R. Heavey; 140 (UP), FotograFFF/SS; 140 (LO), Craig Tuttle/CO; 141 (Background), Dave Bevan/Alamy, 141 (CTR), Brain light/Alamy; 141 (UP), Steven Russell Smith/Alamy; 141 (CTR RT), Joseph Lacy/Alamy; 142 (UP), Ed Reschke/GI; 142 (LOLE), age fotostock RM/GI; 142 (LORT), PR RM/GI; 143 (UPLE), Edwin Giesbers/Nature Picture Library; 143 (UPRT), Claus Meyer/MP/NGC; 143 (CTR RT), Anneka/SS; 143 (LO), Inga Spence/Visuals Unlimited/CO; 144 (UP), AVTG/IS.com; 144 (LO), Brad Wynnyk/SS; 145 (A), Rich Carey/SS; 145 (B), Richard Walters/IS.com; 145 (C), Karen Graham/SS; 145 (D), Michio Hoshino/MP/NationalGeographicStock.com; 146 (UP), Dan Kitwood/GI; 147 (UP), AP Photo/U.S. Forest Service, Mike McMillan; 147 (CTR), AP Photo/Aftab Ahmed; 147 (LO), AP Photo/Dar Yasin; 148 (UP), Lori Mehmen/Associated Press; 148 (LO), Jim Reed; 149 (UP LE), Gene Blevins/LA Daily News/CO; 149 (LO LE), Neil Bookman/National Geographic My Shot; 149 (UP RT), Susan Law Cain/SS; 149 (UP CTR RT), Brian Nolan/IS.com; 149 (RT CTR), Susan Law Cain/SS; 149 (CTR), Judy Kennamer/SS; 149 (LO RT), jam4travel/SS; 149 (LO CTR RT), jam4travel/SS; 150 (Background), Ralf Hettler/GI; 152–153 (UP), Jason Edwards/NationalGeographic Stock.com; 152 (LOLE), Brandon Cole; 152 (LORT), Reinhard Dirscherl/Visuals Unlimited, Inc.; 153 (LOLE), Dray van Beeck/SS; 153 (LORT), Brandon Cole; 153 (LO), Chris Gorgio/IS.com; 153, AVAVA/SS; 154 (UPLE), John Greim/LightRocket/GI; 154 (UPRT), Ljupco Smokov/SS; 154 (UP CTR RT), Vetta/GI; 154 (CTR LE), Feng Yu/SS; 154 (LORT), Karen Gowlett-Holmes/GI; 154 (LOLE), Universal Images Group Editorial/GI; 155 (UPLE), Chad Zuber/SS; 155 (UP CTR LE), Underwater Imaging/Alamy; 155 (UPRT), Tanya Puntti/SS; 155 (UP CTR RT), AFP/GI; 155 (LO CTR LE), Rich Carey/SS; 155 (LO CTR RT), Georgios Kollidas/SS; 155 (LOLE), RHIMAGE/SS; 155 (LORT), Waterframe RM/GI; 156 (UP), Dan Kitwood/GI; 156 (LOLE), Brain light/Alamy; 156 (CTR RT), Vetta/GI/GI

Fun and Games (158–177)

158 (Background), Javier Brosch/SS; 159 (UPRT), Steve Collender/SS; 160 (UPRT), Gerry Ellis/MP; 160 (UPRT), Michael & Patricia Fogden/MP; 160 (CTR LE), Fred Bavendam/MP; 160 (CTR RT), Julie Larsen Maher Wildlife Conservation Society; 160 (LOLE), Gary K. Smith/MP; 160 (LORT), Wild Wonders of Europe/Widstrand/Nature Picture Library; 160 (LOCTR), Ron Sumners/dreamstime; 160 (LORT), Samantha Carrirolo/GI; 161 (UPLE), Yuji Sakai/GI; 161 (UP CTR), Roman Sigaev/SS; 161 (UPRT), MIMAGES/Alamy; 161 (CTR LE), Loskutnikov/SS; 161 (CTR), Pablo Scapinachis/dreamstime; 161 (CTR RT), Ira Heuvelman-Dobrolyubova/GI; 161 (LOLE), Pressmaster/SS;

162 (CTR), Alice Feagan; 163 (Background), Dan Sipple; 164 (4), R H Productions/Brand Harding World Imagery/CO; 164 (6), Tony Savino/CO; 164 (2), Paul Souders/CO; 164 (3), Danita Delimont/GI; 164 (7), Peter Dazeley/GI; 164 (2), vasabii/C; 165 (BACK), Jeff Hendricks and Viktoriya Tsoy; 165 (interior), James Yamasaki; 166 (UPLE), Purestock/GI; 166 (UP CTR), Ken Lucas/Visuals Unlimited, Inc./GI; 166 (UPRT), Ingram Publishing/SPS; 166 (CTR LE), Duffie/Alamy; 166 (CTR), Fred Bavendam/MP; 166 (CTR RT), phototrappist/GI; 166 (LOLE), Chris Newbert/MP; 166 (LOCTR), Sheli Spring Saldana/dreamstime; 166 (LORT), Dorling Kindersley/GI; 167 (UP), Miroslav Hlavko/SS; 167 (CTR LE), RubberBall/SPS; 167 (CTR LE CTR), ALEAIMAGE/IS; 167 (CTR), Kameel/IS; 167 (LO), Eric Isselée/SS; 167 (CTR RT), Krzysztof Wiktor/SS; 168 (Background), Smart Bomb Interactive; 169 (UPRT), Gary Fields; 169 (CTR LE), Gary Fields; 169 (CTR), Chris Ware; 169 (LOLE), Pat Moriarty; 169 (LORT), Gary Fields; 170 (Background), Dan Sipple; 171 (CTR), James Yamasaki; 172 (CTR), Strika Entertainment; 174 (UP), Jurgen & Christine Sohns/MP; 174 (CTR LE BACK), Ber Lybil/Dreamstime; 174 (CTR LE FRONT), Szasz-Fabian Ilka Erika/SS; 174 (CTR BACK), Iulian Gherghel/dreamstime; 174 (CTR FRONT), Mike Flippo/SS; 174 (CTR RT), Pixsooz/SS; 174 (LORT), Andrey_Kuzmin/SS; 174 (LOLE), Valentyn Volkov/SS; 175 (CTR), James Yamasaki; 176–177 (header), Madlen/SS; 176 (UP), Steve Bower/SS; 176 (CTR LE), Stan Fellerman/Alamy; 176 (CTR), Fer Gregory/SS; 176 (CTR RT), Akihito Yokoyama/Alamy; 176 (LOLE), Andrei Shumskiy/SS; 176 (LO CTR RT), Anastasios Kandris/SS; 176 (LO), moneymaker11/SS; 176 (LORT), Eric Isselée/SS; 177 (Background), Dan Sipple

Culture Connection (178–203)

178 (CTR), Amy Toensing/NGC; 178 (CTR RT), Steve Collender/SS; 178, Scott Matthews; 180 (1), Keystone-France/Gamma-Keystone/GI; 180 (2), Holger Leue/CO; 180 (3), IS; 180 (5), SS; 180 (7), Regien Paassen/SS; 180 (8), SS; 181 (9), Vereshchagin Dmitry/SS; 181 (11), EPA/Sergio Barrenechea/CO; 181 (12), Winston Link/SS; 181 (13), Hung Chung Chih/SS; 181 (15), Kc Alfred/U-T San Diego/ZUMAPRESS/Newscom; 181 (16), The British Museum/Trustees of the British Museum/Art Resource, NY; 182 (UP CTR), Guido Daniele; 182 (LOLE), Guido Daniele; 182 (UPLE), Mark Thiessen/NG Staff; 182 (LOCTR), Mark Thiessen/NG Staff; 182 (UPRT), Sari ONeal/SS; 182 (LORT), Meriel Lland/GI; 183 (UP CTR LE), Guido Daniele; 183 (LORT), Guido Daniele; 183 (UPLE), Mark Thiessen/NG Staff; 183 (CTR RT), Mark Thiessen/NG Staff; 183 (LO), Mark Thiessen/NG Staff; 183 (RT), ErinWilkins/GI; 183 (LOLE), Tomaz Kunst/SS; 184, REX USA/Jaime Jacott; 185 (CTR), Reuters/Danish Siddiqui; 185 (LO), Eduardo Longo; 185 (UP), Simon Dale/ZUMAPRESS/Newscom; 186 (4), Tubol Evgeniya/SS; 186 (1), fotohunter/SS; 186 (6), pattarastock/SS; 186 (10), Shamil Zhumatov/Reuters/CO; 186 (9), Supachta Ae/SS; 187 (11), Dinodia/age fotostock; 187 (14), Zee/Alamy; 187 (15), wacpan/SS; 188 (CTR), harper kt/SS; 189 (UP) Elena Schweitzer/SS; 189 (CTR), Michael Piazza; 189 (LO), barbaliss/SS; 191 (RT), Mark Thiessen; 191 (LE), Mark Thiessen, NGS; 192 (B), Paul Harrison/Alamy; 192 (C), Radomir Tarasov/Dreamstime.com; 192 (E), Erwan Galesne/Numista; 192 (F), Michael Mitin/Dreamstime.com; 192 (a), The Trustees of the British Museum; 192 (d), Zoonar GmbH/Alamy; 192 (g), Ninette Maumus/Alamy; 192 (c), GI; 193 (D), Ron Nickel/Design Pics/CO; 193 (d), D. Hurst/Alamy; 193 (f), Nataliya Evmenenko/dreamstime; 193 (b), Comstock/GI; 193 (a), Courtesy of Heritage Auctions; 194 (CTR), Rebecca Hale, NGS;

195 (RT), IS; 195 (CTR), Mark Thiessen, NGS; 196 (UPLE), Ocean/CO; 197 (CTR), Gonzalo Ordoñez; 198 (UPLE), John Hazard; 198 (UPRT), Jose Ignacio Soto/SS; 198 (LO), Photosani/SS; 199 (LE), Corey Ford/Dreamstime; 200 (UP), Randy Olson; 200 (LOLE), Martin Gray/NationalGeographicStock.com; 200 (LORT), Sam Panthaky/AFP/GI; 201 (LOLE), Reza/NationalGeographic Stock.com; 201 (LORT), Richard Nowitz/NationalGeographicStock.com; 201 (UP), Winfield Parks/NationalGeographicStock.com; 202 (UP), Michael Mitin/Dreamstime.com; 202 (CTR), Ocean/CO; 202 (UPRT), John Hazard; 203 (UP), Neftali/SS; 203 (CTR), Ajay Bhaskar/IS.com; 203 (LO), Sunil Menon/IS.com

Going Green (204–221)

204 (Background), Flickr RF/GI; 206 (UPLE), Art by Zac Freeman; 206 (LO), courtesy Crowne Plaza Hotel; 207 (UPLE), courtesy Ducere Technologies; 207 (UPRT), courtesy Settlers Ghost Golf Club; 207 (LO), WENN/Newscom; 207, courtesy Ducere Technologies; 208 (UPRT), David J. Southall; 208 (UP CTR LE), Rod Williams/MP; 208 (RT CTR), Ernie Janes/NHPA/Photoshot; 209 (LO), James R. D. Scott/GI; 209 (UP), Courtesy FWC/Activities were conducted under the USFWS permit number MA770191; 210 (LO), Erlend Kvalsvik/IS.com; 210 (UP), Paul Souders/CO; 211 (LOLE), AP Photo/Extreme Ice Survey, James Balog; 211 (CTR), James Balog/NGC; 212 (LE), Stéphane Bidouze/SS; 212 (Background), Mujka Design Inc./IS.com; 213 (LO), Nick Garbutt/naturepl.com; 213 (UP), Rich Carey/SS; 213, TKTKTKTKTK; 213, Nick Garbutt/naturepl.com; 214 (1), David Kilpatrick/Alamy; 214 (2), Suzanne Long/Alamy; 214 (4), Mgkuijpers/Dreamstime; 214 (3), dk/Alamy; 214 (5), Milous Chab/Dreamstime; 214 (6), Softlightaa/Dreamstime; 214 (LOLE), Photoshot Holdings Ltd/Alamy; 214 (LO CTR), FLPA/Alamy; 214 (9), George H. H. Huey/Alamy; 215 (10), SPS/Alamy; 215 (11), Pete Oxford/MP; 215 (12), Piper Mackay/Nature Picture Library; 215 (13), blickwinkel/Alamy; 215 (14), Morley Read/Alamy; 215 (15), geogphotos/Alamy; 215 (16), ADS/Alamy; 216 (Back), Brian J. Skerry/NGC; 216 (Inset), CuboImages/Alamy; 217 (UP), Michael Piazza; 217 (Inset), Adrian Brooks/Imagewise; 218 (LOLE), Ambient Images Inc./SPS; 218 (UP), moodboard/SPS; 218 (LORT), Rebecca Hale, NGS; 219 (UPRT), Larry Landolfi/Science Source; 219 (LE CTR), Dex Image/Alamy; 219 (LO CTR RT), Courtesy Uncharted Play; 219 (LOLE), FLPA/Gary K Smith/MP; 219 (LORT), Alan Tansey; 220 (UP), James R. D. Scott/GI; 220 (RT), Erlend Kvalsvik/IS.com; 220 (LO), Rod Williams/MP; 221, Albo003/SS

History Happens (222–253)

222, FLICKER RF/GI; 222 (UPLE), Steve Collender/SS; 224 (UP), Victor R. Boswell, Jr./NationalGeographicStock.com; 224 (CTR), DeAgostini/GI; 224 (LO), Sandro Vannini/CO; 225 (UPLE), Leemage/Universal Images Group/GI; 225 (UPRT), Werner Forman/Art Resource, NY; 225 (LOLE), Mark Moffett/NG Stock/MP; 225 (LORT), Photolibrary.com/GI; 225 (RT CTR), Kenneth Garrett/NationalGeographicStock.com; 226 (LO), Fengling/SS; 226 (UPLE), De Agostini/GI; 226 (UPRT), Tuul/Robert Harding Picture Library; 227 (LOLE), Kenneth Garrett/NG Stock; 227 (LORT), Yoshio Tomii/SPS; 227 (UP), Adam Woolfitt/Robert Harding Picture Library; 228–231 (Background), age fotostock/SPS; 229 (LORT), North Wind Picture Archives/Alamy; 230 (UPLE), bbbb/SS; 230 (UPRT), BW Folsom/SS; 230 (UP CTR), Natali Glado/SS; 230 (LOCTR), Pan Xunbin/SS; 230 (LOLE), IS; 230 (LO), SS; 230 (LORT), SS; 231 (UPLE), DeAgostini/GI; 231 (UPRT), Wasan Ritthawon/SS; 231 (UP CTR LE), Turner & de Vries/GI; 231 (UP CTR RT), Joe Raedle/Newsmakers/GI; 231 (LO CTR LE), AFP/GI; 231 (LE CTR RT), Danny Smythe/Alamy; 231 (LO), Jiri Flogel/SS; 232 (LO), M Kathleen Schamel; 232 (LE), Doug Allan/Nature Picture Library; 232 (RT), Atlantide Phototravel/CO; 233 (UP), Art By Mondolithic; 233 (CTR), Art By Mondolithic; 233 (LO), Art By Mondolithic; 234 (Various), Cidepix/dreamstime; 234 (RT), Cloki/dreamstime; 234 (Various), Byjeng/dreamstime; 234 (LO), Andrey57641/dreamstime; 234 (Various), Luba V Nel/dreamstime; 234 (LORT), Kupka/Mauritius/SPS; 235 (LE), Bettmann/CO; 235 (UP CTR), McManus-Young Collection/Library of Congress Prints & Photographs Division; 235 (LORT), Bettmann/CO; 236–237, AP Images/Adam Butler; 237 (UPRT), and Lt. D McLellan/IWM/GI; 238 (UP), Scott Rothstein/SS; 239 (UP), AleksandarNakic/IS.com; 239 (LO), Gary Blakely/SS; 239 (CTR), S. Borisov/SS; 240 (LE), Fred Harper; 240 (UPRT), Fred Harper; 240 (LO), Fred Harper; 241, Prisma/SPS; 242 (F), Michael Schmeling/Alamy; 242 (B), WHHA; 242 (C), WHHA; 242 (E), WHHA; 242 (G), WHHA; 242 (H), WHHA; 242 (I), WHHA; 242 (A), WHHA; 242 (I), Andrea Haase/Dreamstime; 243 (A), WHHA; 243 (B), WHHA; 243 (C), WHHA; 243 (D), WHHA; 243 (E), WHHA; 243 (F), WHHA; 243 (G), WHHA; 243 (H), WHHA; 243 (J), WHHA; 244 (A), WHHA; 244 (B), WHHA; 244 (C), WHHA; 244 (D), WHHA; 244 (E), WHHA; 244 (F), WHHA; 244 (G), WHHA; 244 (H), WHHA; 244 (I), WHHA; 244 (J), WHHA; 245 (LO inset), Hulton-Deutsch Collection/CO; 245 (LO), Winterling/Dreamstime; 245 (A), WHHA; 245 (B), WHHA; 245 (C), WHHA; 245 (D), WHHA; 245 (E), WHHA; 245 (F), WHHA; 245 (G), WHHA; 245 (H), WHHA; 246 (H), MPI/GI; 246 (E), Bjørn Hovdal/Dreamstime; 246 (b), Kiboka/Dreamstime.com; 246 (A), WHHA; 246 (C), WHHA; 246 (D), WHHA; 246 (F), WHHA; 246 (G), WHHA; 246 (J), The White House; 246 (K), The White House; 246 (I), WHHA; 247 (UPLE), Asaf Eliason/SS; 247 (UP CTR), Asaf Eliason/SS; 247 (CTR LE), CreativeWay/Alamy; 247 (CTR), CreativeWay/Alamy; 247 (UPRT), Robynrg/SS; 247 (CTR RT), Brian McEntire/SS; 247 (LORT), Asaf Eliason/SS; 248 (LO), Bettmann/CO; 248 (UP), Bettmann/CO; 249 (Background), Reuters/Mannie Garcia/CO; 249 (CTR), Division of Political History, National Museum of American History, Smithsonian Institution; 249 (LO CTR), Charles Kogod/NGC; 250 (UPLE), Archive Photos/GI; 250 (UPRT), Bettmann/CO; 250 (LOLE), Michael Ochs Archives/GI; 250 (Inset), Underwood & Underwood/CO; 250 (LORT), Patrick Faricy; 250, Stuart, Gilbert (1755–1828)/Art Resource, NY; 251 (UPLE), Bettmann/CO; 251 (UPRT), Jason Reed/Reuters/CO; 251 (LOLE), John Harrelson/GI for NASCAR; 251 (LORT), 2011 Silver Screen Collection/GI; 252 (LE), Kupka/Mauritius/SPS; 252 (LORT), North Wind Picture Archives/Alamy; 252 (UP), Adam Woolfitt/Robert Harding Picture Library; 253 (UPRT), Michael Frost/Disney Publishing Worldwide

Geography Rocks (254–337)

254, IS; 261 (CTR CTR), Maria Stenzel/NationalGeographicStock.com; 261 (LO CTR), Bill Hatcher/NationalGeographicStock.com; 261 (UP), Carsten Peter/NationalGeographicStock.com; 261 (RT CTR), Gordon Wiltsie/NationalGeographicStock.com; 261 (LOLE), James P. Blair/NationalGeographicStock.com; 261 (CTR LE), Thomas J. Abercrombie/NationalGeographicStock.com; 261 (LO RT), Bill Curtsinger/NationalGeographicStock.com; 262, Jurgen & Christine Sohns/Flpa/Robert Harding Picture Library; 263 (UPLE), Pete Oxford/npl/MP; 263 (LE CTR), AWL Images/GI; 263 (UPRT), jsbdueck/SS; 263 (UPRT), Ashraf Shazly/AFP/GI; 263 (UP CTR RT), Flickr RM/GI; 263 (LORT), Glowimages/GI; 266, Geoff Renner/Robert Harding Picture Library; 267 (UPLE), Jack Stein Grove/Danita Delimont.com; 267 (UP CTR RT), McPHOTO MDF/age fotostock; 267 (UPRT), Paul A. Souders/CO; 267 (LE CTR), Pilipenko D/IS; 267 (LO CTR RT), Colin Monteath/Hedgehog House/MP; 267 (LORT), Achim Baque/SS; 270, GI/Robert Harding Picture Library; 271 (UPLE), IS; 271 (UP CTR RT), Ko Chi Keung Alfred/Redlink/CO; 271 (CTR LE), IS; 271 (LO CTR RT), AP Photo/Sherwin Crasto; 271 (LORT), Katherine Feng/MP; 274, Melissa Woods/GI; 275 (UPLE), Cusp/SPS; 275 (LO CTR RT), Jeff Hunter/The Image Bank/GI; 275 (UPRT), Mitsuaki Iwago/MP; 275 (CTR UP RT), Kevin Schafer/MP; 275 (CTR LE), Toru Hanai/Reuters/CO; 275 (LORT), Stanislav Fosenbauer/SS; 278, Gavin Hellier/Robert Harding Picture Library; 279 (UPLE), Steven Vidler/Eurasia Press/CO; 279 (LE CTR), David Osborn/Alamy; 279 (UPRT), NGC/GI; 279 (UP CTR RT), ol/ img/SS; 279 (LO CTR RT), DeAgostini/GI; 279 (LORT), imageBROKER/Alamy; 282, Steve Dunwell/GI; 283 (UPLE), W. Bertsch/Robertstock; 283 (LE CTR), Javier Trueba/MSF/Science Source; 283 (UPRT), G K & Vikki Hart/GI; 283 (UP CTR RT), Tami Freed/SS; 283 (LO CTR RT), FLPA/Chris and Tilde Stuart/MP; 283 (LORT), Chris van Rijswijk/Buitenbeeld/MP; 286, Tui De Roy/MP; 287 (UPLE), Photononstop/SPS; 287 (UPRT), Mike Theiss/NGC; 287 (UP CTR RT), ZUMA Press, Inc./Alamy; 287 (CTR LE), David Tipling/Alamy; 287 (LORT), Hemis.fr RM/GI; 293, Mark Carwardine/Nature Picture Library; 296, Mark Conlin/Alamy; 299 (LO), Dennis Cox/WorldViews; 300, blickwinkel/Alamy; 304 (LO), anshar/SS; 307, Pniesen/Dreamstime; 310 (LO), YAY Media AS/Alamy; 313 (LO), Aurora Creative/GI; 326 (UPRT), Panoramic Images/GI; 326 (UP CTR LE), SS; 326 (UP CTR RT), SS; 326 (LORT), PhotoDisc; 327 (UP), Howiewu/Dreamstime; 327 (UP CTR), Coleong/Dreamstime; 327 (CTR), Aivoges/Dreamstime; 327 (LO CTR), Dolby1985/Dreamstime; 327 (LO), age fotostock/Alamy; 328–329 (UP), Art by CTON; 328 (LOLE), Adrian Dennis/AP Photo; 328–329 (various), Rozaliy/Dreamstime; 328–329 (various), Boykung/Dreamstime; 329 (LORT), Hugo Burnand, Clarence House/AP Photo; 329 (UPRT), Jorg Greuel/Photographer's Choice/GI; 330 (UPLE), Solvin Zanki/Nature Picture Library; 330 (UPRT), jeremy sutton-hibbert/Alamy; 330 (CTR LE), Ivonne Wierink/Dreamstime; 330 (LO CTR), Courtesy of the St. Regis Lhasa Resort; 330 (LOLE), Svetlana Kolpakova/Dreamstime; 330 (CTR RT), Dirk Ercken/SS; 330 (LO RT), Kei Shooting/SS; 330 (CTR UP), ZUMA Press, Inc./Alamy; 331 (UPLE), Ambient Images Inc./Alamy; 331 (LE CTR LO), M. Unal Ozmen/SS; 331 (LE CTR UP), Kelly Shannon Kelly/Alamy; 331 (LOLE), Chris Willson/Alamy; 331 (LORT), Courtesy of Atlantis, Paradise Island; 331 (RT CTR), Margojh/Dreamstime; 331 (UPRT), Panoramic Images/GI; 332 (UPLE), Thorpe Park; 332 (UPRT), Chris Batson/Alamy; 332 (LOLE), Joel A. Rogers; 333 (UPLE), Yasuyoshi Chiba/AFP/GI; 333 (UPRT), Reuters/Andrew Winning; 333 (LO), Reuters/Christian Charisius; 334 (BACK), Frank Hoppe; 334 (INSET), Frank Hoppe; 335 (UP), SnowCastle; 335 (CTR), SnowCastle; 335 (LO), SnowCastle; 335 (BACK), SnowCastle; 336 (LE), Chris Batson/Alamy; 336 (UP), Adrian Dennis/AP Photo; 336 (LO), Solvin Zanki/Nature Picture Library

Want to Learn More?

Find more information about topics in this almanac in these National Geographic Kids resources.

Animal Jam Official Insider's Guide
Katherine Noll
2014
animaljam.com

Funny Fill-In: My Space Adventure
Emily Krieger
2013

Get Outside Guide
Nancy Honovich and Julie Beer
2014

George Washington's Rules to Live By
K. M. Kostyal
2014

How to Speak Dog
Aline Alexander Newman and Gary Weitzman, D.V.M.
2013

Just Joking Series
National Geographic Kids
2012–2016

Mission: Lion Rescue
Ashlee Brown Blewett
With Daniel Raven-Ellison
2014
kids.nationalgeographic.com/mission-animal-rescue

National Geographic Kids Cookbook: A Year-Round Fun Food Adventure
Barton Seaver
2014

This or That?
Crispin Boyer
2014

Ultimate Globetrotting World Atlas
National Geographic Kids
2014

349

Staff for This Book

Shelby Alinsky, *Project Manager*
Mary Varilla Jones, *Project Editor*
James Hiscott, Jr., *Art Director*
Carl Mehler, *Director of Maps*
Hillary Leo, *Photo Editor*
Ruth Ann Thompson, *Designer*
Sarah Wassner Flynn, *Contributing Writer*
Michelle Harris, *Researcher*
Sara Zeglin, *Digital Content Producer*
Paige Towler, *Editorial Assistant*
Erica Holsclaw, *Special Projects Assistant*
David B. Miller, *Map Research*
Michael McNey, *Map Production*
Stuart Armstrong, *Graphics Illustrator*
Sanjida Rashid, *Design Production Assistant*
Colm McKeveny, *Rights Clearance Specialist*
Grace Hill, *Managing Editor*
Joan Gossett, *Senior Production Editor*
Lewis R. Bassford, *Production Manager*
Rachel Faulise, *Production Services*
Susan Borke, *Legal and Business Affairs*

Published by the National Geographic Society

Gary E. Knell,
President and Chief Executive Officer

John M. Fahey,
Chairman of the Board

Melina Gerosa Bellows
Chief Education Officer

Declan Moore
Chief Media Officer
President, Publishing and Travel

Hector Sierra
Senior Vice President and General Manager,
Book Division

Senior Management Team, Kids Publishing and Media

Nancy Laties Feresten, *Senior Vice President*; Jennifer Emmett, *Vice President, Editorial Director, Kids Books*; Julie Vosburgh Agnone, *Vice President, Editorial Operations*; Rachel Buchholz, *Editor and Vice President*, NG Kids *Magazine*; Michelle Sullivan, *Vice President, Kids Digital*; Eva Absher-Schantz, *Design Director*; Jay Sumner, *Photo Director*; Hannah August, *Marketing Director*; R. Gary Colbert, *Production Director*

Digital Anne McCormack, *Director*; Laura Goertzel, Sara Zeglin, *Producers*; Jed Winer, *Special Projects Assistant*; Emma Rigney, *Creative Producer*; Brian Ford, *Video Producer*; Bianca Bowman, *Assistant Producer*; Natalie Jones, *Senior Product Manager*

In Partnership With NATIONAL GEOGRAPHIC KIDS Magazine

Rachel Buchholz, *Editor and Vice President*
Eileen O'Tousa-Crowson, *Art Director*
Catherine D. Hughes, *Senior Editor, Science*
Editorial: Andrea Silen, Kay Boatner, *Associate Editors*; Nick Spagnoli, *Copy Editor*; Rose Davidson, *Special Projects Assistant*
Photo: Kelley Miller, *Senior Editor*; Lisa Jewell, Hillary Leo, *Editors*; Bri Bertoia, *Special Projects Assistant*
Art: Kathryn Robbins, *Designer*; Stephanie Rudig, *Associate Digital Designer*; Rachel Kenny, *Special Projects Assistant*
Production: Sean Philpotts, *Manager*
Administration: Allyson Shaw, *Editorial Assistant and Social Media*

The National Geographic Society is one of the world's largest nonprofit scientific and educational organizations. Founded in 1888 to "increase and diffuse geographic knowledge," the Society's mission is to inspire people to care about the planet. It reaches more than 400 million people worldwide each month through its official journal, *National Geographic,* and other magazines; National Geographic Channel; television documentaries; music; radio; films; books; DVDs; maps; exhibitions; live events; school publishing programs; interactive media; and merchandise. National Geographic has funded more than 10,000 scientific research, conservation, and exploration projects and supports an education program promoting geographic literacy.

For more information, please visit nationalgeographic.com, call 1-800-NGS LINE (647-5463), or write to the following address:

National Geographic Society, 1145 17th Street N.W., Washington, D.C. 20036-4688 U.S.A.

Visit us online at nationalgeographic.com/books

For librarians and teachers: ngchildrensbooks.org

More for kids from National Geographic: kids.nationalgeographic.com

For information about special discounts for bulk purchases, please contact National Geographic Books Special Sales: ngspecsales@ngs.org

For rights or permissions inquiries, please contact National Geographic Books Subsidiary Rights: ngbookrights@ngs.org

Paperback edition ISBN: 978-1-4263-1921-1
Hardcover edition ISBN: 978-1-4263-1922-8
Scholastic edition ISBN: 978-1-4263-2376-8

Printed in the United States of America

15/QGT-CML/1